SCIENCE OF EDUCATION

This edition published by Lector House in 2024

ISBN: 978-93-6138-350-2

Lector House LLP
Registered Office: H. No. 96, Block C, Tomar Colony,
Burari, Delhi – 110084, India
info@lectorhouse.com
www.lectorhouse.com

SCIENCE OF EDUCATION

DEPARTMENT OF EDUCATION, ONTARIO

2024

LECTOR HOUSE LLP

ONTARIO NORMAL SCHOOL MANUALS

SCIENCE OF EDUCATION

AUTHORIZED BY

THE MINISTER OF EDUCATION

CONTENTS

Chapter *Page*

PART I
PRINCIPLES OF EDUCATION

PART II
METHODOLOGY

PART III
EDUCATIONAL PSYCHOLOGY

PART I
PRINCIPLES OF EDUCATION

THE SCIENCE OF EDUCATION

CHAPTER I

NATURE AND PURPOSE OF EDUCATION

Value of Scientific Knowledge.—In the practice of any intelligent occupation or art, in so far as the practice attains to perfection, there are manifested in the processes certain scientific principles and methods to which the work of the one practising the art coforms. In the successful practice, for example, of the art of composition, there are manifested the principles of rhetoric; in that of housebuilding, the principles of architecture; and in that of government, the principles of civil polity. In practising any such art, moreover, the worker finds that a knowledge of these scientific principles and methods will guide him in the correct practice of the art,—a knowledge of the science of rhetoric assisting in the art of composition; of the science of architecture, in the art of housebuilding; and of the science of civil polity, in the art of government.

The Science of Education.—If the practice of teaching is an intelligent art, there must, in like manner, be found in its processes certain principles and methods which may be set forth in systematic form as a science of education, and applied by the educator in the art of teaching. Assuming the existence of a science of education, it is further evident that the student-teacher should make himself acquainted with its leading principles, and likewise learn to apply these principles in his practice of the art of teaching. To this end, however, it becomes necessary at the outset to determine the limits of the subject-matter of the science. We shall, therefore, first consider the general nature and purpose of education so far as to decide the facts to be included in this science.

CONDITIONS OF GROWTH AND DEVELOPMENT

A. Physical Growth.—Although differing in their particular conception of the nature of education, all educators agree in setting the child as the central figure in the educative process. As an individual, the child, like other living organisms, develops through a process of inner changes which are largely conditioned by outside influences. In the case of animals and plants, physical growth, or development, is found to consist of changes caused in the main through the individual responding to external stimulation. Taking one of the simplest forms of animal life, for example, the amoeba, we find that when stimulated by any foreign matter not constituting its food, say a particle of sand, such an organism at once withdraws itself from the stimulating elements. On the other hand, if it comes in contact with suitable food, the amoeba not only flows toward it, but by assimilating it, at once begins to increase in size, or grow, until it finally divides, or reproduces, itself as shown in the following figures. Hence the amoeba as an organism is not only able to react appropriately toward different stimuli, but is also able to change itself, or develop, by its appropriate reactions upon such stimulations.

In plant life, also, the same principle holds. As long as a grain of corn, wheat, etc., is kept in a dry place, the life principle stored up within the seed is unable to manifest itself in growth. When, on the other hand, it is appropriately stimulated by water, heat, and light, the seed awakens to life, or germinates. In other words, the seed reacts upon the external stimulations of water, heat, and light, and manifests the activity known as growth, or development. Thus all physical growth, whether of the plant or the animal, is conditioned on the energizing of the inherent life principle, in response to appropriate stimulation of the environment.

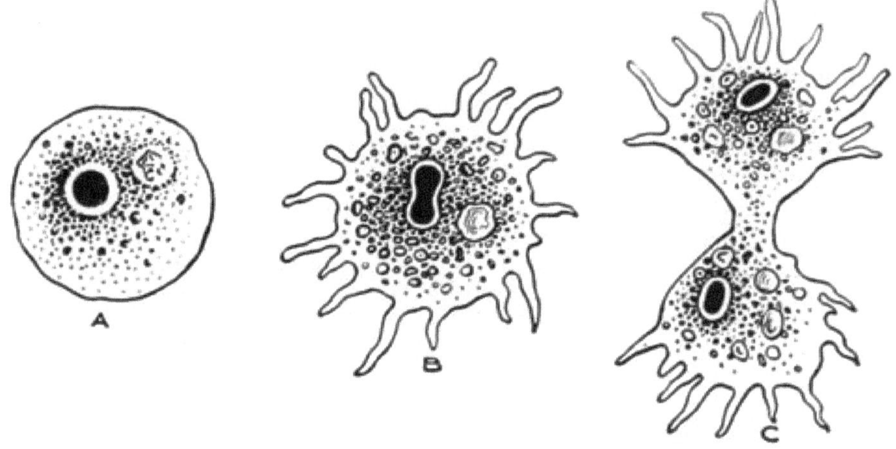

A. Simple amoeba. **B. An amoeba developing as a result of assimilating food.** **C. An amoeba about to divide, or propagate.**

B. Development in Human Life.—In addition to its physical nature, human life has within it a spiritual law, or principle, which enables the individual to respond to suitable stimulations and by that means develop into an intelligent and moral being. When, for instance, waves of light from an external object stimulate the nervous system through the eye, man is able, through his intelligent nature, to react mentally upon these stimulations and, by interpreting them, build up within his experience conscious images of light, colour, and form. In like manner, when the nerves in the hand are stimulated by an external object, the mind is able to react upon the impressions and, by interpreting them, obtain images of touch, temperature, and weight. In the sphere of action, also, the child who is stimulated by the sight of his elder pounding with a hammer, sweeping with a broom, etc., reacts imitatively upon such stimulations, and thus acquires skill in action. So also when stimulated by means of his human surroundings, as, for example, through the kindly acts of his mother, father, etc., he reacts morally toward these stimulations and thus develops such social qualities as sympathy, love, and kindness. Nor are the conditions of development different in more complex intellectual problems. If a child is given nine blocks on which are printed the nine digits, and is asked to arrange them in the form of a square so that each of the horizontal and the vertical columns will add up to fifteen, there is equally an inner growth through stimulation and response. In such a case, since the answer is unknown to the child, the problem serves as a stimulation to his mind. Furthermore, it is only by reacting upon this problem with his present knowledge of the value of the various digits when combined in threes, as 1, 6, 8; 5, 7, 3; 9, 2, 4; 1, 5, 9; etc., that the necessary growth of knowledge relative to the solution of the problem will take place within the mind.

WORTH IN HUMAN LIFE

But the possession of an intellectual and moral nature which responds to appropriate stimulations implies, also, that as man develops intellectually, he will find meaning in human life as realized in himself and others. Thus he becomes able to recognize worth in human life and to determine the conditions which favour its highest growth, or development.

The Worthy Life not a Natural Growth.—Granting that it is thus possible to recognize that "life is not a blank," but that it should develop into something of worth, it by no means follows that the young child will adequately recognize and desire a worthy life, or be able to understand and control the conditions which make for its development. Although, indeed, there is implanted in his nature a spiritual tendency, yet his early interests are almost wholly physical and his attitude impulsive and selfish. Left to himself, therefore, he is likely to develop largely as a creature of appetite, controlled by blind passions and the chance impressions of the moment. Until such time, therefore, as he obtains an adequate development of his intellectual and moral life, his behaviour conforms largely to the wants of his physical nature, and his actions are irrational and wasteful. Under such conditions the young child, if left to himself to develop in accordance with his native tendencies through the chance impressions which may stimulate him from without, must fall short of attaining to a life of worth. For this reason education is designed to control the growth, or development, of the child, by directing his stimulations and responses in such a way that his life may develop into one of worth.

Character of the Worthy Life.—If, however, it is possible to add to the worth of the life of the child by controlling and modifying his natural reactions, the first problem confronting the scientific educator is to decide what constitutes a life of worth. This question belongs primarily to ethics, or the science of right living, to which the educator must turn for his solution. Here it will be learned that the higher life is one made up of moral relations. In other words, the perfect man is a social man and the perfect life is a life made up of social rights and duties, wherein one is able to realize his own good in conformity with the good of others, and seek his own happiness by including within it the happiness of others. But to live a life of social worth, man must gain such control over his lower physical wants and desires that he can conform them to the needs and rights of others. He must, in other words, in adapting himself to his social environment, develop a sense of duty toward his fellows which will cause him to act in co-operation with others. He must refuse, for instance, to satisfy his own want by causing want to others, or to promote his own desires by giving pain to others. Secondly, he must obtain such control over his physical surroundings, including his own body, that he is able to make these serve in promoting the common good. In the worthy life, therefore, man has so adjusted himself to his fellow men that he is able to co-operate with them, and has so adjusted himself to his physical surroundings that he is able to make this co-operation effective, and thus live a socially efficient life.

FACTORS IN SOCIAL EFFICIENCY

A. Knowledge, a Factor in Social Efficiency.—The following simple examples will more fully demonstrate the factors which enter into the socially efficient life. The young child, for instance, who lives on the shore of one of our great lakes, may learn through his knowledge of colour to distinguish between the water and the sky on the horizon line. This knowledge, he finds, however, does not enter in any degree into his social life within the home. When on the same basis, however, he learns to distinguish between the ripe and the unripe berries in the garden, he finds this knowledge of service in the community, or home, life, since it enables him to distinguish the fruit his mother may desire for use in the home. One mark of social efficiency, therefore, is to possess knowledge that will enable us to serve effectively in society.

B. Skill, a Factor in Social Efficiency.—In the sphere of action, also, the child might acquire skill in making stones skip over the surface of the lake. Here, again, however, the acquired skill would serve no purpose in the community life, except perhaps occasionally to enable him to amuse himself or his fellows. When, on the other hand, he acquires skill in various home occupations, as opening and closing the gates, attending to the furnace, harnessing and driving the horse, or playing a musical instrument, he finds that this skill enables him in some measure to serve in the community life of which he is a member. A second factor in social efficiency, therefore, is the possession of such skill as will enable us to co-operate effectively within our social environment.

C. Right Feeling, a Factor in Social Efficiency.—But granting the possession of adequate knowledge and skill, a man may yet fall far short of the socially efficient life. The machinist, for instance, may know fully all that pertains to the making of an excellent engine for the intended steamboat. He may further possess the skill necessary to its actual construction. But through indifference or a desire for selfish gain, this man may build for the vessel an engine which later, through its poor construction, causes the loss of the ship and its crew. A third necessary requisite in social efficiency, therefore, is the possession of a sense of duty which compels us to use our knowledge and skill with full regard to the feelings and rights of others. Thus a certain amount of socially useful knowledge, a certain measure of socially effective skill, and a certain sense of moral obligation, or right feeling, all enter as factors into the socially efficient life.

FORMAL EDUCATION

Assuming that the educator is thus able to distinguish what constitutes a life of worth, and to recognize and in some measure control the stimulations and reactions of the child, it is evident that he should be able to devise ways and means by which the child may grow into a more worthy, that is, into a more socially efficient, life. Such an attempt to control the reactions of the child as he adjusts himself to the physical and social world about him, in order to render him a more socially efficient member of the society to which he belongs, is described as formal education.

CHAPTER II

FORMS OF REACTION

INSTINCTIVE REACTION

Since the educator aims to direct the development of the child by controlling his reactions upon his physical and social surroundings, we have next to consider the forms under which these reactions occur. Even at birth the human organism is endowed with certain tendencies, which enable it to react effectively upon the presentation of appropriate stimuli. Our instinctive movements, such as sucking, hiding, grasping, etc., being inherited tendencies to react under given conditions in a more or less effective manner for our own good, constitute one type of reactive movement. At birth, therefore, the child is endowed with powers, or tendencies, which enable him to adapt himself more or less effectively to his surroundings. Because, however, the child's early needs are largely physical, many of his instincts, such as those of feeding, fighting, etc., lead only to self-preservative acts, and are, therefore, individual rather than social in character. Even these individual tendencies, however, enable the child to adjust himself to his surroundings, and thus assist that physical growth without which, as will be learned later, there could be no adequate intellectual and moral development. But besides these, the child inherits many social and adaptive tendencies—love of approbation, sympathy, imitation, curiosity, etc., which enable him of himself to participate in some measure in the social life about him.

Instinct and Education.—Our instincts being inherited tendencies, it follows that they must cause us to react in a somewhat fixed manner upon particular external stimulation. For this reason, it might be assumed that these tendencies would build up our character independently of outside interference or direction. If such were the case, instinctive reactions would not only lie beyond the province of formal education, but might even seriously interfere with its operation, since our instinctive acts differ widely in value from the standpoint of the efficient life. It is found, however, that human instincts may not only be modified but even suppressed through education. For example, as we shall learn in the following paragraphs, instinctive action in man may be gradually supplanted by more effective habitual modes of reaction. Although, therefore, the child's instinctive tendencies undoubtedly play a large part in the early informal development of his character outside the school, it is equally true that they can be brought under the direction of the educator in the work of formal education. For that reason a more thorough study of instinctive forms of reaction, and of their relation to formal education, will be made in Chapter XXI.

HABITUAL REACTION

A second form of reaction is known as habit. On account of the plastic character of the matter constituting the nervous tissue in the human organism, any act, whether instinctive, voluntary, or accidental, if once performed, has a tendency to repeat itself under like circumstances, or to become habitual. The child, for example, when placed amid social surroundings, by merely yielding to his general tendencies of imitation, sympathy, etc., will form many valuable modes of habitual reaction connected with eating, dressing, talking, controlling the body, the use of household implements, etc. For this reason the early instinctive and impulsive acts of the child gradually develop into definite modes of action, more suited to meet the particular conditions of his surroundings.

Habit and Education.—Furthermore, the formation of these habitual modes of reaction being largely conditioned by outside influences, it is possible to control the process of their formation. For this reason, the educator is able to modify the child's natural reactions, and develop in their stead more valuable habits. No small part of the work of formal education, therefore, must consist in adding to the social efficiency of the child by endowing him with habits making for neatness, regularity, accuracy, obedience, etc. A detailed study of habit in its relation to education will be made in Chapter XXII.

CONSCIOUS REACTION

An Example.—The third and highest form of human reaction is known as ideal, or conscious, reaction. In this form of reaction the mind, through its present ideas, reacts upon some situation or difficulty in such a way as to adjust itself satisfactorily to the problem with which it is faced. As an example of such a conscious reaction, or adjustment, may be taken the case of a young lad who was noticed standing over a stationary iron grating through which he had dropped a small coin. A few moments later the lad was seen of his own accord to take up a rod lying near, smear the end with tar and grease from the wheel of a near by wagon, insert the rod through the grating, and thus recover his lost coin. An analysis of the mental movements involved previously to the actual recovery of the coin will illustrate in general the nature of a conscious reaction, or adjustment.

Factors in process

Factors Involved in Process.—In such an experience the consciousness of the lad is at the outset occupied with a definite problem, or felt need, demanding adjustment—the recovering of the lost coin, which need acts as a stimulus to the consciousness and gives direction and value to the resulting mental activity. Acting under the demands of this problem, or need, the mind displays an intelligent initiative in the selecting of ideas—stick, adhesion, tar, etc., felt to be of value for securing the required new adjustment. The mind finally combines these selected ideas into an organized system, or a new experience, which is accepted mentally as an adequate solution of the problem. The following factors are found, therefore, to enter into such an ideal, or conscious, reaction:

1. *The Problem.*—The conscious reaction is the result of a definite problem, or difficulty, presented in consciousness and grasped by the mind as such—How to recover the coin.

2. *A Selecting Process.*—To meet the solution of this problem use is made of ideas which already form a part of the lad's present experience, or knowledge, and which are felt by him to have a bearing on the presented problem.

3. *A Relating Process.*—These elements of former experience are organized by the child into a mental plan which he believes adequate to solve the problem before him.

4. *Application.*—This resulting mental plan serves to guide a further physical reaction, which constitutes the actual removal of the difficulty—the recovery of the coin.

Significance of Conscious Reactions.—In a conscious reaction upon any situation, or problem, therefore, the mind first uses its present ideas, or experience, in weighing the difficulties of the situation, and it is only after it satisfies itself in theory that a solution has been reached that the physical response, or application of the plan, is made. Hence the individual not only directs his actions by his higher intelligent nature, but is also able to react effectively upon varied and unusual situations. This, evidently, is not so largely the case with instinctive or habitual reactions. For efficient action, therefore, there must often be an adequate mental adjustment prior to the expression of the physical action. For this reason the value of consciousness consists in the guidance it affords us in meeting the demands laid upon us by our surroundings, or environment. This will become more evident, however, by a brief examination into the nature of experience itself.

EXPERIENCE

Its Value.—In the above example of conscious adjustment it was found that a new experience arises naturally from an effort to meet some need, or problem, with which the mind is at the time confronted. Our ideas, therefore, naturally organize themselves into new experiences, or knowledge, to enable us to gain some desired end. It was in order to effect the recovery of the lost coin, for example, that conscious effort was put forth by the lad to create a mental plan which should solve the problem. Primarily, therefore, man is a doer and his ideas, or knowledge, is meant to be practical, or to be applied in directing action. It is this fact, indeed, which gives meaning and purpose to the conscious states of man. Hour by hour new problems arise demanding adjustment; the mind grasps the import of the situation, selects ways and means, organizes these into an intelligent plan, and directs their execution, thus enabling us:

Not without aim to go round
In an eddy of purposeless dust.

Its Theoretic or Intellectual Value.—But owing to the value which thus attaches to any experience, a new experience may be viewed as desirable apart from its immediate application to conduct. Although, for instance, there is no immediate physical need that one should learn how to resuscitate a drowning person, he is nevertheless prepared to make of it a problem, because he feels that such knowledge regarding his environment may enter into the solution of future difficulties. Thus the value of new experience, or knowledge, is often remote and intellectual, rather than immediate and physical, and looks to the acquisition of further experience quite as much as to the directing of present physical movement. Beyond the value they may possess in relation to the removal of present physical difficulty, therefore, experiences may be said to possess a secondary value in that they may at any time enter into the construction of new experiences.

Its Growth: A. Learning by Direct Experience.—The ability to recall and use former experience in the upbuilding of an intelligent new experience is further valuable, in that it enables a person to secure much experience in an indirect rather than in a direct way, and thus avoid the direct experience when such would be undesirable. Under direct experience we include the lessons which may come to us at first hand from our surroundings, as when the child by placing his hand upon a thistle learns that it has sharp prickles, or by tasting quinine learns that it is bitter. In this manner direct experience is a teacher, continually adjusting man to his environment; and it is evident that without an ability to retain our experiences and turn them to use in organizing a new experience without expressing it in action, all conscious adjustments would have to be secured through such a direct method.

B. Learning Indirectly.—Since man is able to retain his experiences and organize them into new experiences, he may, if desirable, enter into a new experience in an indirect, or theoretic, way, and thus avoid the harsher lessons of direct experience. The child, for example, who knows the discomfort of a pin-prick may apply this, without actual expression, in interpreting the danger lurking in the thorn. In like manner the child who has fallen from his chair realizes thereby, without giving it expression, the danger of falling from a window or balcony. It is in this indirect, or theoretic, way that children in their early years acquire, by injunction and reproof, much valuable knowledge which enables them to avoid the dangers and to shun the evils presented to them by their surroundings. By the same means, also, man is able to extend his knowledge to include the experiences of other men and even of other ages.

Relative value of experiences

Relative Value of Experiences.—While the value of experience consists in its power to adjust man to present or future problems, and thus render his action more efficient, it is to be noted that different experiences may vary in their value. Many of these, from the point of their value in meeting future problems or making adjustments, must appear trivial and even useless. Others, though adapted to meet our needs, may do this in a crude and ineffective manner. As an illustration of such difference in value, compare the effectiveness and accuracy of the notation possessed by primitive men as illustrated in the following strokes:

1, 11, 111, 1111, 11111, 111111, etc., with that of our present system of notation as suggested in: 1, 10, 100, 1000, 10000, 100000, 1000000, etc. In like manner to experience that ice is cold is trivial in comparison with experiencing its preservative effects as seen in cold storage or its medicinal effects in certain diseases; to know that soda is white would be trivial in comparison with a knowledge of its properties in baking.

Man Should Participate in Valuable Experiences.—Of the three forms of human reaction, instinctive, habitual, and conscious, or ideal, it is evident that, owing to its rational character, ideal reaction is not only the most effective, but also the only one that will enable man to adjust himself to unusual situations. For this reason, and because of the difference in value of experiences themselves, it is further evident that man should participate in those experiences which are most effective in facilitating desired adjustments or in directing right conduct. It is found, moreover, that this participation can be effected by bringing the child's experiencing during his early years directly under control. It is held by some, indeed, that the whole aim of education is to reconstruct and enrich the experiences of the child and thereby add to his social efficiency. Although this conception of education leaves out of view the effects of instinctive and habitual reaction, it nevertheless covers, as we shall see later, no small part of the purpose of formal education.

INFLUENCE OF CONSCIOUS REACTION

A. On Instinctive Action.—Before concluding our survey of the various forms of reaction, it may be noted that both instinctive and habitual action are subject to the influence of conscious reaction. As a child's early instinctive acts develop into fixed habits, his growing knowledge aids in making these habits intelligent and effective. Consciousness evidently aids, for example, in developing the instinctive movements of the legs into the rhythmic habitual movements of walking, and those of the hands into the later habits of holding the spoon, knife, cup, etc. Greater still would be the influence of consciousness in developing the crude instinct of self-preservation into the habitual reactions of the spearman or boxer. In general, therefore, instinctive tendencies in man are subject to intelligent training, and may thereby be moulded into effective habits of reaction.

B. On Habitual Action.—Further new habits may be established and old ones improved under the direction of conscious reaction. When a child first learns to represent the number four by the symbol, the problem is necessarily met at first through a conscious adjustment. In other words, the child must mentally associate into a single new experience the number idea and certain ideas of form and of muscular movement. Although, however, the child is conscious of all of these factors when he first attempts to give expression to this experience, it is clear that very soon the expressive act of writing the number is carried on without any conscious direction of the process. In other words, the child soon acquires the habit of performing the act spontaneously, or without direction from the mind. Inversely, any habitual mode of action, in whatever way established, may, if we possess the necessary experience, be represented in idea and be accepted or corrected accordingly. A person, for instance, who has acquired the necessary knowledge of the laws of hygiene, may represent ideally both his own and the proper manner of standing, sitting, reclining, etc., and seek to modify his present habits accordingly. The whole question of the relation of conscious to habitual reaction will, however, be considered in Chapter XXII.`

CHAPTER III

THE PROCESS OF EDUCATION

CONSCIOUS ADJUSTMENT

From the example of conscious adjustment previously considered, it would appear that the full process of such an adjustment presents the following characteristics:

1. *The Problem.*—The individual conceives the existence within his environment of a difficulty which demands adjustment, or which serves as a problem calling for solution.

2. *A Selecting Process.*—With this problem as a motive, there takes place within the experience of the individual a selecting of ideas felt to be of value for solving the problem which calls for adjustment.

3. *A Relating Process.*—These relevant ideas are associated in consciousness and form a new experience believed to overcome the difficulty involved in the problem. This new experience is accepted, therefore, mentally, as a satisfactory plan for meeting the situation, or, in other words, it adjusts the individual to the problem in hand.

4. *Expression.*—This new experience is expressed in such form as is requisite to answer fully the need felt in the original problem.

EDUCATION AS ADJUSTMENT

Example from Writing.—An examination of any ordinary educative process taken from school-room experience will show that it involves in some degree the factors mentioned above.

As a very simple example, may be taken the case of a young child learning to form capital letters with short sticks. Assuming that he has already copied letters involving straight lines, such as A, H, etc., the child, on meeting such a letter as C or D, finds himself face to face with a new problem. At first he may perhaps attempt to form the curves by bending the short thin sticks. Hereupon, either through his own failure or through some suggestion of his teacher, he comes to see a short, straight line as part of a large curve. Thereupon he forms the idea of a curve composed of a number of short, straight lines, and on this principle is able to express himself in such forms as are shown here.

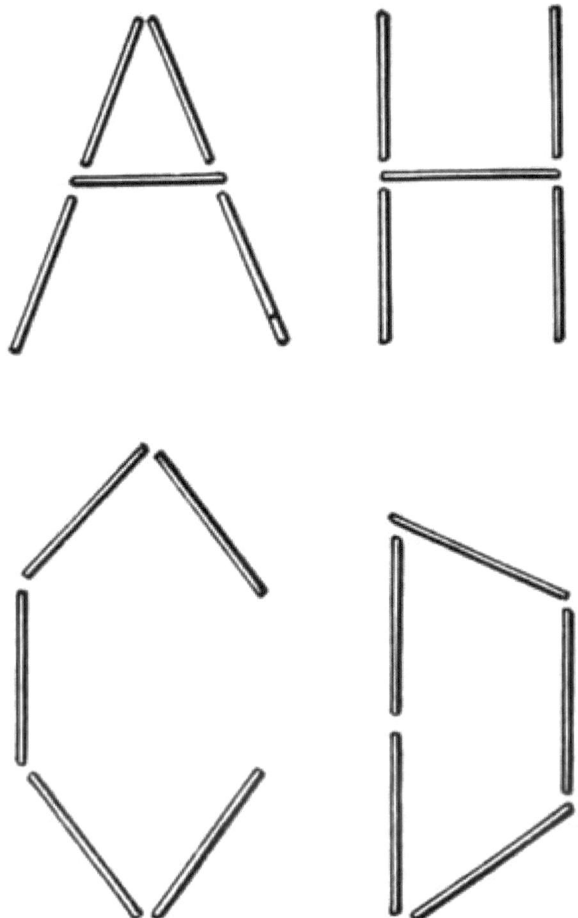

In this simple process of adjustment there are clearly involved the four stages referred to above, as follows:

1. *The Problem.*—The forming of a curved letter by means of straight sticks.

2. *A Selecting Process.*—Selecting of the ideas straight and curved and the fixing of attention upon them.

3. *A Relating Process.*—An organization of the selected ideas into a new experience in which the curve is viewed as made up of a number of short, straight lines.

4. *Expression.*—Working out the physical expression of the new experience in the actual forming of capitals involving curved lines.

Example from Arithmetic.—An analysis of the process by which a child learns that there are four twos in eight, shows also the following factors:

1. *The Problem.*—To find out how many twos are contained in the vaguely

known eight.

2. *A Selecting Process.*—To meet this problem the pupil is led from his present knowledge of the number two, to proceed to divide eight objects into groups of two; and, from his previous knowledge of the number four, to measure the number of these groups of two.

3. *A Relating Process.*—Next the three ideas two, four, and eight are translated into a new experience, constituting a mental solution of the present problem.

4. *Expression.*—This new experience expresses itself in various ways in the child's dealings with the number problems connected with his environment.

Example from Geometry.—Taking as another example the process by which a student may learn that the exterior angle of a triangle is equal to the two interior and opposite angles, there appear also the same stages, thus:

1. *The Problem.*—The conception of a difficulty or problem in the geometrical environment which calls for solution, or adjustment—the relation of the angle *a* to the angles *b* and *c* in Figure 1.

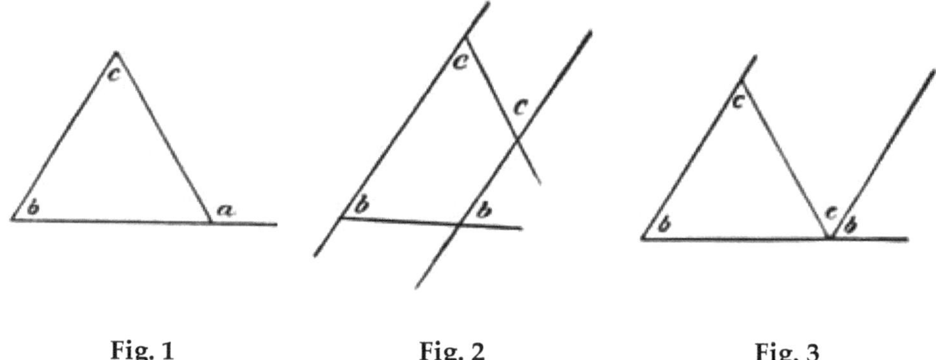

Fig. 1 Fig. 2 Fig. 3

2. *A Selecting Process.*—With this problem as a motive there follows, as suggested by Figure 2, the selecting of a series of ideas from the previous experiences of the pupil which seem relative to, or are considered valuable for solving the problem in hand.

3. *A Relating Process.*—These relative ideas pass into the formation of a new experience, as illustrated in Figure 3, constituting the solution of the problem.

4. *Expression.*—A further applying of this experience may be made in adjusting the pupil to other problems connected with his geometric environment; as, for example, to discover the sum of the interior angles of a triangle.

EDUCATION AS CONTROL OF ADJUSTMENT

The examples of adjustment taken from school-room practice, are found, however, to differ in one important respect from the previous example taken from practical life. This difference consists in the fact that in the recovery of the coin the modification of experience took place wholly without control or direction other than that furnished by the problem itself. Here the problem—the recovery of the coin—presents itself to the child and is seized upon as a motive by his attention solely on account of its own value; secondly, this problem of itself directs a flow of relative images which finally bring about the necessary adjustment. In the examples taken from the school, on the other hand, the processes of adjustment are, to a greater or less extent, directed and regulated through the presence of some type of educative agent. For instance, when a student goes through the process of learning the relation of the exterior angle to the two interior and opposite angles, the control of the process appears in the fact that the problem is directly presented to the student as an essential step in a sequence of geometric problems, or adjustments. The same direction or control of the process is seen again in the fact that the student is not left wholly to himself, as in the first example, to devise a solution, but is aided and directed thereto, first, in that the ideas bearing upon the problem have previously been made known to the student through instruction, and secondly, in that the selecting and adjusting of these former ideas to the solution of the new problem is also directed through the agency of either a text-book or a teacher. A conscious adjustment, therefore, which is brought about without direction from another, implies only a process of learning on the part of the child, while a controlled adjustment implies both a process of learning on the part of the child and a process of teaching on the part of an instructor. For scientific treatment, therefore, it is possible to limit formal education, so far as it deals with conscious adjustment, to those modifications of experience which are directed or controlled through an educative agent, or, in other words, are brought about by means of instruction.

REQUIREMENTS OF THE INSTRUCTOR

Formal education being an attempt to direct the development of the child by controlling his stimulations and responses through the agency of an instructor, we may now understand in general the necessary qualifications and offices of the teacher in directing the educative process.

1. The teacher must understand what constitutes the worthy life; that is, he must have a definite aim in directing the development of the child.

2. He must know what stimulations, or problems, are to be presented to the child in order to have him grow, or develop, into this life of worth.

3. He must know how the physical, intellectual, and moral nature of the child reacts upon these appropriate stimulations.

4. He must have skill in presenting the stimuli, or problems, to the child and in bringing its mind to react appropriately thereon.

5. He must, in the case of conscious reactions, see that the child not only acquires the new experience, but that he is also able to apply it effectively. In other words, he must see that the child acquires not only knowledge, but also skill in the use of knowledge.

CHAPTER IV

THE SCHOOL CURRICULUM

Valuable Experience: Race Knowledge.—Since education aims largely to increase the effectiveness of the moral conduct of the child by adding to the value of his experience, the science of education must decide the basis on which the educator is to select experiences that possess such a value in directing conduct. Now a study of the progress of a nation's civilization will show that this advancement is brought about through the gradual interpretation of the resources at the nation's command, and the turning of these resources to the attainment of human ends. Thus there is gradually built up a community, or race, experience, in which the materials of the physical, economic, political, moral, and religious life are organized and brought under control. By this means is constituted a body of race experience, the value of which has been tested in its direct application to the needs of the social life of the community. It is from the more typical forms of this social, or race, experience that education draws the experience, or problems, for the educative process. In other words, through education the experiences of the child are so reconstructed that he is put in possession of the more typical and more valuable forms of race experience, and thus rendered more efficient in his conduct, or action.

PURPOSES OF CURRICULUM

Represents Race Experiences.—So far as education aims to have the child enter into typical valuable race experiences, this can be accomplished only by placing these experiences before him as problems in such form that he may realize them through a regular process of learning. The purpose of the school curriculum is, therefore, to provide such problems as may, under the direction of the instructor, control the conscious reactions of the child, and enable him to participate in these more valuable race experiences. In this sense arithmetic becomes a means for providing the child with a series of problems which may give him the experiences which the race has found valuable in securing commercial accuracy and precision. In like manner, constructive work provides a series of problems in which the child experiences how the race has turned the materials of nature to human service. History provides problems whose solution gives the experience which enables the pupil to meet the political and social conditions of his own time. Physics shows how the forces of nature have become instruments for the service of man. Geography shows how the world is used as a background for social life; and grammar, what principles control the use of the race language as a medium for the communication of thought.

Classifies Race Experience.—Without such control of the presentation of these racial experiences as is made possible through the school and the school curriculum, the child would be likely to meet them only as they came to him in the actual processes of social life. These processes are, however, so complex in modern society, that, in any attempt to secure experience directly, the child is likely to be overwhelmed by their complex and unorganized character. The message boy in the dye-works, for example, may have presented to him innumerable problems in number, language, physics, chemistry, etc., but owing to the confused, disorganized, and mingled character of the presentation, these are not likely to be seized upon by him as direct problems calling for adjustment. In the school curriculum, on the other hand, the different phases of this seemingly unorganized mass of experiences are abstracted and presented to the child in an organized manner, the different phases being classified as facts of number, reading, spelling, writing, geography, physics, chemistry, etc. Thus the school curriculum classifies for the child the various phases of this race experience and provides him with a comprehensive representation of his environment.

Systematizes Race Experience.—The school curriculum further presents each type of experience, or each subject, in such a systematic order that the various experiences may develop out of one another in a natural way. If the child were compelled to meet his number facts altogether in actual life, the impressions would be received without system or order, now a discount experience, next a problem in fractions, at another time one in interest or mensuration. In the school curriculum, on the other hand, the child is in each subject first presented with the simple, near, and familiar, these in turn forming basic experiences for learning the complex, the remote, and the unknown. Thus he is able in geography, for example, on the basis of his simple and known local experiences, to proceed to a realization of the whole world as the background for human life.

Clarifies Race Experience.—Finally, when a child is given problems by means of the school curriculum, the experiences come to him in a pure form. That is, the trivial, accidental, and distracting elements which are necessarily bound up with these experiences when they are met in the ordinary walks of life are eliminated, and the single type is presented. For instance, the child may every day meet accidentally examples of reflection and refraction of light. But these not being separated from the mass of accompanying impressions, his mind may never seize as distinct problems the important relations in these experiences, and may thus fail to acquire the essential principles involved. In the school curriculum, on the other hand, under the head of physics, he has the essential aspects presented to him in such an unmixed, or pure, form that he finds relatively little difficulty in grasping their significance. Thus the school curriculum renders possible an effective control of the experiencing of the child by presenting in a comprehensive form a classified, systematized, and pure representation of the more valuable features of the race experience. In other words, it provides suitable problems which may lead the child to participate more fully in the life about him. Through the subjects of the school curriculum, therefore, the child may acquire much useful knowledge which would not otherwise be met, and much which, if met in ordinary life, could not be apprehended to an equal degree.

DANGERS IN USE OF CURRICULUM

While recognizing the educational value of the school curriculum, it should be noticed that certain dangers attach to its use as a means of providing problems for developing the experiences of the child. It is frequently argued against the school that the experiences gained therein too often prove of little value to the child in the affairs of practical life. The world of knowledge within the school, it is claimed, is so different from the world of action outside the school, that the pupil can find no connection between them. If, however, as claimed above, the value of experience consists in its use as a means of efficient control of conduct, it is evident that the experiences acquired through the school should find direct application in the affairs of life, or in other words, the school should influence the conduct, or behaviour, of the child both within and without the school.

A. Child may not see Connection with Life.—Now the school curriculum, as has been seen, in representing the actual social life, so classifies and simplifies this life that only one type of experience—number, language, chemistry, geography, etc., is presented to the child at one time. It is evident, however, that when the child faces the problems of actual life, they will not appear in the simple form in which he meets them as represented in the school curriculum. Thus, when he leaves the school and enters society, he frequently sees no connection between the complex social life outside the school and the simplified and systematized representation of that life, as previously met in the school studies. For example, when the boy, after leaving school, is set to fill an order in a wholesale drug store, he will in the one experience be compelled to use various phases of his chemical, arithmetical, writing, and bookkeeping knowledge, and that perhaps in the midst of a mass of other accidental impressions. In like manner, the girl in her home cooking might meet in a single experience a situation requiring mathematical, chemical, and physical knowledge for its successful adjustment, as in the substitution of soda and cream of tartar for baking-powder. This complex character of the problems of actual life may prove so bewildering that the person is unable to see any connection between the outside problem and his school experiences. Thus school knowledge frequently fails to function to an adequate degree in the practical affairs of life.

How to Avoid This Danger.—To meet this difficulty, school work must be related as closely as possible to the practical experiences of the child. This would cause the teacher, for example, to draw his problems in arithmetic, his subjects in composition, or his materials for nature study from the actual life about the child, while his lessons in hygiene would bear directly on the care of the school-room and the home, and the health of the pupils. Moreover, that the work of the school may represent more fully the conditions of actual life, pupils should acquire facility in correlating different types of experience upon the same problem. In this way the child may use in conjunction his knowledge of arithmetic, language, geography, drawing, nature study, etc., in school gardening; and his arithmetic, language, drawing, art, etc., in conjunction with constructive occupations.

Value of Typical Forms of Expression.—A chief cause in the past for the lack of connection between school knowledge and practical life was the comparative absence from the curriculum of any types of human activity. In other words, though the ideas controlling human activity were experienced by the child within the school, the materials and tools involved in the physical expression of such ideas were almost entirely absent. The result was that the physical habits connected with the practical use of knowledge were wanting. Thus, in addition to the lack of any proper co-ordinating of different types of knowledge in suitable forms of activity, the knowledge itself became theoretic and abstract. This danger will, however, be discussed more fully at a later stage.

B. Curriculum May Become Fossilized.—A second danger in the use of the school curriculum consists in the fact that, as a representation of social life, it may not keep pace with the social changes taking place outside the school. This may result in the school giving its pupils forms of knowledge which at the time have little functional value, or little relation to present life about the child. An example of this was seen some years ago in the habit of having pupils spend considerable time and energy in working intricate problems in connection with British currency. This currency having no practical place in life outside the school, the child could see no connection between that part of his school work and any actual need. Another marked example of this tendency will be met in the History of Education in connection with the educational practice of the last two centuries in continuing the emphasis placed on the study of the ancient languages, although the functional relation of these languages to everyday life was on the decline, and scientific knowledge was beginning to play a much more important part therein. While the school curriculum may justly represent the life of past periods of civilization so far as these reflect on, and aid in the interpreting of, the present, it is evident that in so far as the child experiences the past without any reference to present needs, the connection which should exist between the school and life outside the school must tend to be destroyed.

C. May be Non-progressive.—As a corollary to the above, is the fact that the school, when not watchful of the changes going on without the school, may fail to represent in its curriculum new and important phases of the community life. At the present time, for example, it is a debatable question whether the school curriculum is, in the matter of our industrial life, keeping pace with the changes taking place in the community. It is in this connection that one of the chief dangers of the school text-book is to be found. The text is too often looked upon as a final authority upon the particular subject-matter, rather than being treated as a mode of representing what is held valuable and true in relation to present-day interests and activities. The position of authority which the text-book thus secures, may serve as a check against even necessary changes in the attitude of the school toward any particular subject.

D. May Present Experience in too Technical Form.—Lastly, the school curriculum, even when representing present life, may introduce it in a too highly technical form. So far at least as elementary education is concerned, each type of knowledge, or each subject, should find a place on the curriculum from a consideration of its influence upon the conduct and, therefore, upon the present life of the child. There is always a danger, however, that the teacher, who may be a specialist in the subject, will wish to stress its more intellectual and abstract phases, and thus force upon the child forms of knowledge which he is not able to refer to his life needs in any practical way. This tendency is illustrated in the desire of some teachers to substitute with young children a technical study of botany and zoology, in place of more concrete work in nature study. Now when the child approaches these phases of his surroundings in the form of nature study, he is able to see their influence upon his own community life. When, on the other hand, these are introduced to him in too technical a form, he is not able, in his present stage of learning, to discover this connection, and the so-called knowledge remains in his experience, if it remains at all, as uninteresting, non-significant, and non-digested information. In the elementary school at least, therefore, knowledge should not be presented to the child in such a technical and abstract way that it will seem to have no contact with daily life.

CHAPTER V

EDUCATIONAL INSTITUTIONS

THE SCHOOL

As man, in the progress of civilization, became more fully conscious of the worth of human life and of the possibilities of its development through educational effort, the providing of special instruction for the young naturally began to be recognized as a duty. As this duty became more and more apparent, it gave rise, on the principle of the division of labour, to corporate, or institutional, effort in this direction. By this means there has been finally developed the modern school as a fully organized corporate institution devoted to educational work, and supported as an integral part of our civil or public obligations.

Origin of the School.—To trace the origin of the school, it will be necessary to look briefly at certain marked stages of the development of civilization. The earliest and simplest forms of primitive life suggest a time when the family constituted the only type of social organization. In such a mode of life, the principle of the division of labour would be absent, the father or patriarch being the family carpenter, butcher, doctor, judge, priest, and teacher. In the two latter capacities, he would give whatever theoretic or practical instruction was received by the child. As soon, however, as a tribal form of life is met, we find the tribe or race collecting a body of experience which can be retained only by entrusting it to a selected body. This experience, or knowledge, is at first mainly of a religious character, and is possessed and handed on by a body of men forming a priesthood. Such priestly bodies, or colleges, may be considered the earliest special organizations devoted to the office of teaching. As civilization gradually advanced, a mass of valuable practical knowledge relative to man's environment was secured and added to the more theoretic forms. As this practical knowledge became more complex, there was felt a greater need that the child should be made acquainted with it in some systematic manner during his early years. Thus developed the conception of the school as an instrument by which such educative work might be carried on more effectively. On account of the constant increase of practical knowledge and its added importance in directing the political and economic life of the people, the civil authorities began in time to assume control of secular education. Thus the government of the school as an institution gradually passed to the state, the teacher taking the place of the priest as the controlling agent in the education of the young.

OTHER EDUCATIVE AGENTS

The church

The Church.—But notwithstanding the organization of the present school as a civic institution, it is to be noticed that the church still continues to act as an educative agent. In many communities, in fact, the church is still found to retain a large control of education even of a secular type. Even in communities where the church no longer exercises control over the school, she still does much, though in a more indirect way, to mould the thought and character of the community life; and is still the chief educational agent concerned in the direct attempt to enrich the religious experiences of the race.

The home

The Home.—While much of the knowledge obtained by the child within his own home necessarily comes through self, or informal, education, yet in most homes the parent still performs in many ways the function of a teacher, both by giving special instruction to the child and by directing the formation of his habits. In certain forms of experience indeed, it is claimed by the school that the instruction should be given by the parent rather than by the teacher. In questions of morals and manners, the natural tie which unites child and parent will undoubtedly enable much of the necessary instruction to be given more effectively in the home. It is often claimed, in fact, that parents now leave too much to the school and the teacher in relation to the education of the child.

The vocation

The Vocation.—Another agent which may directly control the experiences of the young is found in the various vocations to which they devote themselves. This phase of education was very important in the days of apprenticeship. One essential condition in the form of agreement was that the master should instruct the apprentice in the art, or craft, to which he was apprenticed. Owing to the introduction of machinery and the consequent more complex division of labour, this type of formal education has been largely eliminated. It may be noted in passing that it is through these changed conditions that night classes for mechanics, which are now being provided by our technical schools, have become an important factor in our educational system.

Other institutions

Other Educational Institutions.—Finally, many clubs, institutes, and societies attempt, in a more accidental way, to convey definite instruction, and therefore serve in a sense as educational institutions. Prominent among such institutions is the modern Public Library, which affords opportunity for independent study in practically every department of knowledge. Our Farmers' Institutes also attempt to convey definite instruction in connection with such subjects as dairying, horticulture, agriculture, etc. Many Women's Clubs seek to provide instruction for young women, both of a practical and also of a moral and religious character. Various societies of a scientific character have also done much to spread a knowledge of nature and her laws and are likewise to be classed as educational institutions. Such movements as these, while taking place without the limits of the school, may not unreasonably claim a certain recognition as educational factors in the community and should receive the sympathetic co-operation of the teacher.

CHAPTER VI

THE PURPOSE OF THE SCHOOL

CIVIC VIEWS

Since the school of to-day is organized and supported by the state as a special corporate body designed to carry on the work of education, it becomes of public interest to know the particular purpose served through the maintenance of such a state institution. We have already seen that the school seeks to interpret the civilized life of the community, to abstract out of it certain elements, and to arrange them in systematic or scientific order as a curriculum of study, and finally to give the child control of this experience, or knowledge. We have attempted to show further that by this means education so increases the effectiveness of the conscious reactions of the child and so modifies his instincts and his habits as to add to his social efficiency. As, however, many divergent and incomplete views are held by educators and others as to the real purpose of public instruction, it will be well at this stage to consider briefly some of the most important types of these theories.

Aristocratic View.—It may be noted that the experience, or knowledge, represented in the curriculum cannot exist outside of the knowing mind. In other words, arithmetic, grammar, history, geography, etc., are not something existing apart from mind, but only as states of consciousness. Text-books, for instance, do not contain knowledge but merely symbols of knowledge, which would have no significance and give no light without a mind to interpret them. Some, therefore, hold that the school, in seeking to translate this social experience into the consciousness of the young, should have as its aim merely to conserve for the future the intellectual and moral achievements of the present and the past. This they say demands of the school only that it produce an intellectual priesthood, or a body of scholars, who may conserve wisdom for the light and guidance of the whole community. Thus arises the aristocratic view of the purpose of education, which sees no justification in the state attempting to provide educational opportunities for all of its members, but holds rather that education is necessary only for the leaders of society.

Democratic View.—Against the above view, it is claimed by others that, while public education should undoubtedly be conducted for the benefit of the state as a whole; yet, since a chain cannot be stronger than its weakest link, the efficiency of the state must be measured by that of its individual units. The state, therefore, must aim, by means of education, to add to its own efficiency by adding to that of each and all of its members. This demands, however, that every individual should be able to meet in an intelligent way such situations as he is likely to encounter in his community life. Although carried on, therefore, for the good of the state, yet education should be democratic, or universal, and should fit every individual to become a useful member of society.

These Views Purely Civic.—It is to be noted that though the latter view provides for the education of all as a duty of the state, yet both of the above views are purely civic in their significance, and hold that education exists for the welfare of the state as a whole and not for the individual. If, therefore, the state could be benefited by having the education of any class of citizens either limited or extended in an arbitrary way, nothing in the above conception of the purpose of state education would forbid such a course.

INDIVIDUALISTIC VIEWS

Opposed to the civic view of education, many hold, on the other hand, that education exists for the child and not for the state, and therefore, aims primarily to promote the welfare of the individual. By these educators it is argued that, since each child is created with a separate and distinct personality, it follows that he possesses a divine right to have that personality developed independently of the claims of the community to which he belongs. According to this view, therefore, the aim of education should be in each case solely to effect some good for the individual child. These educators, however, are again found to differ concerning what constitutes this individual good.

The Culture Aim.—According to the practice of many educators, education is justified on the ground that it furnishes the individual a degree of personal culture. According to this view, the worth of education is found in the fact that it puts the learner in possession of a certain amount of conventional knowledge which is held to give a polish to the individual; this polish providing a distinguishing mark by which the learned class is separated from the ignorant. It is undoubtedly true that the so-called culture of the educated man should add to the grace and refinement of social life. In this sense, culture is not foreign to the conception of individual and social efficiency. A narrow cultural view, however, overlooks the fact that man's experience is significant only when it enables him to meet the needs and problems of the present, and that, as a member of a social community, he must apply himself to the actual problems to be met within his environment. To acquire knowledge, therefore, either as a mere possession or as a mark of personal superiority, is to give to experience an unnatural value.

The Utilitarian Aim.—Others express quite an opposite view to the above, declaring that the aim of education is to enable the individual to get on in the world. By this is meant that education should enable us to be more successful in our business, and thus live more comfortable lives. Now, so far as this practical success of the individual can be achieved in harmony with the interests of society as a whole, we may grant that education should make for individual betterment. Indeed it may justly be claimed that an advancement in the comfort of the individual under such conditions really implies an increase in the comfort of society as a whole; for the man who is not able to provide for his own welfare must prove, if not a menace, at least a burden to society. If, however, it is implied that the educated man is to be placed in a position to advance his own interests irrespective of, or in direct opposition to, the rights and comforts of others, then the utilitarian view of the end of education must appear one-sided. To emphasize the good of the individual irrespective of the rights of others, and to educate all of its members with such an end in view, society would tend to destroy the unity of its own corporate life.

The Psychological Aim.—According to others, although education aims to benefit the child, this benefit does not come from the acquisition of any particular type of knowledge, but is due rather to a development which takes place within the individual himself as a result of experiencing. In other words, the child as an intelligent being is born with certain attributes which, though at first only potential, may be developed into actual capacities or powers. Thus it is held that the real aim of education is to develop to the full such capacities as are found already within the child. Moreover, it is because the child has such possibilities of development within him, and because he starts at the very outset of his existence with a divine yearning to develop these inner powers, that he reaches out to experience his surroundings. For this reason, they argue that every individual should have his own particular capacities and powers fully and harmoniously developed. Thus the true aim of education is said to be to unfold the potential life of each individual and allow it to realize itself; the purpose of the school being primarily not to make of the child a useful member of society, but rather to study the nature of the child and develop whatever potentialities are found within him as an individual. Because this theory places such large emphasis on the natural tendencies and capacities of the child, it is spoken of as the psychological aim of education.

Limitations of the Aim.—This view evidently differs from others in that it finds the justification for education, not primarily in the needs or rights of a larger society of which the child is a member, but rather in those of the single individual. Here, however, a difficulty presents itself. If the developing of the child's capacities and tendencies constitute the real purpose of public education, may not education at times conflict with the good of the state itself? Now it is evident that if a child has a tendency to lie, or steal, or inflict pain on others, the development of such tendencies must result in harm to the community at large. On the other hand, it is clear that in the case of other proclivities which the child may possess, such as industry, truthfulness, self-sacrifice, etc., the development of these cannot be separated from the idea of the good of others. To apply a purely individual aim to education, therefore, seems impossible; since we can have no standard to distinguish between good and bad tendencies, unless these are measured from a social standpoint or from a consideration of the good of others, and not from the mere tendencies and capacities of the individual. Moreover, to attempt the harmonious development of all the child's tendencies and powers is not justifiable, even in the case of those tendencies which might not conflict with the good of others. As already noted, division of labour has now gone so far that the individual may profitably be relieved from many forms of social activity. This implies as a corollary, however, that the individual will place greater stress upon other forms of activity.

THE SOCIAL, OR ECLECTIC, VIEW

Moreover, because, as already noted, the child is by his very nature a social being, it follows that the good of the individual can never in reality be opposed to the good of society, and that whenever the child has in his nature any tendencies which conflict with the good of others, these do not represent his true, or social, nature. For education to suppress these, therefore, is not only fitting the child for society but also advancing the development of the child so far as his higher, or true, nature is concerned. Thus the true view of the purpose of the school and of education will be a social, or eclectic, one, representing the element of truth contained in both the civic and the individualistic views. In the first place, such a view may be described as a civic one, since it is only by considering the good of others, that is of the state, that we can find a standard for judging the value of the child's tendencies. Moreover, it is only by using the forms of experience, or knowledge, that the community has evolved, that conditions can be provided under which the child's tendencies may realize themselves. Secondly, the true view is equally an individualistic view, for while it claims that the child is by his nature a social being, it also demands a full development of the social or moral tendencies of the individual, as being best for himself as well as for society.

This View Dynamic.—In such an eclectic view of the aim of education, it is to be noted further that society may turn education to its own advancement. By providing that an individual may develop to his uttermost such good tendencies as he may possess, education not only allows the individual to make the most of his own higher nature, but also enables him to contribute something to the advancement, or elevation, of society itself. Such a conception of the aim of education, therefore, does not view the present social life as some static thing to which the child must be adapted in any formal sense, but as dynamic, or as having the power to develop itself in and through a fuller development of the higher and better tendencies within its individual members.

A Caution.—While emphasizing the social, or moral, character of the aim of education, it is to be borne in mind by the educator that this implies more than a passive possession by the individual of a certain moral sentiment. Man is truly moral only when his moral character is functioning in goodness, or in *right action*. This is equivalent to declaring that the moral man must be individually efficient in action, and must likewise control his action from a regard for the rights of others. There is always a danger, however, of assuming that the development of moral character consists in giving the child some passive mark, or quality, without any necessity of having it continually functioning in conduct. But this reduces morality to a mere sentiment. In such a case, the moral aim would differ little from the cultural aim mentioned above.

CHAPTER VII

DIVISIONS OF EDUCATIONAL STUDY

CONTROL OF EXPERIENCE

Significance of Control.—From our previous inquiry into the nature of education, we may notice that at least two important problems present themselves for investigation in connection with the educative process. Our study of the subject-matter of education, or the school curriculum, has shown that its function as an educational instrumentality is to furnish for the child experiences of greater value, this enhanced value consisting in the greater social significance of the race experiences, or knowledge, embodied within the curriculum, when compared with the more individual experiences of the average child. It has been noted further, however, that the office of education is not merely to have the child translate this race experience into his own mind, but rather to have him add to his social efficiency by gaining an adequate power of control over these experiences. It is not, for instance, merely to know the number combinations, but to be able to meet his practical needs, that the child must master the multiplication tables. Control of experience, however, as we have seen from our analysis of the learning process, implies an ability to hold an aim, or problem, in view, and a further ability to select and arrange the means of gaining the desired end. In relation to the multiplication table, therefore, control of experience implies that a person is able to apprehend the present number situation as one that needs solution, and also that he can bring, or apply, his knowledge of the table to its solution.

Nature of Growth of Control.—The young child is evidently not able at first to exercise this power of control over his experiences. When a very young child is aroused, say by the sound proceeding from a bell, the impression may give rise to certain random movements, but none of these indicate on his part any definite experience or purpose. When, however, under the same stimulation, in place of these random movements, the child reacts mentally in a definite way, it signifies on his part the recognition of an external object. This recognition shows that the child now has, in place of the first vague image, a more or less definite idea of the external thing. Before it was vague noise; now it is a bell. But a yet more valuable control is gained by the child when he gives this idea a wider meaning by organizing it as an element into more complex experiences, as when he relates it with the idea of a fire, of dinner, or of a call to school. Before it was merely a bell; now it is an alarm of fire. So far, however, as the child is lacking in the control of his experiences, he remains largely a mere creature of impulse and instinct, and is occupied with present impressions only. This implies also an inability to set up problems and solve them through a regular process of adjustment, and a consequent lack of power to arrange experiences as guides to action. In the educative process, however, as previously exemplified, we find that the child is not a slave to the passing transient impressions of the present, but is able to secure a control over his experience which enables him to set up intelligent aims, devise plans for their attainment, and apply these plans in gaining the end desired. Growth of control takes place, therefore, to the extent to which the child thus becomes able to keep an end in view and to select and organize means for its realization.

Elements of Control.—In the growth of control manifested in the learning process, the child, as we have noticed, becomes able to judge the value, or worth, of experience. In other words, he becomes able to distinguish between the important and the trivial, and to see the relative values of various experiences when applied to practical ends. Further, he gains right feeling or an emotional warmth toward that which his intelligence affirms to be worthy, or grows to appreciate the right. Thirdly, he secures a power in execution that enables him to attain to that which his judgment and feeling have set up as a desirable end. In fine, the educative process implies for the child a growth of control by which he becomes able (1) to select worthy ends; (2) to devise plans for their attainment; and (3) to put these plans into successful execution.

THE INSTRUCTOR'S PROBLEMS

The end in any learning process being to set the pupils a problem which may stimulate them to gain such an efficient control of useful experience, or knowledge, we may note two important problems confronting the teacher as an instructor:

1. *Problem of Matter.*—The teacher must be so conversant with the subject-matter of the curriculum and with its value in relation to actual life, that he may select therefrom the problems and materials which will enable the child to come into possession of the desirable experiences. This constitutes the question of the subject-matter of education.

2. *Problem of Method.*—The teacher must further be conversant with the process by which the child gets command of experience or with the way in which the mind of the child, in reacting upon any subject-matter, selects and organizes his knowledge into new experience and puts the same into execution. In other words, the teacher must fully understand how to direct the child successfully through the four stages of the learning process.

General method

(*a*) *General Method.*—In a scientific study of education it is usually assumed that the student-teacher has mastered academically the various subjects of the curriculum. In the professional school, therefore, the subject-matter of education is studied largely from the standpoint of method. In his study of method the student of education seeks first to master the details of the process of education outlined in the opening Chapters under the headings of problem, selecting process, relating process, and application. By this means the teacher comes to understand in greater detail how the mind of the child reacts upon the presented problems of the curriculum in gaining control over his experiences, or, in other words, how the process of learning actually takes place within the consciousness of the child. This sub-division is treated under the head of *General Method*.

Special methods

(*b*) *Special Methods.*—In addition to General Method, the student-teacher must study each subject of the curriculum from the standpoint of its use in setting problems, or lessons, which shall enable the child to gain control of a richer experience. This sub-division is known as *Special Methods,* since it considers the particular problems involved in adapting the matter of each subject to the general purpose of the educative process.

School management

3. *Problem of Management.*—From what has been seen in reference to the school as an institution organized for directing the education of the child, it is apparent that in addition to the immediate and direct control of the process of learning as involved in the method of instruction, there is the more indirect control of the process through the systematic organization and management of the school as a corporate institution. These more indirect problems connected with the control of education within the school will include, not only such topics as the organization and management of the pupils, but also the legal ways and means for providing these various educational instrumentalities. These indirect elements of control constitute a third phase of the problem of education, and their study is known as *School Organization and Management.*

History of education

4. *An Historic Problem.*—It has been noted that the corporate institution known as the school arose as the result of the principle of the division of labour, and thus took to itself duties previously performed under other less effective conditions. Thus the school presents on its organic side a history with which the teacher should be more or less familiar. On its historical side, therefore, education presents a fourth phase for study. This division of the subject is known as the *History of Education*.

SUMMARY

The facts of education, as scientifically considered by the student-teacher, thus arrange themselves under four main heads:

1. General Method
2. Special Methods
3. School Organization and Management
4. History of Education

The third and fourth divisions of education are always studied as separate subjects under the above heads. In dealing with Special Methods, also, it is customary in the study of education to treat each subject of the curriculum under its own head in both a professional and an academic way. There is left, therefore, for scientific consideration, the subject of General Method, to a study of which we shall now proceed.

PART II
METHODOLOGY

CHAPTER VIII

GENERAL METHOD

Meaning of Method.—In the last Chapter it was seen that, in relation to the child, education involves a gaining of control over experiences. It has been seen further, that the child gains control of new experience whenever he goes through a process of learning involving the four steps of problem, selecting activity, relating activity, and expression. Finally it has been decided that the teacher in his capacity as an instructor, by presenting children with suitable problems, may in a sense direct their selecting and relating activities and thus exercise a certain control over their learning processes. To the teacher, therefore, method will mean an ability to control the learning process in such a way that the children shall, in their turn, gain an adequate control over the new experience forming the subject-matter of any learning process. Thus a detailed study by student-teachers of the various steps of the learning process, with a view to gaining knowledge and skill relative to directing pupils in their learning, constitutes for such teachers a study of General Method.

SUBDIVISIONS OF METHOD

Subdivisions of Method.—For the student-teacher, the study of general method will involve a detailed investigation of how the child is to gain control of social experiences as outlined above, and how the teacher may bring about the same through instruction.

Tn such an investigation, he must examine in detail the various steps of the educative process to discover:

1. How the knowledge, or social experience, contained in the school curriculum should be presented to the child. This will involve an adequate study of the first step of the learning process—the problem.

2. How the mind, or consciousness, of the child reacts during the learning process upon the presented materials in gaining control of this knowledge. This will embrace a study of the second and third steps of the process—the selecting and relating activities.

3. How the child is to acquire facility in using a new experience, or in applying it to direct his conduct. This involves a particular study of the fourth step of the process—the law of expression.

4. How the teacher may use any outside agencies, as maps, globes, specimens,

experiments, etc., to assist in directing the learning process. This involves a study of various classes of educational instrumentalities.

5. How the principles of general method are to be adapted to the different modes by which the learner may gain new experience, or knowledge. This will involve a study of the different kinds of lessons, or a knowledge of lesson types.

METHOD IMPLIES KNOWLEDGE OF MIND

Before we proceed to such a detailed study of the educative process as a process of teaching, it should be noted that the existence of a general method is possible only provided that the growth of conscious control takes place in the mind of the child in a systematic and orderly manner. All children, for instance, must be supposed to respond in the same general way in the learning process when they are confronted with the same problem. Without this they could not secure from the same lesson the same experiences and the same relative measure of control over these experiences. But if our conscious acts are so uniform that the teacher may expect from all of his pupils like responses and like states of experience under similar stimulations, then a knowledge on the part of the teacher of the orderly modes in which the mind works will be essential to an adequate control of the process of learning. Now a full and systematic account of mind and its activities is set forth in the Science of Psychology. As the Science of Consciousness, or Experience, psychology explains the processes by which all experience is built up, or organized, in consciousness. Thus psychology constitutes a basic science for educational method. It is essential, therefore, that the teacher should have some knowledge of the leading principles of this science. For this reason, frequent reference will be made, in the study of general method, to underlying principles of psychology. The more detailed examination of these principles and of their application to educational method will, however, be postponed to a later part of the text. Each of the four important steps of the learning process will now be treated in order, beginning in the next Chapter with the problem.

CHAPTER IX

THE LESSON PROBLEM

Problem, a Motive.—The foregoing description and examples of the educative process have shown that new knowledge necessarily results whenever the mind faces a difficulty, or need, and adjusts itself thereto. In other words, knowledge is found to possess a practical value and to arise as man faces the difficulties, or problems, with which he is confronted. The basis of conscious activity in any direction is, therefore, a feeling of *need*. If one analyses any of his conscious acts, he will find that the motive is the satisfaction of some desire which he more or less consciously feels. The workman exerts himself at his labour because he feels the need of satisfying his artistic sense or of supplying the necessities of those who are dependent upon him; the teacher prepares the lessons he has to present and puts forth effort to teach them successfully, because he feels the need of educating the pupils committed to his care; the physician observes symptoms closely and consults authorities carefully, because he feels the need of curing his patients; the lawyer masters every detail of the case he is pleading, because he feels the need of protecting the interests of his client. What is true of adults is equally true of children in school. The pupil puts forth effort in school work because he feels that this work is meeting some of his needs.

NATURE OF PROBLEM

Nature of Problem.—It is not to be assumed, however, that the only problem which will prompt the individual to put forth conscious effort must be a purely physical need, such as hunger, thirst, or a distinct desire for the attainment of a definite object, as to avoid danger or to secure financial gain or personal pleasure. Nor is it to be understood that the learner always clearly formulates the problem in his own mind. Indeed, as will be seen more fully later, one very important motive for mastering a presented problem is the instinct of curiosity. As an example of such may be noted a case which came under the observation of the writer, where the curiosity of a small child was aroused through the sight of a mud-turtle crawling along a walk. After a few moments of intense investigation, he cried to those standing by, "Come and see the bug in the basket." Here, evidently, the child's curiosity gave the strange appearance sufficient value to cause him to make it an object of study. Impelled by this feeling, he must have selected ideas from his former experience (bug—crawling thing; basket—incasing thing), which seemed of value in interpreting the unknown presentation. Finally by focusing these upon this strange object, he formed an idea, or mental picture, which gave him a reasonable control over the new vague presentation. Such a motive as curiosity may not imply to the same degree as some others a personal need, nor does it mean that the child consciously says to himself that this new material or activity is satisfying a specific need, but in some vague way he knows that it appeals to him because of its attractiveness in itself or because of its relation to some other attractive object. In brief, it interests him, and thus creates a tendency on the part of an individual to give it his attention. In such situations, therefore, the learner evidently feels to a greater or less degree a necessity, or a practical need, for solving the problem before him.

NEED OF PROBLEM

Knowledge Gained Accidentally.—It is evident, however, that at times knowledge might be gained in the absence of any set problem upon which the learner reacts. For example, a certain person while walking along a road intent upon his own personal matters observed a boy standing near a high fence. On passing further along the street, he glanced through an opening and observed a vineyard within the inclosure. On returning along the street a few minutes later, he saw the same boy standing at a near by corner eating grapes. Hereupon these three ideas at once co-ordinated themselves into a new form of knowledge, signifying stealing-of-fruit. In such a case, the experience has evidently been gained without the presence of a problem to guide the selecting and relating of the ideas entering into the new knowledge. In like manner, a child whose only motive is to fill paper with various coloured crayon may accidentally discover, while engaged on this problem, that red and yellow will combine to make orange, or that yellow and blue will combine to make green. Here also the child gains valuable experience quite spontaneously, that is, without its constituting a motive, or problem, calling for adjustment.

Learning without Motive.—In the light of the above, a question suggests itself in relation to the lesson problem, or motive. Granting that a regular school recitation must contain some valuable problem for which the learning process is to furnish a solution, and granting that the teacher must be fully conscious both of the problem and of its mode of solution, the question might yet be asked whether a problem is to be realized by the child as a felt need at the beginning of the lesson. For example, if the teacher wishes his pupils to learn how to compose the secondary colour purple, might he have them blend in a purely arbitrary way, red and blue, and finally ask them to note the result? Or again, if he wishes the pupils to learn the construction of a paper-box or fire-place, would he not be justified in directing them to make certain folds, to do certain cutting, and to join together the various sections in a certain way, and then asking them to note the result? If such a course is permissible, it would seem that, so far at least as the learner is concerned, he may gain control of valuable experience, or knowledge, without the presence of a problem, or motive, to give the learning process value and direction.

Problem Aids Control.—It is true that in cases like the above, the child may gain the required knowledge. The cause for this is, no doubt, that the physical activity demanded of the pupil constitutes indirectly a motive for attending sufficiently to gain the knowledge. But in many cases no such conditions might exist. It is important, therefore, to have the pupil as far as possible realize at the outset a definite motive for each lesson. The advantage consists in the fact that the motive gives a value to the ideas which enter into the new knowledge, even before they are fully incorporated into a new experience. For example, if in a lesson in geometrical drawing, the teacher, instead of having the child set out with the problem of drawing a pair of parallel lines, merely orders him to follow certain directions, and then requests him to measure the shortest distance between the lines at different points, the child is not likely to grasp the connections of the various steps involved in the construction of the whole problem. This means, however, that the learner has not secured an equal control over the new experience.

Pupils Feel Its Lack.—A further objection to conducting a lesson in such a way that the child may find no motive for the process until the close of the lesson, is the fact that he is himself aware of its lack. In school the child soon discovers that in a lesson he selects and gives attention to various ideas solely in order to gain control over some problem which he may more or less definitely conceive in advance. For this reason, if the teacher attempts, as in the above examples, to fix the child's attention on certain facts without any conception of purpose, the pupil nevertheless usually asks himself the question: "What does the teacher intend me to do with these facts?" Indeed, without at least that motive to hold such disconnected ideas in his mind, it is doubtful whether the pupil would attend to them sufficiently to organize them into a new item of knowledge. When, therefore, the teacher proposes at the outset an attractive problem to solve, he has gone a long way toward stimulating the intellectual activity of the pupil. The setting of problems, the supplying of motives, the giving of aims, the awakening of needs—this constitutes a large part of the business of the teacher.

PUPIL'S MOTIVE

Pupil's Problem versus Teacher's.—But it is important that the problem before the pupil at the beginning of the lesson should really be the pupil's and not the teacher's merely. The teacher should be careful not to impose the problem on the pupils in an arbitrary way, but should try to connect the lesson with an interest that is already active. The teacher's motive in teaching the lesson and the pupil's motive in attending to it are usually quite different. The teacher's problem should, of course, be identical with the real problem of the lesson. Thus in a literature lesson on "Hide and Seek" (*Ontario Third Reader*), the teacher's motive would be to lead the pupil to appreciate the music of the lines, the beauty of the images, and the pathos of the ideas; and in general, to increase the pupil's capacities of constructive imagination and artistic appreciation. The pupil's motive might be to find out how the poet had described a familiar game. In a nature study lesson on "The Rabbit," the teacher's motive would be to lead the pupil to make certain observations and draw certain inferences and thus add something to his facility in observation and inference. The pupil's motive in the same lesson would be to discover something new about a very interesting animal. In general, the teacher's motive will be (1) to give the pupil a certain kind of useful knowledge; (2) to develop and strengthen certain organs; or (3) to add something to his mechanical skill by the forming of habitual reactions. In general, the pupil's motive will be to learn some fact, to satisfy some instinct, or perform some activity that is interesting either in itself or because of its relation to some desired end. That is, the pupil's motive is the satisfaction of an interest or the promotion of a purpose.

Pupil's Motive May Be Indirect.—It is evident from the foregoing that the pupil's motive for applying himself to any lesson may differ from the real lesson problem, or motive. For instance, in mastering the reading of a certain selection, the pupil's chief motive in applying himself to this particular task may be to please and win the approbation of the teacher. The true lesson problem, however, is to enable the learner to give expression to the thoughts and feelings of the author. When the aim, or motive, is thus somewhat disconnected from the lesson problem itself, it becomes an *indirect* motive. While such indirect motives are undoubtedly valuable and must often be used with young children, it is evident that when the pupil's motive is more or less directly associated with the real problem of the lesson, it will form a better centre for the selecting and organizing of the ideas entering into the new experience.

Relation to Pupil's Feeling.—A chief essential in connection with the pupil's motive, or attitude, toward the lesson problem, is that the child should *feel* a value in the problem. That is, his apprehension of the problem should carry with it a desire to secure a complete mastery of the problem from a sense of its intrinsic value. The difference in feeling which a pupil may have toward the worth of a problem would be noticed by comparing the attitude of a class in the study of a military biography or a pioneer adventure taken from Canadian or United States sources respectively. In the case of the former, the feeling of patriotism associated with the lesson problem will give it a value for the pupils entirely absent from the other topic. The extent to which the pupil feels such a value in the lesson topic will in most cases also measure the degree of control he obtains over the new experience.

AWAKENING INTEREST IN PROBLEMS

As will be seen in Chapter XXIX, where our feeling states will be considered more fully, feeling is essentially a personal attitude of mind, and there can be little guarantee that a group of pupils will feel an equal value in the same problem. At times, in fact, even where the pupil understands fairly well the significance of a presented lesson problem, he may feel little personal interest in it. One of the most important questions of method is, therefore, how to awaken in a class the necessary interest in the lesson problem with which they are being presented.

1. **Through Physical Activity.**—It is a characteristic of the young child to enjoy physical activity for the sake of the activity itself. This is true even of his earliest acts, such as stretching, smiling, etc. Although these are merely impulsive movements without conscious purpose, the child soon forms ideas of different acts, and readily associates these with other ideas. Thus he takes a delight in the mere functioning of muscles, hands, voice, etc., in expressive movements. As he develops, however, on account of the close association, during his early years, between thought and movement, the child is much interested in any knowledge which may

be presented to him in direct association with motor activity. This fact is especially noticeable in that the efforts of a child to learn a strange object consist largely in endeavouring to discover what he can do with it. He throws, rolls, strikes, strives *to* open it, and in various other ways makes it a means of physical expression. Whenever, especially, he can discover the use of an object, as to cut with knife or scissors, to pound with a hammer, to dip with a ladle, or to sweep with a broom, this social significance of the object gives him full satisfaction, and little attention is paid to other qualities. For these reasons the teacher will find it advantageous, whenever possible, to associate a lesson problem directly with some form of physical action. In primary number work, for example, instead of presenting the child with mere numbers and symbols, the teacher may provide him with objects, in handling which he may associate the number facts with certain acts of grouping objects. It is in this way that a child should approach such problems as:

How many fours are there in twelve?
How many feet in a yard?
How many quarts in a peck? etc.

The teaching of fractions by means of scissors and cardboard; the teaching of board measure by having boards actually measured; the teaching of primary geography by means of the sand-table; the teaching of nature study by excursions to fields and woods; these are all easy because we are working in harmony with the child's natural tendency to be physically active. The more closely the lesson problem adjusts itself to these tendencies, the greater will be the pupil's activity and hence the more rapid his progress.

2. Through Constructive Instinct.—The child's delight in motor expression is closely associated with his instinctive tendency to construct. When, therefore, new knowledge can be presented to the child in and through constructive exercises, he is more likely to feel its value. Thus it is possible, by means of such occupations as paper folding or stick-laying, to provide interesting problems for teaching number and geometric forms. In folding the check-board, for example, the child will master necessary problems relating to the numbers, 2, 4, 8, and 16. In learning colour, it is more interesting for the child to study different colours through painting leaves, flowers, and fruits, than to learn them through mere sense impressions, or even through comparing coloured objects, as in the Montessori chromatic exercises. A study of the various kindergarten games and occupations would give an abundance of examples illustrative of the possibility of presenting knowledge in direct association with various types of constructive work.

A. Activity must be Directly Connected with Problem.—It may be noted, however, that certain dangers associate themselves with these methods. One danger consists in the fact that, if care is not taken, the physical activity may not really involve the knowledge to be conveyed, but may be only very indirectly associated with it. Such a danger might occur in the use of the Montessori colour tablets for teaching tints and shades. In handling those, kindergarten children show a strong inclination to build flat forms with the tablets. Now unless these building exercises involve the distinguishing of the various tints and shades, the constructive activity will be likely to divert the attention of the pupil away from the colour problem which the tablets are supposed to set for the pupils.

B. Not too much Emphasis on Manual Skill.—Again, in expressive exercises intended merely to impart new knowledge, it may happen that the teacher will lay too much stress on perfect form of expression. In these exercises, however, the purpose should be rather to enable the child to realize the ideas in his expressive actions. When, for example, a child, in learning such geographical forms as island, gulf, mountain, etc., uses sand, clay, or plasticine as a medium of expression, too much striving after accuracy of form in minor details may tend to draw the pupil's attention from the broader elements of knowledge to be mastered. In other words, it is the gaining of certain ideas, or knowledge, and not technical perfection, that is being aimed at in such expressive movements.

3. Instinct of Curiosity as Motive.—The value of the instinct of curiosity in setting a problem for the young child has been already referred to. From what was there seen, it is evident that to the extent to which the teacher awakens wonder and curiosity in his presentation of a lesson problem, the child will be ready to enter upon the further steps of the learning process. For example, by inserting two forks and a large needle into a cork, as illustrated in the accompanying Figure, and then apparently balancing the whole on a small hard surface, we may awaken a deep interest in the problem of gravity. In the same manner, by calling the pupils' attention to the drops on the outside of a glass pitcher filled with water, we may have their curiosity aroused for the study of condensation. So also the presentation of a picture may arouse curiosity in places or people.

4. Ownership as Motive.—The natural pleasure which children take in collection and ownership may often be associated with presented problems in a way to cause them to take a deeper interest in the knowledge to be acquired. For example, in presenting a lesson on the countries of Europe, the collection of coins or stamps representative of the different countries will add greatly to the interest, compared with a mere outline study of the political divisions from a map. A more detailed examination of the instincts and tendencies of the child and their relation to the educative process will, however, be found in Chapter XXI.

5. Acquired Interest as Motive.—Finally, in the case of individual pupils, a knowledge of their particular, or special, interests is often a means of awakening in them a feeling of value for various types of school work. As an example, there might be cited the experience of a teacher who had in his school a pupil whom it seemed impossible to interest in reading. Thereupon the teacher made it his object to learn what were this pupil's chief interests outside the school. Using these as a basis for the selecting of simple reading matter for the boy, he was soon able to create in him an interest in reading for its own sake. The result was that in a short time this pupil was rendered reasonably efficient in what had previously seemed to him an uninteresting and impossible task.

6. Use of Knowledge as Motive.—In the preceding cases, interest in the problem is made to rest primarily upon some native instinct, or tendency. It is to be noted, however, that as the child advances in the acquisition of knowledge, or experience, there develops in him also a desire for mental activity. In other words, the normal child takes a delight in the use of any knowledge over which he possesses adequate control. It is to be noted further, that the child masters the new problem by bringing to bear upon it suitable ideas selected out of his previously acquired experiences. It is evident, therefore, that, when a lesson problem is presented to the child in such a way that he sees a connection between it and his present knowledge and feels, further, that the problem may be mastered by a use of knowledge over which he has complete mastery, he will take a deeper interest in the learning process. When, on the other hand, he has imperfect control over the old knowledge from which the interpreting ideas are selected, his interest in the problem itself will be greatly reduced. Owing to this fact, the teacher may adapt his lesson problems, or motives, to the stage of development of the pupils. In the case of young children, since they have little knowledge, but possess a number of instinctive tendencies, the lesson problem should be such as may be associated with their instinctive tendencies. Since, however, the expressing of these tendencies necessarily brings to the child ideas, or increases his knowledge, the pupil will in time desire to use his growing knowledge for its own sake. Here the child becomes able to grasp a problem consciously, or in idea, and, so far as it appeals to his past experience, will desire to work for its solution. Thus any problem which is recognized as having a vital connection with his own experience constitutes for the child a strong motive. For older pupils, therefore, the lesson problem which constitutes the strongest motive is the one that is consciously recognized and felt to have some direct connection with their present knowledge.

KNOWLEDGE OF PROBLEM

Relation to Pupil's Knowledge.—Since the conscious apprehension of the problem by the pupil in its relation to his present knowledge constitutes the best motive for the learning process, a question arises how this problem is to be grasped by the pupil. First, it is evident that the problem is not a state of knowledge, or a complete experience. If such were the case, there would be nothing for him to learn. It is this partial ignorance that causes a problem to exist for the learner as a felt need, or motive. On the other hand it is not a state of complete ignorance, otherwise the learner could not call up any related ideas for its solution. When, for example, the child, after learning the various physical features, the climate, and people of Ontario, is presented with the problem of learning the chief industries, he is able by his former knowledge to realize the existence of these industries sufficiently to feel the need of a fuller realization. In the same way the student who has traced the events of Canadian History up to the year 1791, is able to know the Constitutional Act as a problem for study, that is, he is able to experience the existence of such a problem and to that extent is able to know it. His mental state is equally a state of ignorance, in that he has not realized in his own consciousness all the facts relative to the Act. In the orderly study of any school subject, therefore, the mastery of the previous lesson or lessons will in turn suggest problems for further lessons. It is this further development of new problems out of present knowledge that demands an orderly sequence of topics in the different school subjects, a fact that should be fully realized by the teacher.

Recognition of Problem: A. Prevents Digressions.—An adequate recognition of the lesson problem by the pupil in the light of his own experience is useful in preventing the introduction of irrelevant material into the lesson. Young children are particularly prone (and, under certain circumstances, older students also) to drag into the lessons interesting side issues that have been suggested by some phase of the work. As a rule, it is advisable to follow closely the straight and narrow road that leads to the goal of the lesson and not to permit digressions into attractive by-paths. If a pupil attempts to introduce irrelevant matter, he should be asked what the problem of the lesson is and whether what he is speaking of will be of any value in attaining that end. The necessity of this will, however, be seen more fully in our consideration of the next division of the learning process.

B. Organizes the Lesson Facts.—The adequate recognition of the lesson problem is valuable in helping the pupil to organize his knowledge. If you take a friend for a walk along the streets of a strange city engaging him in interesting conversation by the way, and if, when you have reached a distant point, you tell him that he must find his way back alone, he will probably be unable to do so without assistance. But if you tell him at the outset what you are going to do, he will note carefully the streets traversed, the corners turned, the directions taken, and will likely find his way back easily. This is because he had a clearly defined problem before him. The conditions are much the same in a lesson. When the pupil starts out with no definite problem and is led along blindly to some unknown goal, he will be unable to retrace his route; that is, he will be unable to reproduce the matter over which he has been taken. But with a clearly defined problem he will be able to note the order of the steps of the lesson, their relation to one another and to the problem, and when the lesson is over he will be able to go over the same course again. The facts of the lesson will have become organized in his mind.

HOW TO SET LESSON PROBLEM

Precautions.—If the teacher expects his pupils to become interested in a problem by immediately recognizing a connection between it and their previous knowledge, he must avoid placing the problem before them in a form in which they cannot readily apprehend this connection. The teacher who announced at the beginning of the grammar lesson, "To-day we are going to learn about Mood in verbs" started the problem in a form that was meaningless to the class. The simplest method in such a lesson would be to draw attention to examples in sentences of verbs showing this change and then say to the class, "Let us discover why these verbs are changed." Similarly, to propose as the problem of the history lesson "the development of parliamentary government during the Stuart period" would be to use terms too difficult for the class to interpret. It would be better to say: "We are going to find out how the Stuart kings were forced by Parliament to give up control of certain things." Instead of saying, "We shall study in this lesson the municipal government of Ontario," it would be much better to proceed in some such way as the following: "A few days ago your father paid his taxes for the year. Now we are going to learn by whom, and for what purposes, these taxes are spent." Similarly, "Let us find out all we can about the cat," would be inferior to, "Of what use to the cat are his sharp claws, padded feet, and rough tongue?"

On the other hand, it is evident that, in attempting to present the problem in a form in which the pupils may recognize its connection with their previous experiences, care must be taken not to tell outright the whole point of the lesson. In a lesson on the adverb, for instance, it would not do to say: "You have learned how adjectives modify, or change the meaning of, nouns. To-day we shall study words that modify verbs." A more satisfactory way of proceeding in such a lesson would be to have on the black-board two sets of sentences exactly alike except that the second would contain adverbs and the first would not. Then ask: "What words are in the second group of sentences that are not in the first? Let us examine the use of these words." In the same way, to state the problem of an arithmetic lesson as the discovery of "how to add fractions by changing them to equivalent fractions having the same denominator" is open to the objection of telling too much. In this case a better method would be to present a definite problem requiring the use of addition of fractions. The pupil will see that he has not the necessary arithmetical knowledge to solve the problem and will then be in the proper mental attitude for the lesson.

EXAMPLES OF MOTIVATION

A few additional examples, drawn from different school subjects, are here added to illustrate further what is meant by setting a problem as a need, or motive.

A. History.—The members of a Form IV class were about to take up the study of the influence of John Wilkes upon parliamentary affairs during the reign of George III. As most of the pupils had visited the Canadian Parliament Buildings and had watched from the galleries the proceedings of the House of Commons, the teacher took this as the point of departure for the lesson. First, he obtained from the class the facts that the members of the Commons are elected by the different constituencies of the Dominion and that nobody has any power to interfere with the people's right to elect whomsoever they wish to represent them. The same conditions exist to-day in England, but this has not always been the case there. There was a time when the people's choice of a representative was sometimes set aside. The teacher then inquired regarding the men who sit in the gallery just above the Speaker's chair. These are the parliamentary reporters for the important daily newspapers throughout the Dominion. They send telegraphic despatches regarding the debates in the House to their respective newspapers. These despatches are published the following day, and the people of the country are thus enabled to know what is going on in Parliament. Nobody has any right to prevent these newspapers from publishing what they wish regarding the proceedings, provided, of course, the reports are not untruthful. These conditions prevail also in England now, but have not always done so.

The work of the lesson was to see how these two conditions, freedom of elections and liberty of the press, have been brought about. The pupils were thus placed in a receptive attitude to hear the story of John Wilkes.

B. Arithmetic.—A Form IV class had been studying decimals and knew how to read and write, add and subtract them. The teacher suggested a situation requiring the use of multiplication, and the pupils found themselves without the necessary means to meet the situation. For instance, "Mary's mother sent her to buy 2.25 lb. tea which cost $.375 per lb. What would she have to pay for it?" Or, "Mr. Brown has a field containing 8.72 acres. Last year it yielded 21.375 bushels of wheat to the acre. Wheat was worth 97.5 cents per bushel. What was the crop from the field worth?" The pupils saw that, in order to solve these questions, they must know how to multiply decimals. Multiplication of decimals became the problem of the lesson, the goal to be attained.

C. Grammar.—The teacher wished to show the meaning of *case* as an inflection of nouns and pronouns. He had written on the black-board such sentences as:

> I dropped my book when John pushed me.
> When the man passed, he had his dog with him.

He asked the pupils what words in these sentences refer to the same person, and obtained the answer that *I, my,* and *me* all refer to one person, and *he, his,* and *him* to another. Then, he proposed the problem, "Let us find out why we have three different forms of a word all meaning the same person." The problem was adapted to animate the curiosity of the pupils and call into activity their capacity for perceiving relationships.

D. Literature.—The teacher was about to present the poem, "Hide and Seek," to a Form III class. He said, "You have all played 'hide and seek.' How do you play it? You will find on page 50 of your *Ontario Third Reader* a beautiful poem describing a game of 'hide and seek' that is rather a sad one. Let us see how the poet has described this game." The pupils were at once interested in what the poet had to say about what was to them a very familiar diversion, and, while the lesson was in progress, their capacity for sympathy and for artistic appreciation was appealed to.

E. Geography.—A Form III class was to study some of the more important commercial centres of Canada. Speaking of Montreal, the teacher proposed the problem, "Do you think we can find out why a city of half a million people has grown up at this particular point?" The pupils' instinct of curiosity was here appealed to and their capacity for perceiving relationships was challenged.

F. Composition.—The teacher wished to take up the writing of letters of application with a class of Form IV pupils. He wrote on the black-board an advertisement copied from a recent newspaper, for example, "Wanted—A boy about fifteen to assist in office; must be a good writer and accurate in figures; apply by letter to Martin & Kelly, 8 Central Chambers, City." Then he said, "Some day in the near future many of you will be called upon to answer such an advertisement as this. Now what should a letter of application in reply to this contain?" The class at once proceeded, with the teacher's assistance, to work out a satisfactory letter. Here, a purpose for the future was the principal need promoted.

G. Nature Study.—The pupils of a Form II class had been making observations regarding a pet rabbit that one of their number had brought to school. After reporting these observations, the pupils were asked, "What good do you think these long ears, large eyes, strong hind legs, split upper lip, etc., are to the rabbit?" Here the problem set was related to the children's instinctive interest in a living animal, appealed to the instinct of curiosity, and challenged their capacity to draw inferences.

CHAPTER X

LEARNING AS A SELECTING ACTIVITY OR PROCESS OF ANALYSIS

Knowledge Obtained Through Use of Ideas.—As already noted, the presented problem of a lesson is neither a state of complete knowledge nor a state of complete ignorance. On the other hand, its function is to provide a starting-point and guide for the calling up of a number of suitable ideas which the pupil may later relate into a single experience, constituting the new knowledge. Take, for example, a person without a knowledge of fractions, who approaches for the first time the problem of sharing as found in such a question as:

Divide $15 between John and William, giving John $3 as often as William gets $2.

In gaining control of this situation, the pupil must select the ideas $3 and $2, the knowledge that $3 and $2 = $5, and the further knowledge that $15 contains $5 three times. These various ideas will constitute data for organizing the new experience of $9 for John and $6 for William. In the same manner, when the student in grammar is first presented with the problem of interpreting the grammatical value of the word *driving* in the sentence, "The boy *driving* the horse is very noisy," he is compelled to apply to its interpretation the ideas noun, adjectival relation, and adjective, and also the ideas object, objective relation, and verb. In this way the child secures the mental elements which he may organize into the new experience, or knowledge (participle), and thus gain control of the presented word.

Interpreting Ideas Already Known.—It is to be noticed at the outset that all ideas selected to aid in the solution of the lesson problem have their origin in certain past experiences which have a bearing on the subject in hand. When presented with a strange object (guava), a person fixes his attention upon it, and thereupon is able, through his former sensation experiences, to interpret it as an unknown thing. He then begins to select, out of his experiences of former objects, ideas that bear upon the thing before him. By focusing thereon certain ideas with which he is perfectly familiar, as rind, flesh, seed, etc., he interprets the strange thing as a kind of fruit. In the same way, when the student is first presented in school with an example of the infinitive, he brings to bear upon the vague presentation various ideas already contained within his experience through his previous study of the noun and the verb. To the extent also to which he possesses and is able to recall these necessary old ideas, will he be able to adjust himself to the new and unfamiliar presented example (infinitive). It is evident, therefore, that a new presentation can have a meaning for us only as it is related to something in our past experience.

Further Examples.—The mind invariably tries to interpret new presentations in terms of old ideas. A newspaper account of a railway wreck will be intelligible to us only through the revival and reconstruction of those past experiences that are similar to the elements described in the account. The grief, disappointment, or excitement of another will be appreciated only as we have experienced similar feelings in the past. New ideas are interpreted by means of related old ideas; new feelings and acts are dependent upon and made possible by related old feelings and acts. Moreover, the meaning assigned to common objects varies with different persons and even with the same person under different circumstances. A forest would be regarded by the savage as a place to hide from the attacks of his enemies; by the hunter as a place to secure game; by the woodcutter as affording firewood; by the lumberman as yielding logs for lumber; by the naturalist as offering opportunity for observing insects and animals; by the artist as a place presenting beautiful combinations of colours. This ability of the mind to retain and use its former knowledge in meeting and interpreting new experiences is known in psychology as *apperception*. A more detailed study of apperception as a mental process will be made in Chapter XXVI.

THE SELECTING PROCESS

Learner's Mind Active.—A further principle of method to be deduced from the foregoing is, that the process of bringing ideas out of former experiences to bear upon a presented problem must take place within the mind of the learner himself. The new knowledge being an experience organized from elements selected out of former experiences, it follows that the learner will possess the new knowledge only in so far as he has himself gone through the process of selecting the necessary interpreting ideas out of his own former knowledge and finally organizing them into new knowledge. This need for the pupil to direct mental effort, or attention, upon the problem in order to bring upon it, out of his former knowledge, the ideas relative to the solution of the question before him, is one of the most important laws of method. From the standpoint of the teacher, this law demands that he so direct the process of learning that the pupil will clearly call up in consciousness the selected interpreting ideas as portions of his old knowledge, and further feel a connection between these and the new problem before him.

Learner's Experience Analysed.—The second stage of the learning process is found to involve also a breaking up of former experience. This appears in the fact that the various ideas which are necessary to interpret the new problem are to be selected out of larger complexes of past experience. For example, in a lesson whose problem is to account for the lack of rainfall in the Sahara desert, the pupil may have a complex of experiences regarding the position of the desert. Out of this mass of experience he must, however, select the one feature—its position in relation to the equator. In the same way, he may have a whole body of experience regarding the winds of Africa. This body must, however, be analysed, and the attention fixed upon the North-east trade-wind. Again, he may know many things about these winds, but here he selects out the single item of their coming from a land source. Again, from the complex of old knowledge which he possesses regarding the land area from which the wind blows, he must analyse out its temperature, and compare it with that of the areas toward which the wind is blowing. Thus it will be seen that, step by step, the special items of old knowledge to be used in the apperceptive process are selected out of larger masses of experience. For this reason this phase of the learning process is frequently designated as a process of analysis.

Problem as Object of Analysis.—Although the second step of the learning process has been described as a selecting of elements from past experience, it might be supposed that the various elements which the mind has been said to select from its former experiences to interpret the new problem, come in a sense from the presentation itself. Thus it is often said, in describing the present step in the learning process, that the presentation embodies a certain aggregate of experience, which the learner can master by analysing it into its component parts and recombining the analysed parts into a better known whole.

Analysis Depends upon Selection.—It is not in the above sense, however, that the term analysis is to be applied in the learning process. It is not true, for instance, when a person is presented with a strange object, say an *ornithorhynchus*, and realizes it in only a vague way, that any mere analysis of the object will discover for him the various characteristics which are to synthesize into a knowledge of the animal. This would imply that in analysis the mind merely breaks up a vaguely known whole in order to make of it a definitely known whole. But the learner could not discover the characteristics of such an object unless the mind attended to it with certain elements of its former experiences. Unless, for instance, the person already knew certain characteristics of both birds and animals, he could not interpret the ornithorhynchus as a bird-beaked animal. In the case of the child and the mud-turtle, also, there could have been no analysis of the problem in the way referred to, had the child not had the ideas, bug and basket, as elements of former experience. These characteristics, therefore, which enter into a definite knowledge of the object, do not come out of the object by a mere mechanical process of analysis, but are rather read into the object by the apperceptive process. That is, the learner does not get his new experience directly out of the presented materials, but builds up his new experience out of elements of his former knowledge. In other words, the learner sees in the new object, or problem, only such characteristics as his former knowledge and interest enable him to see. Thus while the learner may be said from one standpoint to analyse the new problem, this is possible only because he is able to break up, or analyse, his former experience and read certain of its elements into the new presentation. To say that the mind analyses the unknown object, or topic, in any other sense, would be to confound mental interpretation with physical analysis.

A Further Example.—The following example will further show that the learner can analyse a presented problem only to the extent that he is able to put characteristics into it by this process of analysing or selecting from his past experience. Consider how a young child gains his knowledge of a triangle. At first his control of certain sensations enables him to read into it two ideas, three-sidedness and three-angledness, and only these factors, therefore, organize themselves into his experience triangle. Nor would any amount of mere attention enable him at this stage to discover another important quality in the thing triangle. Later, however, through the growth of his geometric experience, he may be able to read another quality into a triangle, namely two-right-angledness. This new quality will then, and only then, be organized with his former knowledge into a more complete knowledge of a triangle. Here again it is seen that analysis as a learning process is really reading into a new presentation something which the mind already possesses as an element of former experience, and not gaining something at first hand out of the presented problem.

Problem Directs Selection.—It will be well to note here also that the selecting of the interpreting ideas is usually controlled by the problem with which the mind is engaged. This is indicated from the various ways in which the same object may be interpreted as the mind is confronted with different problems. The round stone, for instance, when one wishes to crack the filbert, is viewed as a hammer; when he wishes to place his paper on the ground, it becomes a weight; when he is threatened by the strange dog, it becomes a weapon of defence. In like manner the sign *x* suggests an unknown quantity in relation to the algebraic problem; in relation to phonics it is a double sound; in relation to numeration, the number ten. It is evident that in all these cases, what determines the meaning given to the presented object is the *need,* or *problem,* that is at the moment predominant. In the same way, any lesson problem, in so far as it is felt to be of value, forms a starting-point for calling up other ideas, and therefore starts in the learner's mind a flow of ideas which is likely to furnish the solution. Moreover, the mind has the power to measure the suitability of various ideas and select or reject them as they are felt to stand related to the problem in hand. For example, when a pupil is engaged in a study of the grammatical value of the word *driving* in the sentence, "The boy driving the horse is very noisy," it is quite possible that he may think of the horse at his own home, or the shouting of his father's hired man, or even perhaps the form of the word *driving,* if he has just been viewing it in a writing lesson. The mind is able, however, to reject these irrelevant ideas, and select only those that seem to adjust themselves to the problem in hand. The cause of this lies in the fact that the problem is at the outset at least partly understood by the learner, which fact enables him to determine whether the ideas coming forward in consciousness are related in any way to this partially known topic. Thus in the example cited, the learner knows the problem sufficiently to realize that it is a question of grammatical function, and is able, therefore, to feel the value, or suitability, of any knowledge which may be applied to it, even before he is fully aware of its ultimate relation thereto.

LAW OF PREPARATION

Control of Old Knowledge Necessary.—But notwithstanding the direction given the apperceptive process through the aim, or problem, it is evident that if the pupil is to select from his former experiences the particular elements which bear upon the problem in hand, he must have a ready and intelligent control over such former knowledge. It is too evident, however, that pupils frequently do not possess sufficient control over the old knowledge which will bear upon a presented problem. In endeavouring, for example, to grasp the relation of the exterior angle to the two interior and opposite angles, the pupil may fail because he has not a clear knowledge of the equality of angles in connection with parallel lines. For this reason teachers will often find it necessary (before bringing old knowledge to bear upon a new problem) to review the old knowledge, or experience, to be used during the apperceptive process. Thus a lesson on the participle may begin with a review of the pupils' knowledge of verbs and adjectives, a lesson on the making of the colours orange and green for painting a pumpkin with its green stem may begin with a recognition of the standard colours, red, yellow, and blue, and the writing of a capital letter with a review of certain movements.

Preparation Recalls Interpreting Ideas.—It must be noted that this review of former knowledge always implies, either that the pupil is likely to have forgotten at least partially this former knowledge, or that without such review he is not likely to recall and apply it readily when the new problem is placed before him. For this reason the teacher is usually warned that his lesson should always begin with a review of such of the pupil's old knowledge as is to be used in mastering the new experiences.

Value of Preparation

A. Aids the Understanding.—The main advantage of this preparatory work is that it brings into clear consciousness that group of ideas and feelings best suited to give meaning to the new presentation. Without it, the pupil may not understand, or only partially understand, or entirely misunderstand the lesson. (1) He may not understand the new matter at all because he does not bring any related facts from his past experience to bear upon it. Multiplication of decimals would in all probability be a merely mechanical process if the significance of decimals and the operation of multiplying fractions were not brought to bear upon it, the pupil not understanding it at all as a rational process. (2) He may only partially understand the new matter because he does not see clearly the relation between his old ideas and the new facts, or because he does not bring to the new facts a sufficient equipment of old ideas to make them meaningful. The adverbial objective would be imperfectly understood if it were not shown that its functions are exactly parallel with those of the adverb. The pupil would have only a partial understanding of it. (3) He may entirely misunderstand the new facts because he uses wrong old experiences to give them meaning. Such was evidently the difficulty in the case of the young pupil who, after a lesson on the equator, described it as a menagerie lion running around the earth. Many of the absurd answers that a pupil gives are due to his failure to use the correct old ideas to interpret the new facts. He has misunderstood because his mind was not prepared by making the proper apperceiving ideas explicit.

B. Saves Time.—There is the further advantage of economy of time, when an adequate preparation of the mind has been made. When the appropriate ideas are definitely in the forefront of consciousness, they seize upon kindred impressions as soon as these are presented and give them meaning. On the other hand, when sufficient preparation has not been made, time must be taken during the presentation of the new problem to go back in search of those experiences necessary to make it meaningful. Frequent interruptions and consequent waste of time will be inevitable. Time will be saved by having the apperceiving ideas ready and active.

C. Provides for Review.—One of the most important values of the preparatory step is the opportunity given for the review of old ideas. These have to be revived, worked over, and reconstructed, and in consequence they become the permanent possessions of the mind. The pupil's knowledge of the functions of the adverb is reviewed when he learns the adverb phrase and adverb clause, and is still further illuminated when he comes to study the adverbial objective. Further, the apperceiving ideas become more interesting to the pupil, when he finds that he can use them in the conquest of new fields. He has a consciousness of power, which in itself is a source of satisfaction and pleasure.

Precautions regarding Preparation

Must not be too Long.—Two precautions seem advisable in the preparatory step. The first is that too long a time should not be spent over it. There is sometimes a tendency to go back too far and drag forward ideas that are only remotely connected with the new ideas to be presented. Under such conditions much irrelevant material is likely to be introduced, and often a train of associations out of harmony with the meaning and spirit of the lesson is started. This is especially dangerous in lessons in literature and history. Only those experiences should be revived which are necessary to a clear apprehension of the ideas or a full appreciation of the emotions to be presented in the new lesson.

Must Recall Vital Ideas.—The most active, vivid, and powerful ideas in the pupil's mind are those which are closely connected with his life. This suggests the second precaution, namely, the use wherever possible of the ideas associated with his surroundings, his games, his occupations. When this is done, not only will the new knowledge have a much greater interest attached to it but it will also be much more vividly apprehended. This will be referred to further in connection with the use of illustrations in teaching.

Necessity of Preparation

Teachers, however, are not always agreed as to the amount of time or emphasis to be given to this preparatory step. If the teacher can assure himself that a lesson is following in easy sequence upon something with which the children are undoubtedly familiar, he may, many argue, safely omit such preparatory work. Indeed it is evident that after leaving school the child will have no personal monitor to call up beforehand the ideas that he must apply in solving the problems continually presenting themselves in practical life. On the other hand, however, it is to be remembered that the young child is, at the best, feeling his way in the process of adjusting himself to new experiences. For this reason, the first work for the teacher in any lesson is to ascertain whether the pupils are in a proper attitude for the new knowledge, and, so far as is necessary, prepare their minds through the recall of such knowledge as is related to the new experiences to be presented. Although, therefore, the step of preparation is not an essential part of the learning process, since it constitutes for the pupil merely a review of knowledge acquired through previous learning processes, it may be accepted as a step in the teacher's method of controlling the learning process.

Examples of Preparation

The following additional examples as to the mode and form of the step of preparation may be considered by the student-teacher:

In a lesson in phonic reading in a primary class, the preparation should consist of a review of those sounds and those words which the pupil already knows that are to be used in the new lesson. In a nature study lesson on "The Rabbit," in a Form II class, the preparation should include a recall of any observations the pupils may have made regarding the wild rabbit. They may have observed its timidity, its manner of running, what it feeds upon, where it makes its home, its colour during the winter and during the summer, the kind of tracks it makes in the snow, etc. All these facts will be useful in interpreting the new observations and in assisting the pupils to make new inferences. In a lesson in a Form III class on "Ottawa as a Commercial Centre," the preparation consists of a recall of the pupil's knowledge regarding the position of the city; the adjacent rivers, the Ottawa, Gatineau, Rideau, Lièvre, Madawaska; the waterfalls of the Rideau and Chaudière; the forests to the north and west, with their immense supplies of pine, spruce, and hemlock; and the fact that it is the Dominion capital. All these facts are necessary in inferring the causes of the importance of Ottawa. In a literature lesson in a Form III class on *The Charge of the Light Brigade,* the preparation would involve a recall of some deed of personal heroism with which the pupils are familiar, such as that of John Maynard, Grace Darling, or any similar one nearer home. Recall how such a deed is admired and praised, and the memory of the doer is cherished and revered. Then the teacher should tell the story of Balaklava with all the dramatic intensity he is master of, in order that the pupils may be in a proper mood to approach the study of the poem. In a grammar lesson on "The Adverbial Objective" the preparation should consist of a review of the functions of the adverb as modifying a verb, an adjective, and sometimes another adverb. Upon this knowledge alone can a rational idea of the adverbial objective be built. In an arithmetic lesson on "Multiplication of Decimals," in a Form IV class, the preparation should involve a review of the meaning of decimals, of the interconversion of decimals and fractions (for example, .05 = 5 hundredths; 27 ten-thousandths = .0027, etc.); and of the multiplication of fractions. Unless the pupil can do these operations, it is obviously impossible to make his knowledge of multiplication of decimals anything more than a merely mechanical process.

PREPARATION MERELY AIDS SELECTION

Before closing our consideration of preparation as a stage of method, it will be well again to call attention to the fact that this is not one of the four recognized stages of the learning process, but rather a subsidiary feature of the second, or apperceptive stage. In other words, actual advance is made by the pupil toward the control of a new experience, not through a review of former experience, but by an active relating of elements selected from past experience to the interpretation of the new problem.

CHAPTER XI

LEARNING AS A RELATING ACTIVITY
OR
PROCESS OF SYNTHESIS

Learning a Unifying Process.—It has been seen that the learner, in gaining control of new knowledge, must organize into the new experience elements selected from former experiences. For instance, when a person gains a knowledge of a new fruit (guava), he not only brings forward in consciousness from his former knowledge the ideas—rind, flesh, seed, etc.,—to interpret the strange object, but also associates these into a single experience, a new fruit. So long also as the person referred to in an earlier chapter retained in his consciousness as distinct factors three experiences—seeing a boy at the fence, seeing the vineyard, and finally, seeing the boy eating grapes—these would not, as three such distinct experiences, constitute a knowledge of grape-stealing. On the other hand, as soon as these are combined, or associated by a relating act of thought, the different factors are organized into a new idea symbolized by the expression, *grape-stealing*.

Examples From School-room Procedure.—A similar relating process is involved when the learner faces a definite school problem. When, for instance, the pupil gains a knowledge of the sign ÷, he must not only bring forward in consciousness from his former knowledge distinct ideas of a line, of two dots, and of a certain mathematical process, but must also associate these into a new idea, division-sign. So also a person may know that air takes up more moisture as it becomes warmer, that the north-east trade-winds blow over the Sahara from land areas, and that the Sahara is situated just north of the equator. But the mind must unify these into a single experience in order to gain a knowledge of the condition of the rainfall in that quarter.

NATURE OF SYNTHESIS

Deals with Former Experiences.—This mental organizing, or unifying, of the elements of past experiences to secure control of the new experience, is usually spoken of as a process of synthesis. The term synthesis, however, must be used with the same care as was noted in regard to the term analysis. Synthesis does not mean that totally *new* elements are being unified, but merely that whatever selected elements of old knowledge the mind is able to read into a presented problem, are built, or organized, into a new system; and constitute, for the time being, one's knowledge and control of that problem. This is well exemplified by noting the growth of a person's knowledge of any object or topic. Thus, so long as the child is able to apperceive only the three sides and three angles of a triangle, his idea of triangle includes a synthesis of these. When later, through the building up of his geometric knowledge, he is able to apperceive that the interior angles equal two right angles, his knowledge of a triangle expands through the synthesis of this with the former knowledge.

All Knowledge a Synthesis.—The fact that all knowledge is an organization from earlier experiences becomes evident by looking at the process from the other direction. The adult who has complete knowledge of an orange has it as a single experience. This experience is found, however, to represent a co-ordination of other experiences, as touch, taste, colour, etc. Moreover, each of these separate characteristics is an association of simpler experiences. Experiencing the touch of the orange, for instance, is itself a complex made up of certain muscular, touch, and temperature sensations. From this it is evident that the knowledge of an orange, although a unity of experience in adult life, is really a complex, or synthesis, made up of a large number of different elements.

What is true of our idea of an orange is true of every other idea. Whether it be the understanding of a plant, an animal, a city, a picture, a poem, an historical event, an arithmetical problem, or a scientific experiment, the process is always the same. The apperceptive process of interpreting the new by selecting and relating elements of former experience, or the process of analysis-synthesis, is universal in learning. Expressed in another form, what is at first indistinct and indefinite becomes clear and defined through attention selecting, for the interpretation of the new presentation, suitable old ideas and setting up relationships among them. Analysis, or selection, is incomplete without an accompanying unification, or synthesis; synthesis, or organization, is impossible without analysis, or selection. It is on account of the mind's ability to unify a number of mental factors into a single experience, that the process of unification, or synthesis, is said to imply economy within our experiences. This fact will become even more evident, however, when later we study such mental processes as sense perception and conception.

INTERACTION OF PROCESSES

It is to be noted, however, that the selecting and the relating of the different interpreting ideas during the learning process are not necessarily separate and distinct parts of the lesson. In other words, the mind does not first select out of its former knowledge a whole mass of disconnected elements, and then later build them up into a new organic experience. There is, rather, in almost every case, a continual interplay between the selecting and relating activity, or between analysis and synthesis, throughout the whole learning process. As soon, for instance, as a certain feature, or characteristic, is noted, this naturally relates itself to the central problem. When later, another characteristic is noted, this may relate itself at once both with the topic and with the formerly observed characteristic into a more complete knowledge of the object. Thus during a lesson we find a gradual growth of knowledge similar to that illustrated in the case of the scholar's knowledge of the triangle, involving a continual interplay of analysis and synthesis, or of selecting and relating different groups of ideas relative to the topic. This would he illustrated by noting a pupil's study of the cat. The child may first note that the cat catches and eats rats and mice, and picks meat from bones. These facts will at once relate themselves into a certain measure of knowledge regarding the food of the animal. Later he may note that the cat has sharp claws, padded feet, long pointed canines, and a rough tongue; these facts being also related as knowledge concerning the mouth and feet of the animal. In addition to this, however, the latter facts will further relate themselves to the former as cases of adaptation, when the child notes that the teeth and tongue are suited to tearing food and cleaning it from the bones, and that its claws and padded feet are suited to surprising and seizing its living prey.

Example from Study of Conjunctive Pronoun.—This continuous selecting and relating throughout a process of learning is also well illustrated in the pupil's process of learning the *conjunctive pronoun*. By bringing his old knowledge to bear on such a sentence as "The men *who* brought it returned at once"; the pupil may be asked first to apperceive the subordinate clause, *who brought it*. This will not likely be connected by the pupil at first with the problem of the value of *who*. From this, however, he passes to a consideration of the value of the clause and its relation. Hereupon, these various ideas at once co-ordinate themselves into the larger idea that *who* is conjunctive. Next, he may be called upon to analyse the subordinate clause. This, at first, also may seem to the child a disconnected experience. From this, however, he passes to the idea of *who* as subject, and thence to the fact that it signifies man. Thereupon these ideas unify themselves with the word *who* under the idea *pronoun*. Thereupon a still higher synthesis combines these two co-ordinated systems into the more complex system, or idea—*conjunctive pronoun*.

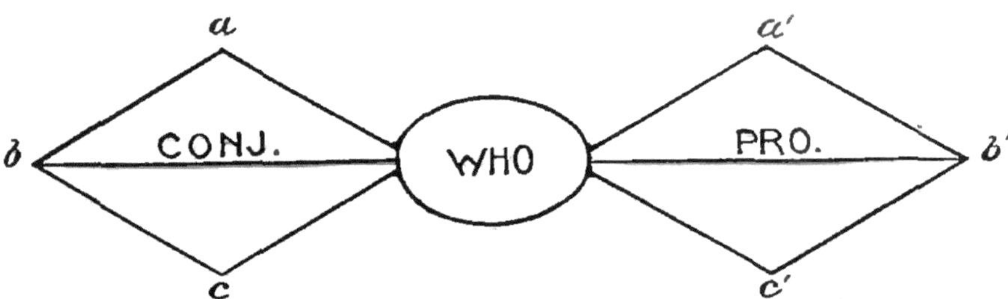

This progressive interaction of analysis and synthesis is illustrated by the accompanying figure, in which the word *who* represents the presented unknown problem; *a*, *b*, and *c*, the selecting and relating process which results in the knowledge, *conjunction*; *a'*, *b'*, and *c'*, the building up of the *pronoun* notion; and the circle, the final organization of these two smaller systems into a single notion, *conjunctive pronoun*.

The learning of any fact in history, the mastery of a poem, the study of a plant or animal, will furnish excellent examples of these subordinate stages of analysis and synthesis within a lesson. It is to be noted further that this feature of the learning process causes many lessons to fall into certain well marked sub-divisions. Each of these minor co-ordinations clustering around a sub-topic of the larger problem, the whole lesson separates itself into a number of more or less distinct parts. Moreover, the child's knowledge of the whole lesson will largely depend upon the extent to which he realizes these parts both as separate co-ordinations and also as related parts of the whole lesson problem.

All Knowledge Unified

Nor does this relating activity of mind confine itself within the single lesson. As each lesson is organized, it will, if fully apprehended, be more or less directly related with former lessons in the same subject. In this way the student should discover a unity within the lessons of a single subject, such as arithmetic or grammar. In like manner, various groups of lessons organize themselves into larger divisions within the subject, in accordance with important relations which the pupil may read into their data. Thus, in grammar, one sequence of lessons is organized into a complete knowledge of sentences; another group, into a complete knowledge of inflection; a smaller group within the latter, into a complete knowledge of tense or mood. It is thus that the mind is able to construct its mass of knowledge into organized groups known as sciences, and the various smaller divisions into topics.

CHAPTER XII

APPLICATION OF KNOWLEDGE OR LAW OF EXPRESSION

Practical Significance of Knowledge.—In our consideration of the fourth phase of the learning process, or the law of expression, it is necessary at the outset to recall what has already been noted regarding the correlation of knowledge and action. In this connection it was learned that knowledge arises naturally as man faces a difficulty, or problem, and that it finds significance and value in so far as it enables him to meet the practical and theoretical difficulties with which he may be confronted. In other words, man is primarily a doer, and knowledge is intended to guide the conduct of the individual along certain recognized lines. This being the case, while instruction aims to control the process by which the child is to acquire valuable social experience, or knowledge, it is equally important that it should promote skill by correlating that knowledge with expression, or should strive to influence action while forming character. To apperceive, for instance, the rules of government and agreement in grammar will have a very limited value if the student is not able to give expression to these in his own conversation. It becomes imperative, therefore, that as far as possible, expression should enter as a factor in the learning process.

Examples of Expression.—Man's expressive acts are found, however, to differ greatly in their form. When one is hurt, he distorts his face and cries aloud; when he hears a good speech he claps his hands and shouts approval; when he reads an amusing story he laughs; when he learns of the death of a friend he sheds tears; when he is affronted his face grows red, his muscles tense, and he strikes a blow or breaks into a torrent of words; when he has seen a striking incident he tells some one about it or writes an account to a distant friend. When his feelings are stirred by a patriotic address, he springs to his feet and sings, "God Save the King." The desire that his team should carry the foot-ball to the southern goal causes the spectator to lean and push in that direction. When he conceives how he may launch a successful venture, the business man at once proceeds to carry it into effect. These are all examples of *expression*. Every impression, idea, or thought, tends sooner or later to work itself out in some form of motor expression.

TYPES OF ACTION

A. Uncontrolled Actions.—Passing to an examination of such physical, or motor, activities, we find that man's expressive acts fall into three somewhat distinct classes. A young child is found to engage in many movements which seem destitute of any conscious direction. Some of these movements, such as breathing, sneezing, winking, etc., are found to be useful to the child, and imply what might be termed inherited control of conduct, though they do not give expression to any consciously organized knowledge, or experience. At other times, his bodily movements seem to be mere random, or impulsive, actions. These latter actions at times arise in a spontaneous way as a result of native bodily vigour, as, for instance, stretching, kicking, etc., as seen in a baby. At other times these uncontrolled acts have their origin in the various impressions which the child is receiving from his surroundings, or environment, as when the babe impulsively grasps the object coming in contact with his hand. Although, moreover, these instinctive movements may come in time under conscious control, such actions do not in themselves imply conscious control or give expression to organized knowledge.

B. Actions Subject to Intelligent Control.—To a second class of actions belong the orderly movements which are both produced and directed by consciousness. When, in distinction to the movements referred to above, a child pries open the lid to see what is in the box, or waves his hand to gain the attention of a companion, a conscious aim, or intention, produces the act, and conscious effort sustains it until the aim is reached. The distinction between mere impulsive and instinctive actions on the one hand, and guided effort on the other, will be considered more fully in Chapter XXX.

C. Habitual Actions.—Thirdly, as has been noted in Chapter II, both consciously directed and uncontrolled action may, by repetition, become so fixed that it practically ceases to be directed by consciousness, or becomes habitual.

Our expressive actions may be classified, therefore, into three important groups as follows:

1. Instinctive, reflex, and impulsive action
2. Consciously controlled, or directed action
3. Habitual action.

NATURE OF EXPRESSION

Implies Intelligent Control.—It is evident that as a stage in the learning process, expression must deal primarily with the second class of actions, since its real purpose is to correlate the new conscious knowledge with action. Expression in education, therefore, must represent largely consciously produced and consciously directed action.

Conscious Expression may Modify A. Instinctive Acts.—While this is true, however, expression, as a stage in the educative process, will also have a relation to the other types of action. As previously noted, the expression stage of the learning process may be used as a means to bring instinctive and impulsive acts under conscious control. This is indeed an important part of a child's education. For instance, it is only by forming ideas of muscular movements and striving to express them that the child can bring his muscular movements under control. It is evident, therefore, that the expressive stage of the lesson can be made to play an important part in bringing many instinctive and impulsive acts under conscious direction. By expressing himself in the games of the kindergarten, the child's social instinct will come under conscious control. By directing his muscular movements in art and constructive work, he gains the control which will in part enable him to check the impulse to strike the angry blow. These points will, however, be considered more fully in a study of the inherited tendencies in Chapter XXI.

B. Habits.—Further, many of our consciously directed acts are of so great value that they should be made more permanent through habituation. Expression must, therefore, in many lessons be emphasized, not merely to test and render clear present conscious knowledge, but also to lead to habitual control of action, or to create skill. This would be especially true in having a child practise the formation of figures and letters. Although at the outset we must have him form the letter to see that he really knows the outline, the ultimate aim is to enable him to form these practically without conscious direction. In language work, also, the child must acquire many idiomatic expressions as habitual modes of speech.

TYPES OF EXPRESSION

Since the tendency to express our impressions in a motor way is a law of our being, it follows that the school, which is constantly seeking to give the pupil intelligent impressions, or valuable knowledge, should also provide opportunity for adequate expression of the same. The forms most frequently adopted in schools are speech and writing. Pupils are required to answer questions orally or in writing in almost every school subject, and in doing so they are given an opportunity for expression of a very valuable kind. In fact, it would often be much more economical to try to give pupils fewer impressions and to give them more opportunities for expression in language. But written or spoken language is not the only means of expression that the school can utilize. Pupils can frequently be required to express themselves by means of manual activity. In art, they represent objects and scenes by means of brush and colour, or pencil, or crayon; in manual training, they construct objects in cardboard and wood; in domestic science, they cook and sew. The primary object of these so-called "new" subjects of the school programme is not to make the pupils artists, carpenters, or house-keepers, but partly to acquaint them with typical forms of human activity and partly to give them means of expression having an educative value. In arithmetic, the pupils express numerical facts by manipulating blocks and splints, and measure quantities, distances, surfaces, and solids. In geography, they draw maps of countries, model them in sand or clay, and make collections to illustrate manufactures at various stages of the process. In literature, they dramatize stories and illustrate scenes and situations by a sketch with pencil or brush. In nature study, they illustrate by drawings and make mounted collections of plants and insects.

VALUE OF EXPRESSION

A. Influences Conduct.—In nature study, history, and literature, the most valuable kind of expression is that which comes through some modification of future conduct. That pupil has studied the birds and animals to little purpose who needlessly destroys their lives or causes them pain. He has studied the reign of King John to little purpose if he is not more considerate of the rights of others on the playground. He has gained little from the life of Robert Bruce, Columbus, or La Salle, if he does not manfully attack difficulties again and again until he has overcome them. He has not read *The Heroine of Verchères*, or *The Little Hero of Haarlem* aright, if he does not act promptly in a situation demanding courage. He has learned little from the story of Damon and Pythias if he is not true to his friends under trying circumstances, and he has not imbibed the spirit of *The Christmas Carol* if he is not sympathetic and kindly toward those less fortunate than himself. From the standpoint of the moral life, therefore, right knowledge is valuable only as it expresses itself in right action.

B. Aids Impression.—Apart from the fact that it satisfies a demand of our being, expression is most important in that it tests the clearness of the applied knowledge. We often think that our impression is clear, only to discover its vagueness when we attempt to express it in some form. People often say that they understand a fact thoroughly, but they cannot exactly express it. Such a statement is usually incorrect. If the impression were clear, the expression under ordinary circumstances would also be clear. In this connection a danger should be pointed out. Pupils sometimes express themselves in language with apparent clearness, when in reality they are merely repeating words that they have memorized and that are quite meaningless to them. The alert teacher can, however, by judicious questioning, avoid being deceived in this regard.

C. Adds to Clearness of Knowledge.—Not only does expression test the clearness of the apperceived new knowledge, but at the same time it gives the knowledge greater clearness. We learn to know by doing. A pupil realizes a story more fully when he has reproduced it for somebody else. He images a scene described in a poem more clearly when he has drawn it. He has a clearer idea of the volume of a cord when he has actually measured out a cord of wood. He has a more accurate conception of the difficulties attending the discoveries of La Salle when he has drawn a map and traced the routes of his various expeditions. There is much truth in the statement that one never fully knows some things until he has taught them to somebody else. The teacher in grammar and geography will often have occasion to realize this. Greater clearness of impression means, of course, greater permanence. We remember best those facts of which our impression was most vivid.

DANGERS OF OMITTING EXPRESSION

A. Knowledge not Practical.—It is apparent, then, that if the pupil is not given opportunity for expression, his ideas are vague and evanescent. Further than this, his capacities for *knowing* will be developed but his capacities for *doing* ignored. His *intellectual* powers will be exercised and his *volitional* powers neglected. The pupil is thus likely to develop into a mere *theorist*; and as the tendencies of childhood are accentuated in later life, he becomes an *impractical* man. There are many men in the world who apparently know a great deal, but who, through inability to make practical application of their knowledge, are unsuccessful in life. It is, however, seriously to be doubted whether knowledge is ever *real* until it has been worked out in practice and conduct. To avoid the danger of becoming impractical, a pupil should have every opportunity for expression.

B. Feelings Weakened.—A second serious danger of neglecting expression lies in the field of the emotions. To have generous emotions continually aroused and never to act upon them, to have one's sympathies frequently stirred and never to perform a kindly act, to experience feelings of love and never to express them in acts of service, is to cultivate a weakness of character. A classic instance of this is that of the lady who wept bitterly over the imaginary sorrows of the heroine in the play while her coachman was freezing to death outside the theatre. If worthy emotions are ever to be of the slightest moral value to us, they must be expressed in action. The pupil frequently has his emotions stirred in the lessons in literature, history, and nature study, and there are situations constantly arising in the school room, on the playground, on the street, and in the home, that afford opportunity for expression. To give a single instance, there is a story in the *Ontario Third Reader* by Elizabeth Phelps Ward, called "Mary Elizabeth." No pupil could read that story without being stirred with a deep pity and yet profound admiration for the pathetic figure of poor little Mary Elizabeth. The natural expression for such emotions would be a more kindly and sympathetic attitude towards some unfortunate child in the school.

RELATION OF EXPRESSION TO IMPRESSION

Knowledge Tends Toward Expression.—On account of the evident connection between knowledge and action, the law of expression has formulated itself into a well-known pedagogical law of method—no impression without expression. Like many other educational maxims, however, this law may be interpreted in too wide a sense. The law of expression in education claims only that valuable experiences, or valuable forms of new knowledge, should not be built up in the child's mind without adequate accompanying expression. In the first case, as already seen, many impressions come to us which are never seized upon sufficiently by our consciousness to become intelligent rules for conduct, or action. It is true, of course that, so far as such impressions stimulate us, they tend toward expression, and to that extent the maxim is true. For instance, when a child is impressed, say, by a sudden strange sound, he has a tendency to express himself by straining his attention, and when the man imagines an enemy is before him, he finds his arms and fists assuming the fighting attitude.

Expression at Times Inhibited.—It is to be noted that the child should early learn to form intelligent plans of action and postpone or even condemn them as forms of expression. In other words, a child should early learn to select and co-ordinate ideas into an orderly system independently of their actual expression in physical action. Without this power to suppress, or inhibit, expression, the child would be unable adequately to weigh and compare alternative courses of action and suppress such as seem undesirable. Such indeed is the weakness of the man who possesses an impulsive nature. Although, therefore, it is true that all knowledge is intended to serve in meeting actual needs, or to function in the control of expression, it is equally true that not every organized experience should find expression in action. Part at least of man's efficiency must consist in his ability to organize a new experience in an indirect way and condemn it as a rule of action. While, therefore, we emphasize the importance, under ordinary conditions, of having the child's knowledge function as directly as possible in some form of actual expression, it is equally important to recognize that in actual life many organized plans should not find expression in outer physical action. This being the case, the divorce between organized experience, or knowledge, and practical expression, which at times takes place in school work, is not necessarily unsound, since it tends to make the child proficient in separating the mental organizing of experience from its immediate expression, and must, therefore, tend to make him more capable of weighing plans before putting them into execution. This will in turn habituate the child to taking the necessary time for reflection between "the acting of a thing and the first purpose." This question will be considered more fully in Chapter XXX, which treats of the development of voluntary control.

It should be noted in conclusion that the law of expression as a fourth stage of the learning process differs in purpose from the use of physical action as a means of creating interest in the problem, as referred to on page 38. When, for instance, we set a pupil who has no knowledge of long measure to use the inch in interpreting the yard stick, expressive action is merely a means of putting the problem before the child in an interesting form on account of his liking for physical action. When, on the other hand, the child later uses the foot or yard as a unit to measure the perimeter of the school-room, he is applying his knowledge of long measure, which has been acquired previously to this expressive act.

CHAPTER XIII

FORMS OF LESSON PRESENTATION

The chief office of the teacher, in controlling the pupils' process of learning, being to direct their self-activity in making a selection of ideas from their former knowledge which shall stand in vital connection with the problem, and lead finally to its solution, the question arises in what form the teacher is to conduct the process in order to obtain this desired result. Three different modes of directing the selecting activity of the student are recognized and more or less practised by teachers. These are usually designated the lecture method, the text-book method, and the developing method.

THE LECTURE METHOD

Example of Lecture Method.—In the lecture method so-called, the teacher tells the students in direct words the facts involved in the new problem, and expects these words to enable the pupils to call up from their old knowledge the ideas which will give the teacher's words meaning, and thus lead to a solution of the problem. For example, in teaching the meaning of alluvial fans in geography, a teacher might seek to awaken the interpreting ideas by merely stating in words the characteristic of a fan. This would involve telling the pupils that an alluvial fan is a formation on the floor of a main river valley, resulting from the depositing of detritus carried down the steep side of the valley by a tributary stream and deposited in the form of a fan, when the force of the water is weakened as it enters the more level floor of the valley. To interpret this verbal description, however, the pupil must first interpret the words of the teacher as sounds, and then convert these into ideas by bringing his former knowledge to bear upon the word symbols. If we could take it for granted that the pupil will readily grasp the ideas here signified by such words as, formation, main river valley, depositing, detritus, steep side, etc., and at once feel the relation of these several ideas to the more or less unknown object—alluvial fan—this method would undoubtedly give the pupil the knowledge required.

The Method Difficult.—To expect of young children a ready ability in thus interpreting words would, however, be an evident mistake. To translate such sound symbols into ideas, and immediately adjust them to the problem, demands a power of language interpretation and of reflection not usually found in school children. The purely lecture method, therefore, has very small place with young children, whatever may be its value with advanced students. Pupils in the primary grades have not sufficient power of attention to listen to a long lecture on any subject, and no teacher should think of conducting a lesson by that method alone. The purpose of the lecture is merely to give information, and that is seldom the sole purpose of a lesson in elementary classes. There the more important purposes are to train pupils to acquire knowledge by thinking for themselves, and to express themselves, both of which are well-nigh impossible if the purely lecture method is followed.

Does not Insure Selection.—The weakness of such a method is well illustrated in the case of the young teacher who, in giving her class a conception of the equator, followed the above method, and carefully explained to the pupils that the equator is an imaginary line running around the earth equally distant from the two poles. When the teacher came later to review the work with the class, one bright lad described the equator as a menagerie lion running around the earth. Here evidently the child, true to the law of apperception, had interpreted, or rather misinterpreted, the words of the teacher, by means of the only ideas in his possession which seemed to fit the uttered sounds. It is evident, therefore, that too often in this method the pupils will either thus misinterpret the meaning of the teacher's words, or else fail to interpret them at all, because they are not able to call up any definite images from what the teacher may be telling them.

When to be Used.—It may be noted, however, that there is some place for the method in teaching. For example, when young children are presented with a suitable story, they will usually have no difficulty in fitting ideas to words, and thus building up the story. It requires, in fact, the continuity found in the telling method to keep the children's attention on the story, the tone of voice and gesture of the reciter going a long way in helping the child to call up the ideas which enable him to construct the story plot. Moreover, some telling must be done by the teacher in every lesson. Everything cannot be discovered by the pupils themselves. Even if it were possible, it would often be undesirable. Some facts are relatively unimportant, and it is much better to tell these outright than to spend a long time in trying to lead pupils to discover them. The lecture method, or telling method, should be used, then, to supply pupils with information they could not find out for themselves, or which they could find out only by spending an amount of time disproportionate to the importance of the facts. The teacher must use good judgment in discriminating between those facts which the pupils may reasonably be expected to find out for themselves and those facts which had better be told. Many teachers tell too much and do not throw the pupils sufficiently on their own resources. On the other hand, many teachers tell too little and waste valuable time in trying to "draw" from the pupils what they do not know, with the result that the pupils fall back upon the pernicious practice of guessing. The teacher needs to be on his guard against "the toil of dropping buckets into empty wells, and growing old in drawing nothing up."

It may be added further that, in practical life, man is constantly required to interpret through spoken language. For this reason, therefore, all children should become proficient in securing knowledge through spoken language, that is, by means of the lecture, or telling, method.

THE TEXT-BOOK METHOD

Nature of Text-book Method.—In the text-book method, in place of listening to the words of the teacher, the pupil is expected to read in a text-book, in connection with each lesson problem, a series of facts which will aid him in calling up, or selecting, the ideas essential to the mastery of the new knowledge. This method is similar, therefore, in a general way, to the lecture method; since it implies ability in the pupil to interpret language, and thus recall the ideas bearing upon the topic being presented. Although the text-book method lacks the interpretation which may come through gesture and tone of voice, it nevertheless gives the pupil abundance of time for reflecting upon the meaning of the language without the danger of losing the succeeding context, as would be almost sure to happen in the lecture method. Moreover, the language and mode of presentation of the writer of the text-book is likely to be more effective in awakening the necessary old knowledge, than would be the less perfect descriptions of the ordinary teacher. On the whole, therefore, the text-book seems more likely to meet the conditions of the laws of apperception and self-activity, than would the lecture method.

Method Difficult for Young Children.—The words of the text-book, however, like the words of the teacher, are often open to misinterpretation, especially in the case of young pupils. This may be illustrated by the case of the student, who upon reading in her history of the mettle of the defenders of Lacolle Mill, interpreted it as the possession on their part of superior arms. An amusing illustration of the same tendency to misinterpret printed language, in spite of the time and opportunity for studying the text, is seen in the case of the student who, after reading the song entitled "The Old Oaken Bucket," was called upon to illustrate in a drawing his interpretation of the scene. His picture displayed three buckets arranged in a row. On being called upon for an explanation, he stated that the first represented "The old oaken bucket"; the second, "The iron-bound bucket"; and the third, "The moss-covered bucket." Another student, when called upon to express in art his conception of the well-known lines:

> All at once I saw a crowd,
> A host of golden daffodils;
> Beside the lake, beneath the trees,
> Fluttering and dancing in the breeze;

represented on his paper a bed of daffodils blooming in front of a platform, upon which a number of female figures were actively engaged in the terpsichorean art.

Pupil's Mind Often Passive.—As in the lecture method, also, the pupil may often go over the language of the text in a passive way without attempting actively to call up old knowledge and relate it to the problem before him. It is evident, therefore, that without further aid from a teacher, the text-book could not be depended upon to guide the pupil in selecting the necessary interpreting ideas. As with the lecture method, however, it is to be recognized that, both in the school and in after life, the student must secure much information by reading, and that he should at some time gain the power of gathering information from books. The use of the text-book in school should assist in the acquisition of this power. The teacher must, therefore, distinguish between the proper *use* of the text-book and the *abuse* of it. There are several ways in which the text-book may be effectively used.

Uses of text-book

1. After a lesson has been taught, the pupils may be required by way of review to read the matter covered by the lesson as stated by the text-book. This plan is particularly useful in history and geography lessons. The text-book strengthens and clarifies the impression made by the lesson.

2. Before assigning the portion to be read in the text-book, the teacher may prepare the way by presenting or reviewing any matter upon which the interpretation of the text depends. This preparatory work should be just sufficient to put the pupils in a position to read intelligently the portion assigned, and to give them a zest for the reading. Sometimes in this assignment, it is well to indicate definitely what facts are sufficiently important to be learned, and where these are discussed in the text-book.

3. The mastery of the text by the pupils may sometimes be aided by a series of questions for which answers are to be found by a careful reading. Such questions give the pupils a definite purpose. They constitute a set of problems which are to be solved. They are likely to be interesting, because problems within the range of the pupils' capacity are a challenge to their intelligence. Further, these questions will emphasize the things that are essential, and the pupils will be enabled to grasp the main points of the lesson assigned. Occasionally, to avoid monotony, the pupils should be required, as a variation of this plan, to make such a series of questions themselves. In these cases, the pupil with the best list might be permitted, as a reward for his effort, to "put" his questions to the class.

4. In the more advanced classes, the pupils should frequently be required to make a topical outline of a section or chapter of the text-book. This demands considerable analytic power, and the pupil who can do it successfully has mastered the art of reading. The ability is acquired slowly, and the teacher must use discretion in what he exacts from the pupil in this regard. If the plan were followed persistently, there would be less time wasted in cursory reading, the results of which are fleeting. What is read in this careful way will become the real possession of the mind and, even if less material is read, more will be permanently retained.

The facts thus learned from the text-book should be discussed by the teacher and pupils in a subsequent recitation period. This may be done by the question and answer method, the teacher asking questions to which the pupils give brief answers; or by the topical recitation method, the pupils reporting in connected form the facts under topics suggested by the teacher. The teacher has thus an opportunity of emphasizing the important facts, of correcting misconceptions, and of amplifying and illustrating the facts given in the text-book. Further, the pupils are given an opportunity of expressing themselves, and have thus an exercise in language which is a valuable means of clarifying their impressions.

Abuse of text-book

As instances of the abuse of the text-book, the following might be cited:

1. The memorization by the pupils of the words of the text-book without any understanding of the meaning.

2. The assignment of a certain number of pages or sections to be learned by the pupils without any preliminary preparation for the study.

3. The employment of the text-book by the teacher during the recitation as a means of guiding him in the questions he is to ask—a confession that he does not know what he requires the pupils to know.

Limitation of Text-book.—The chief limitation of the text-book method of teaching is that the pupil makes few discoveries on his own account, and is, therefore, not trained to think for himself. The problems being largely solved for him by the writer, the knowledge is not valued as highly as it would be if it came as an original discovery. We always place a higher estimation on that knowledge which we discover for ourselves than on that which somebody else gives us.

THE DEVELOPING METHOD

Characteristics of the Method.—The third, or developing, method of directing the selecting activity of the learner, is so called because in this method the teacher as an instructor aims to keep the child's mind actively engaged throughout each step of the learning process. He sees, in other words, that step by step the pupil brings forward whatever old knowledge is necessary to the problem, and that he relates it in a definite way to this problem. Instead of telling the pupils directly, for instance, the teacher may question them upon certain known facts in such a way that they are able themselves to discover the new truth. In teaching alluvial fans, for example, the teacher would begin questioning the pupil regarding his knowledge of river valleys, tributary streams, the relation of the force of the tributary water to the steepness of the side of the river valley, the presence of detritus, etc., and thus lead the pupil to form his own conclusion as to the collecting of detritus at the entrance to the level valley and the probable shape of the deposit. So also in teaching the conjunctive pronoun from such an example as:

He gave it to a boy *who* stood near him;

the teacher brings forward, one by one, the elements of old knowledge necessary to a full understanding of the new word, and tests at each step whether the pupil is himself apprehending the new presentation in terms of his former grammatical knowledge. Beginning with the clause "who stood near him," the teacher may, by question and answer, assure himself that the pupil, through his former knowledge of subordinate clauses, apprehends that the clause is joined adjectively to *boy*, by the word *who*. Next, he assures himself that the pupil, through his former knowledge of the conjunction, apprehends clearly the consequent *conjunctive* force of the word *who*. Finally, by means of the pupil's former knowledge of the subjective and pronoun functions, the teacher assures himself that the pupil appreciates clearly the *pronoun* function of the word *who*. Thus, step by step, throughout the learning process, the teacher makes certain that he has awakened in the mind of the learner the exact old knowledge which will unify into a clearly understood and adequately controlled new experience, as signified by the term *conjunctive pronoun*.

Question and Answer.—On account of the large use of questioning as a means of directing and testing the pupils' selecting of old knowledge, or interpreting ideas, the developing method is often identified with the question and answer method. But the real mark of the developing method of teaching is the effort of an instructor to assure himself that, step by step, throughout the learning process, the pupil himself is actively apprehending the significance of the new problem by a use of his own previous experience. It is true, however, that the method of interrogation is the most universal, and perhaps the most effective, mode by which a teacher is able to assure himself that the learner's mind is really active throughout each step of the learning process. Moreover, as will be seen later, the other subsidiary methods of the developing method usually involve an accompanying use of question and answer for their successful operation. It is for this reason that the question is sometimes termed the teacher's best instrument of instruction. For the same reason, also, the young teacher should early aim to secure facility in the art of questioning. An outline of the leading principles of questioning will, therefore, be given in Chapter XVIII.

Other Forms of Development.—Notwithstanding the large part played by question and answer in the developing method, it must be observed that there are other important means which the teacher at times may use in the learning process in order to awaken clear interpreting ideas in the mind of the learner. In so far, moreover, as any such methods on the part of the teacher quicken the apperceptive process in the child, or cause him to apply his former knowledge in a more active and definite way to the problem in hand, they must be classified as phases of the developing method. Two of these subsidiary methods will now be considered.

THE OBJECTIVE METHOD

Characteristics of the Objective Method.—One important sub-section of the developing method is known as the objective method. In this method the teacher seeks, as far as possible, (1) to present the lesson problem through the use of concrete materials, and (2) to have the child interpret the problem by examining this concrete material. A child's interest and knowledge being largely centred in objects and their qualities and uses, many truths can best be presented to children through the medium of objective teaching. For example, in arithmetic, weights and measures should be taught by actually handling weights and measures and building up the various tables by experiment. Tables of lengths, areas, and volumes may be taught by measurements of lines, surfaces, and solids. Geographical facts are taught by actual contact with the neighbouring hills, streams, and ponds; and by visits to markets and manufacturing plants. In nature study, plants and animals are studied in their natural habitat or by bringing them into the class-room.

Advantages of the Objective Method.—The advantages of this method in such cases are readily manifest. Although, for instance, the pupil who knows in a general way an inch space and the numbers 144, 9, 30¼, 40, and 4, might be supposed to be able to organize out of his former experiences a perfect knowledge of surface measure, yet it will be found that compared with that of the pupil who has worked out the measure concretely in the school garden, the control of the former student over this knowledge will be very weak indeed. In like manner, when a student gains from a verbal description a knowledge of a plant or an animal, not only does he find it much more difficult to apply his old knowledge in interpreting the word description than he would in interpreting a concrete example, but his knowledge of the plant or animal is likely to be imperfect. Objective teaching is important, therefore, for two reasons:

1. It makes an appeal to the mind through the senses, the avenue through which the most vivid images come. Frequently several senses are brought to bear and the impressions thereby multiplied.

2. On account of his interest in objects, the young child's store of old experiences is mainly of objects and of their sensuous qualities and uses. To teach the abstract and unfamiliar through these, therefore, is an application of the law of apperception, since the object makes it easier for the child's former knowledge to be related to the presented problem.

Limitations of Objective Method.—It must be recognized, however, that objective teaching is only a means to a higher end. The concrete is valuable very often only as a means of grasping the abstract. The progress of humanity has ever been from the sensuous and concrete to the ideal and abstract. Not the objects themselves, but what the objects symbolize is the important thing. It would be a pedagogical mistake, then, to make instruction begin, continue, and end in the concrete. It is evident, moreover, that no progress could be made through object-teaching, unless the question and answer method is used in conjunction.

THE ILLUSTRATIVE METHOD

Characteristics of the Illustrative Method.—In many cases it is impossible or impracticable to bring the concrete object into the school-room, or to take the pupils to see it outside. In such cases, somewhat the same result may be obtained by means of some form of graphic illustration of the object, as a picture, sketch, diagram, map, model, lantern slide, etc. The graphic representation of an object may present to the eye most of the characteristics that the actual object would. For this reason pictures are being more and more used in teaching, though it is a question whether teachers make as good use of the pictures of the text-book, in geography for instance, as might be made.

Illustrative Method Involves Imagination.—In the illustrative method, however, the pupil, instead of being able to apply directly former knowledge obtained through the senses, in interpreting the actual object, must make use of his imagination to bridge over the gulf between the actual object and the representation. When, for example, the child is called upon to form his conception of the earth with its two hemispheres through its representation on a globe, the knowledge will become adequate only as the child's imagination is able to picture in his mind the actual object out of his own experience of land, water, form, and space, in harmony with the mere suggestions offered by the model. It is evident, for the above reason, that the illustrative method often demands more from the pupil than does the more concrete objective method. For instance, the child who is able to see an actual mountain, lake, canal, etc., is far more likely to obtain an accurate idea of these, than the student who learns them by means of illustrations. The cause for this lies mainly in the failure of the child to form a perfect image of the real object through the exercise of his imagination. In fact it sometimes happens that he makes very little use of his imagination, his mental picture of the real object differing little from the model placed before him. The writer was informed of a case in which a teacher endeavoured to give some young pupils a knowledge of the earth by means of a large school globe. When later the children were questioned thereon, it was discovered that their earth corresponded in almost every particular with the large globe in the school. The successful use of the illustrative method, therefore, demands from the teacher a careful test by the question and answer method, to see that the learner has properly bridged over, through his imagination, the gulf separating the actual object from its illustration. For this reason an acquaintance with the mental process of imagination is of great value to the teacher. The leading facts connected with this process will be set forth in Chapter XXVII.

Precautions in Use of Materials

In the use of objective and illustrative materials the following precautions are advisable:

1. Their use in the lesson should not be continued too long. It should be remembered that their office is illustrative, and the aim of the teacher should be to have the pupils think in the abstract as soon as possible. To make pupils constantly dependent on the concrete is to make their thinking weak.

2. The pupils must be mentally active while the concrete object or illustrative material is being used, and not merely gaze in a passive way upon the objects. It requires mental activity to grasp the abstract facts that the objects or illustrations typify. A tellurion will not teach the changes of the seasons; bundles of splints, notation; nor black-board examples, the law of agreement; unless these are brought under the child's mental apprehension. The sole purpose of such materials is, therefore, to start a flow of imagery or ideas which bear upon the presented problem.

3. The objects should not be so intrinsically interesting that they distract the attention from what they are intended to illustrate. It would be injudicious to use candies or other inherently attractive objects to illustrate number facts in primary arithmetic. The objects, not the number facts, would be of supreme interest. The teacher who used a heap of sand and some gunpowder to teach what a volcano is, found his pupils anxious for "fireworks" in subsequent geography classes. The science teacher may make his experiments so interesting that his students neglect to grasp what the experiments illustrate. The preacher who uses a large number of anecdotes to illustrate the points of his sermon, would be probably disappointed to know that the only part of his discourse remembered by the majority of his hearers was these very anecdotes. In his enthusiasm for objective teaching, the

teacher may easily make the objects so attractive that the pupils fail altogether to grasp what they signify.

4. In the case of pictures, maps, and sketches, it is well to present those that are not too detailed. A map drawn on the black-board by the teacher is usually better for purposes of illustration than a printed wall map. The latter shows so many details that it is often difficult for the pupil to single out those required in the lesson. The black-board map, on the other hand, will emphasize just those details that are necessary. For the same reason the sketch is often better than the printed picture or photograph. Any one who can sketch rapidly and accurately has at his disposal a valuable means of communicating knowledge, and every teacher should strive to cultivate this power.

MODES OF PRESENTATION COMPARED

The relative clearness of different modes of presenting knowledge may be seen from the following:

If a teacher stated to his pupils that he saw a guava yesterday, possibly no information would be conveyed to them other than that some unknown object has been referred to. Merely to name any object of thought, therefore, does not guarantee any real understanding in the mind of the pupil. If the teacher describes the object as a fruit, fragrant, yellow, fleshy, and pear-shaped, the mental picture of the pupil is likely to be much more definite. If, on the other hand, a picture of the fruit is shown, it is likely that the pupil will more fully realize at least some of the features of the fruit. If the pupil is given the object and allowed to bring all his senses to bear upon it, his knowledge will become both more full and more definite. If he were allowed to express himself through drawing and modelling, his knowledge would become still more thorough, while if he grew, marketed, and manufactured the fruit into jelly, his knowledge of the fruit might be considered complete.

CHAPTER XIV

CLASSIFICATION OF KNOWLEDGE

Before passing to a consideration of the various types or classes into which school lessons may be divided, it is necessary to note a certain distinction in the way the mind thinks of objects, or two classes into which our experiences are said to divide themselves. When the mind experiences, or is conscious of, this particular chair on the platform, that tree outside the window, the size of this piece of stone, or the colour and shape of this bonnet, it is said to be occupied with a particular experience, or to be gaining particular knowledge.

ACQUISITION OF PARTICULAR KNOWLEDGE

Through senses

A. Through the Senses.—These particular experiences may arise through the actual presentation of a thing to the senses. I *see* this chair; *taste* this sugar; *smell* this rose; *hear* this bell; etc. As will be seen later, the senses provide the primary conditions for revealing to the mind the presence of particular things, that is, for building up particular ideas, or, as they are frequently called, particular notions. Neither does a particular experience, or notion, necessarily represent a particular concrete object. It may be an idea of some particular state of anger or joy being experienced by an individual of the beauty embodied in this particular painting, etc.

Through imagination

B. Through the Imagination.—Secondly, by an act of constructive imagination, one may image a picture of a particular object as present here and now. Although never having had the actual particular experience, a person can, with the eye of the imagination, picture as now present before him any particular object or event, real or imaginary, such as King Arthur's round table; the death scene of Sir Isaac Brock or Captain Scott; the sinking of the *Titanic;* the Heroine of Verchères; or the many-headed Hydra.

By deduction

C. By Inference, or Deduction.—Again, knowledge about a particular individual, or particular knowledge, may be gained in what seems a yet more indirect way. For instance, instead of standing beside Socrates and seeing him drink the hemlock and die, and thus, by actual sense observation, learn that Socrates is mortal; we may, by a previous series of experiences, have gained the knowledge that all men are mortal. For that reason, even while he yet lives, we may know the particular fact that Socrates, being a man, is also mortal. In this process the person is supposed to start with the known general truth, "All men are mortal"; next, to call to mind the fact that Socrates is a man; and finally, by a comparison of these statements or thoughts, reason out, or deduce, the inference that therefore Socrates is mortal. This process is, therefore, usually illustrated in what is called the syllogistic form, thus:

All men are mortal.
Socrates is a man.
Socrates is mortal.

When particular knowledge about an individual thing or event is thus inferred by comparing two known statements, it is said to be secured by a process of *deduction*, or by inference.

GENERAL KNOWLEDGE

In all of the above examples, whether experienced through the senses, built up by an act of imagination, or gained by inference, the knowledge is of a single thing, fact, organism, or unity, possessing a real or imaginary existence. In addition to possessing its own individual unity, however, a thing will stand in a more or less close relation with many other things. Various individuals, therefore, enter into larger relations constituting groups, or classes, of objects. In addition, therefore, to recognizing the object as a particular experience, the mind is able, by examining certain individuals, to select and relate the common characteristics of such classes, or groups, and build up a general, or class, idea, which is representative of any member of the class. Thus arise such general ideas as book, man, island, county, etc. These are known as universal, or class, notions. Moreover, such rules, or definitions, as, "A noun is the name of anything"; "A fraction is a number which expresses one or more equal parts of a whole," are general truths, because they express in the form of a statement the general qualities which have been read into the ideas, noun and fraction. When the mind, from a study of particulars, thus either forms a class notion as noun, triangle, hepatica, etc., or draws a general conclusion as, "Air has weight," "Any two sides of a triangle are together greater than the third side," it is said to gain general knowledge.

ACQUISITION OF GENERAL KNOWLEDGE

By conception

A. Conception.—In describing the method of attaining general knowledge, it is customary to divide such knowledge into two slightly different types, or classes, and also to distinguish between the processes by which each type is attained. When the mind, through having experienced particular dogs, cows, chairs, books, etc., is able to form such a general, or class, idea as, dog, cow, chair, or book, it is said to gain a class notion, or concept; and the method by which these ideas are gained is called *conception*.

By induction

B. Induction.—When the mind, on the basis of particular experiences, arrives at some general law, or truth, as, "Any two sides of a triangle are together greater than the third side"; "Air has weight"; "Man is mortal"; "Honesty is the best policy"; etc., it is said to form a universal judgment, and the process by which the judgment is formed is called a process of *induction.*

Examples of General and Particular Knowledge.—When a pupil learns the St. Lawrence River system as such, he gains a particular experience, or notion; when he learns of river basins, he obtains a general notion. In like manner, for the child to realize that here are eight blocks containing two groups of four blocks, is a particular experience; but that 4 + 4 = 8, is a general, or universal, truth. To notice this water rising in a tube as heat is being applied, is a particular experience; to know that liquids are expanded by heat is a general truth. *The air above this radiator is rising* is a particular truth, but *heated air rises* is a general truth. *The English people plunged into excesses in Charles II's reign after the removal of the stern Puritan rule* is particular, but a *period of license follows a period of repression* is general.

Distinction is in Ideas, not Things.—It is to be noted further that the same object may be treated at one time as a particular individual, at another time as a member of a class, and at still another time as a part of a larger individual. Thus the large peninsula on the east of North America may be thought of now, as the individual, Nova Scotia; at another time, as a member of the class, province; and at still another time, as a part of the larger particular individual, Canada.

Only Two Types of Knowledge.—It is evident from the foregoing that no matter what subject is being taught, so far as any person may aim *to develop a new experience* in the mind of the pupil, that experience will be one or other of the two classes mentioned above. If the aim of our lesson is to have the pupils know the facts of the War of 1812-14, to study the rainfall of British Columbia, to master the spelling of a particular word, or to image the pictures contained in the story *Mary Elizabeth,* then it aims primarily to have pupils come into possession of a particular fact, or a number of particular facts. On the other hand, if the lesson aims to teach the pupils the nature of an infinitive, the rule for extracting square root, the law of gravity, the classes of nouns, etc., then the aim of the lesson is to convey some general idea or truth.

Applied Knowledge General

Before proceeding to a special consideration of such type lessons, it will be well to note that the mind always applies general knowledge in the learning process. That is, the application of old knowledge to the new presentation is possible only because this knowledge has taken on a general character, or has become a general way of thinking. The tendency for every new experience, whether particular or general, to pass into a general attitude, or to become a standard for interpreting other presentations, is always present, at least after the very early impressions of infancy. When, for instance, a child observes a strange object, dog, and perceives its four feet, this idea does not remain wholly confined to the particular object, but tends to take on a general character. This consists in the fact that the characteristic perceived is vaguely thought of as a quality distinct from the dog. This quality, *four-footedness*, therefore, is at least in some measure recognized as a quality that may occur in other objects. In other words, it takes on a general character, and will likely be applied in interpreting the next four-footed object which comes under the child's attention. So also when an adult first meets a strange fruit, guava, he observes perhaps that it is *pear-shaped, yellow-skinned, soft-pulped*, of *sweet taste*, and *aromatic flavour*. All such quality ideas as pear-shaped, yellow, soft, etc., as here applied, are general ideas of quality taken on from earlier experiences. Even in interpreting the qualities of particular objects, therefore, as this rose, this machine, or this animal, we apply to its interpretation general ideas, or general forms of thought, taken on from earlier experiences.

The same fact is even more evident when the mind attempts to build up the idea of a particular object by an act of imagination. One may conceive as present, a sphere, red in colour, with smooth surface, and two feet in diameter. Now this particular object is defined through the qualities spherical, red, smooth, etc. But these notions of quality are all general, although here applied to building up the image of a particular thing.

PROCESSES OF ACQUIRING KNOWLEDGE SIMILAR

If what has already been noted concerning the law of universal method is correct, and if all learning is a process of building up a new experience in accordance with the law of apperception, then all of the above modes of gaining either particular or general knowledge must ultimately conform to the laws of general method. Keeping in view the fact that applied knowledge is always general in character, it will not be difficult to demonstrate that these various processes do not differ in their essential characteristics; but that any process of acquiring either particular or general knowledge conforms to the method of selection and relation, or of analysis-synthesis, as already described in our study of the learning process. To demonstrate this, however, it will be necessary to examine and illustrate the different modes of learning in the light of the principles of general method already laid down in the text.

CHAPTER XV

MODES OF LEARNING

DEVELOPMENT OF PARTICULAR KNOWLEDGE

A. Learning through the Senses

In many lessons in nature study, elementary science, etc., pupils are led to acquire new knowledge by having placed before them some particular object which they may examine through the senses. The knowledge thus gained through the direct observation of some individual thing, since it is primarily knowledge about a particular individual, is to be classified as particular knowledge. As an example of the process by which a pupil may gain particular knowledge through the senses, a nature lesson may be taken in which he would, by actual observation, become acquainted with one of the constellations, say the Great Dipper. Here the learner first receives through his senses certain impressions of colour and form. Next he proceeds to read into these impressions definite meanings, as stars, four, corners, bowl, three, curve, handle, etc. In such a process of acquiring knowledge about a particular thing, it is to be noted that the acquisition depends upon two important conditions:

1. The senses receive impressions from a particular thing.

2. The mind reacts upon these impressions with certain phases of its old knowledge, here represented by such words as four, corner, bowl, etc.

Analysis of Process.—When the mind thus gains knowledge of a particular object through sense perception, the process is found to conform exactly to the general method already laid down; for there is involved:

1. *The Motive.*—To read meaning into the strange thing which is placed before the pupil as a problem to stimulate his senses.

2. *Selection, or Analysis.*—Bringing selected elements of former knowledge to interpret the unknown impressions, the elements of his former knowledge being represented in the above example by such words as, four, bowl, curve, handle, etc.

3. *Unification, or Synthesis.*—A continuous relating of these interpreting factors into the unity of a newly interpreted object, the Dipper.

SENSE PERCEPTION IN EDUCATION

A. Gives Knowledge of Things.—In many lessons in biology, botany, etc., although the chief aim of the lesson is to acquire a correct class notion, yet the learning process is in large part the gaining of particular knowledge through the senses. In a nature lesson, for instance, the pupil may be presented with an insect which he has never previously met. When the pupil interprets the object as six-legged, with hard shell-like wing covers, under wings membranous, etc., he is able to gain knowledge about this particular thing:

1. Because the thing manifests itself to him through the senses of sight and touch.

2. Because he is able to bring to bear upon these sense impressions his old knowledge, represented by such words as six, wing, shell, hard, membranous, etc. So far, therefore, as the process ends with knowledge of the particular object presented, the learning process conforms exactly to that laid down above, for there is involved:

1. *The Motive.*—To read meaning into the new thing which is placed before the pupil as a problem to stimulate his senses.

2. *Selection, or Analysis.*—Bringing selected elements of former knowledge to interpret the unknown problem, the elements of his former knowledge being represented above by such words as six, leg, wing, hard, shell, membranous, etc.

3. *Unification, or Synthesis.*—A continuous relating of these interpreting factors into the unity of a better known object, the insect.

B. Is a Basis for Generalization.—It is to be noted, however, that in any such lesson, although the pupil gains through his senses a knowledge of a particular individual only, yet he may at once accept this individual as a sign, or type, of a class of objects, and can readily apply the new knowledge in interpreting other similar things. Although, for example, the pupil has experienced but one such object, he does not necessarily think of it as a mere individual—this thing—but as a representative of a possible class of objects, a beetle. In other words the new particular notion tends to pass directly into a general, or class, notion.

B. Learning through imagination

As an example of a lesson in which the pupil secures knowledge through the use of his imagination, may be taken first the case of one called upon to image some single object of which he may have had no actual experience, as a desert, London Tower, the sphinx, etc. Taking the last named as an example, the learner must select certain characteristics as, woman, head, lion, body, etc., all of which are qualities which have been learned in other past experiences. Moreover, the mind must organize these several qualities into the representation of a single object, the sphinx. Here, evidently, the pupil follows fully the normal process of learning.

1. The term—the sphinx—suggests a problem, or felt need, namely, to read meaning into the vaguely realized term.

2. Under the direction of the instructor or the text-book, the pupil selects, or analyses out of past experience, such ideas as, woman, head, body, lion, which are felt to have a value in interpreting the present problem.

3. A synthetic, or relating, activity of mind unifies the selected ideas into an ideally constructed object which is accepted by the learner as a particular object, although never directly known through the senses.

Nor is the method different in more complex imagination processes. In literary interpretation, for instance, when the reader meets such expressions as:

> The curfew tolls the knell of parting day,
> The lowing herd winds slowly o'er the lea,
> The ploughman homeward plods his weary way
> And leaves the world to darkness and to me;

the words of the author suggest a problem to the mind of the reader. This problem then calls up in the mind of the student a set of images out of earlier experience, as bell, evening, herd, ploughman, lea, etc., which the mind unifies into the representation of the particular scene depicted in the lines. It is in this way that much of our knowledge of various objects and scenes in nature, of historical events and characters, and of spiritual beings is obtained.

Imagination Gives Basis for Generalization.—It should be noted by the student-teacher that in many lessons we aim to give the child a notion of a class of objects, though he may in actual experience never have met any representatives of the class. In geography, for instance, the child learns of deserts, volcanoes, etc., without having experienced these objects through the senses. It has been seen, however, that our general knowledge always develops from particular experience. For this reason the pupil who has never seen a volcano, in order to gain a general notion of a volcano, must first, by an act of constructive imagination, image a definite picture of a particular volcano. The importance of using in such a lesson a picture or a representation on a sand-board, lies in the fact that this furnishes the necessary stimulus to the child's imagination, which will cause him to image a particular individual as a basis for the required general, or class, notion. Too often, however, the child is expected in such lessons to form the class notion directly, that is, without the intervention of a particular experience. This question will be considered more fully in Chapter XXVII, which treats of the process of imagination.

C. Learning by Inference, or Deduction

Instead of placing himself in British Columbia, and noting by actual experience that there is a large rainfall there, a person may discover the same by what is called a process of inference. For example, one may have learned from an examination of other particular instances that air takes up moisture in passing over water; that warm air absorbs large quantities of moisture; that air becomes cool as it rises; and that warm, moist air deposits its moisture as rain when it is cooled. Knowing this and knowing a number of particular facts about British Columbia, namely that warm winds pass over it from the Pacific and must rise owing to the presence of mountains, we may infer of British Columbia that it has an abundant rainfall. When we thus discover a truth in relation to any particular thing by inference, we are said to go through a process of deduction. A more particular study of this process will be made in Chapter XXVIII, but certain facts may here be noted in reference to the process as a mode of acquiring knowledge. An examination will show that the deductive process follows the ordinary process of learning, or of selecting certain elements of old knowledge, and organizing them into a new particular experience in order to meet a certain problem.

Deduction as Formal Reasoning.—It is usually stated by psychologists and logicians that in this process the person starts with the general truth and ends with the particular inference, or conclusion, for example:

> Winds coming from the ocean are saturated with moisture.
>
> The prevailing winds in British Columbia come from the Pacific.
>
> Therefore these winds are saturated with moisture.
>
> All winds become colder as they rise.
>
> The winds of British Columbia rise as they go inland.
>
> Therefore, the winds (atmosphere) in British Columbia become colder as they go inland.
>
> The atmosphere gives out moisture as it becomes colder.
>
> The atmosphere in British Columbia becomes colder as it goes inland.
>
> Therefore, the atmosphere gives out moisture in British Columbia.

Steps in Process.—The various elements involved in a deductive process are often analysed into four parts in the following order:

1. *Principles.* The general laws which are to be applied in the solution of the problem. These, in the above deductions, constitute the first sentence in each, as,

> The air becomes colder as it rises.
> Air gives out its moisture as it becomes colder, etc.

2. *Data.* This includes the particular facts already known relative to the problem. In this lesson, the data are set forth in the second sentences, as follows:

> The prevailing winds in British Columbia come from the Pacific; the wind rises as it goes inland, etc.

3. *Inferences.* These are the conclusions arrived at as a result of noting relations between data and principles. In the above lesson, the inferences are:

> The atmosphere, or trade-winds, coming from the Pacific rise, become colder, and give out much moisture.

4. *Verification.* In some cases at least the learner may use other means to verify his conclusions. In the above lesson, for example, he may look it up in the geography or ask some one who has had actual experience.

Deduction Involves a Problem.—It is to be noted, however, that in a deductive learning process, the young child does not really begin with the general principle. On the contrary, as noted in the study of the learning process, the child always begins with a particular unsolved problem. In the case just cited, for instance, the child starts with the problem, "What is the condition of the rainfall in British Columbia?" It is owing to the presence of this problem, moreover, that the mind calls up the principles and data. These, of course, are already possessed as old knowledge, and are called up because the mind feels a connection between them and the problem with which it is confronted. The principles and data are thus both involved in the selecting process, or step of analysis. What the learner really does, therefore, in a deductive lesson is to interpret a new problem by selecting as interpreting ideas the principles and data. The third division, inference, is in reality the third step of our learning process, since the inference is a new experience organized out of the selected principles and data. Moreover, the verification is often found to take the form of ordinary expression. As a process of learning, therefore, deduction does not exactly follow the formal outline of the psychologists and logicians of (1) principles, (2) data, (3) inference, and (4) verification; but rather that of the learning process, namely, (1) problem, (2) selecting activity, including principles and data, (3) relating activity=inference, (4) expression=verification.

Examples for study

Example of Deduction as Learning Process.—A simple and interesting lesson, showing how the pupil actually goes through the deductive process, is found in paper cutting of forms balanced about a centre, say the letter X.

1. *Problem.* The pupil starts with the problem of discovering a way of cutting this letter by balancing about a centre.

2. *Selection.* Principles and Data. The pupil calls up as data what he knows of this letter, and as principles, the laws of balance he has learned from such letters as, A, B, etc.

3. *Organization or Inference.* The pupil infers from the principle involved in cutting the letter A, that the letter X (Fig. A) may be balanced about a vertical diameter, as in Fig. B.

Repeating the process, he infers further from the principle involved in cutting the letter B, that this result may again be balanced about a horizontal diameter, as in Fig. C.

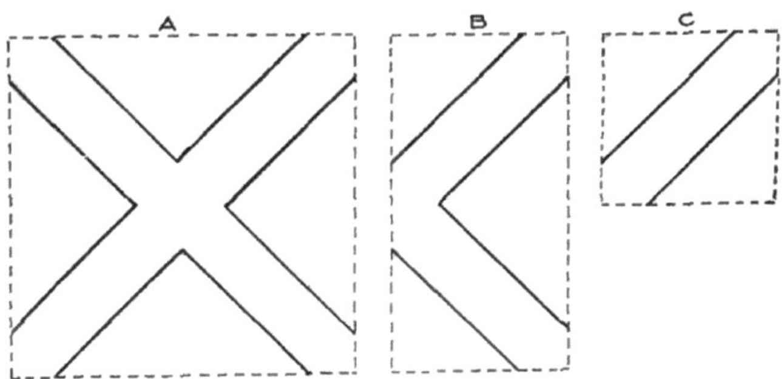

4. *Expression or Verification.* By cutting Figure D and unfolding Figures E and F, he is able to verify his conclusion by noting the shape of the form as it unfolds, thus:

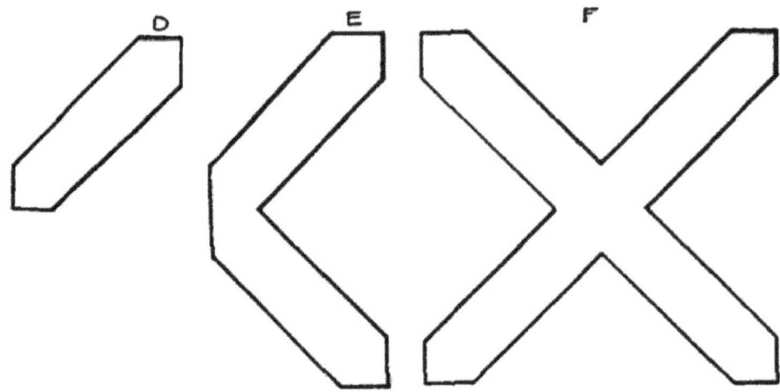

FURTHER EXAMPLES FOR STUDY

The following are given as further examples of deductive processes.

The materials are here arranged in the formal or logical way. The student-teacher should rearrange them as they would occur in the child's learning process.

I. DIVISION OF DECIMALS

1. *Principles*:

(*a*) Multiplying the dividend and divisor by the same number does not alter the quotient.

(*b*) To multiply a decimal by 10, 100, 1000, etc., move the decimal point 1, 2, 3, etc., places respectively to the right.

2. *Data*:

Present knowledge of facts contained in such an example as .0027 divided by .05.

3. *Inferences*:

(*a*) The divisor (.05) may be converted into a whole number by multiplying it by 100.

(*b*) If the divisor is multiplied by 100, the dividend must also be multiplied by 100 if the quotient is to be unchanged.

(*c*) The problem thus becomes .27 divided by 5, for which the answer is .054.

4. *Verification*:

Check the work to see that no mistakes have been made in the calculation. Multiply the quotient by the divisor to see if the result is equal to the dividend.

II. TRADE-WINDS

1. *Principles*:

(*a*) Heated air expands, becomes lighter, and is pushed upward by cooler and heavier currents of air.

(*b*) Air currents travelling towards a region of more rapid motion have a tendency to "lag behind," and so appear to travel in a direction opposite to that of the earth's rotation.

2. *Data*:

(*a*) The most heated portion of the earth is the tropical region.

(*b*) The rapidity of the earth's motion is greatest at the equator and least at the poles.

(*c*) The earth rotates on its axis from west to east.

3. *Inferences*:

(*a*) The heated air in equatorial regions will be constantly rising.

(*b*) It will be pushed upward by colder and heavier currents of air from the north and south.

(*c*) If the earth did not rotate, there would be constant winds towards the south, north of the equator; and towards the north, south of the equator.

(*d*) These currents of air are travelling from a region of less motion to a region of greater motion, and have a tendency to lag behind the earth's motion as they approach the equator.

(*e*) Hence they will seem to blow in a direction contrary to the earth's rotation, namely, towards the west.

(*f*) These two movements, towards the equator and towards the west, combine to give the currents of air a direction towards the south-west north of the equator, and towards the north-west south of the equator.

4. *Verification*:

Read the geography text to see if our inferences are correct.

THE DEVELOPMENT OF GENERAL KNOWLEDGE

The conceptual lesson

The Conceptual Lesson.—As an example of a lesson involving a process of conception, or classification, may be taken one in which the pupil might gain the class notion *noun*. The pupil would first be presented with particular examples through sentences containing such words as John, Mary, Toronto, desk, boy, etc. Thereupon the pupil is led to examine these in order, noting certain characteristics in each. Examining the word *John*, for instance, he notes that it is a word; that it is used to name and also, perhaps, that it names a person, and is written with a capital letter. Of the word *Toronto*, he may note much the same except that it names a place; of the word *desk*, he may note especially that it is used to name a thing and is written without a capital letter. By comparing any and all the qualities thus noted, he is supposed, finally, by noting what characteristics are common to all, to form a notion of a class of words used to name.

The inductive lesson

The Inductive Lesson.—To exemplify an inductive lesson, there may be noted the process of learning the rule that to multiply the numerator and denominator of any fraction by the same number does not alter the value of the fraction.

Conversion of fractions to equivalent fractions
with different denominators

The teacher draws on the black-board a series of squares, each representing a square foot. These are divided by vertical lines into a number of equal parts. One or more of these parts are shaded, and pupils are asked to state what fraction of the whole square has been shaded. The same squares are then further divided into smaller equal parts by horizontal lines, and the pupils are led to discover how many of the smaller equal parts are contained in the shaded parts.

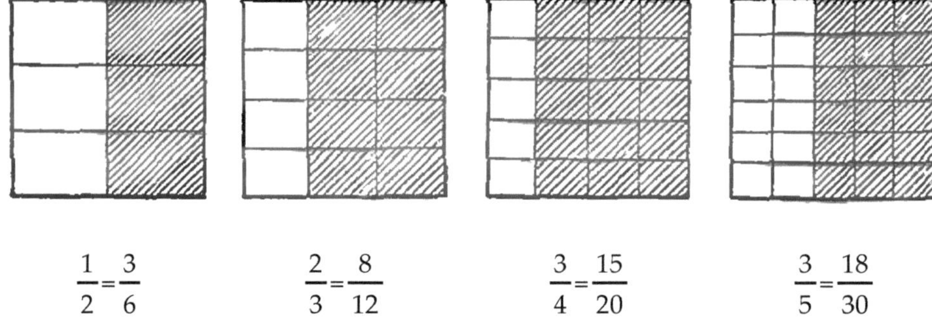

$$\frac{1}{2}=\frac{3}{6} \qquad \frac{2}{3}=\frac{8}{12} \qquad \frac{3}{4}=\frac{15}{20} \qquad \frac{3}{5}=\frac{18}{30}$$

Examine these equations one by one, treating each after some such manner as follows:

How might we obtain the numerator 18 from the numerator 3? (Multiply by 6.)

The denominator 30 from the denominator 5? (Multiply by 6.)

$$\frac{1x3}{2x3}=\frac{3}{6};\ \frac{2x4}{3x4}=\frac{8}{12};\ \frac{3x5}{4x5}=\frac{15}{20};\ \frac{3x6}{5x6}=\frac{18}{30}.$$

If we multiply both the numerator and the denominator of the fraction $3/5$ by 6, what will be the effect upon the value of the fraction? (It will be unchanged.)

What have we done with the numerator and denominator in

every case? How has the fraction been affected? What rule may we infer from these examples? (Multiplying the numerator and denominator by the same number does not alter the value of the fraction.)

The formal steps

In describing the process of acquiring either a general notion or a general truth, the psychologist and logician usually divide it into four parts as follows:

1. The person is said to analyse a number of particular cases. In the above examples this would mean, in the conceptual lesson, noting the various characteristics of the several words, John, Toronto, desk, etc.; and in the second lesson, noting the facts involved in the several cases of shading.

2. The mind is said to compare the characteristics of the several particular cases, noting any likenesses and unlikenesses.

3. The mind is said to pick out, or abstract, any quality or quantities common to all the particular cases.

4. Finally the mind is supposed to synthesise these common characteristics into a general notion, or concept, in the conceptual process, and into a general truth if the process is inductive.

Thus the conceptual and inductive processes are both said to involve the same four steps of:

1. *Analysis.*—Interpreting a number of individual cases.

2. *Comparison.*—Noting likenesses and differences between the several individual examples.

3. *Abstraction.*—Selecting the common characteristics.

4. *Generalization.*—Synthesis of common characteristics into a general truth or a general notion, as the case may be.

Criticism.—Here again it will be found, however, that the steps of the logician do not fully represent what takes place in the pupil's mind as he goes through the learning process in a conceptual or inductive lesson. It is to be noted first that the above outline does not signify the presence of any problem to cause the child to proceed with the analysis of the several particular cases. Assuming the existence of the problem, unless this problem involves all the particular examples, the question arises whether the learner will suspend coming to any conclusion until he has analysed and compared all the particular cases before him. It is here that the actual learning process is found to vary somewhat from the outline of the psychologist and logician. As will be seen below, the child really finds his problem in the first particular case presented to him. Moreover, as he analyses out the characteristics of this case, he does not really suspend fully the generalizing process until he has examined a number of other cases, but, as the teacher is fully aware, is much more likely to jump at once to a more or less correct conclusion from the one example. It is true, of course, that it is only by going on to compare this with other cases that he assures himself that this first conclusion is correct. This slight variation of the actual learning process from the formal outline will become evident if one considers how a child builds up any general notion in ordinary life.

Conception as a Learning Process

A. In Ordinary Life.—Suppose a young child has received a vague impression of a cow from meeting a first and only example; we find that by accepting this as a problem and by applying to it such experience as he then possesses, he is able to read some meaning into it, for instance, that it is a brown, four-footed, hairy object. This idea, once formed, does not remain a mere particular idea, but becomes a general means for interpreting other experiences. At first, indeed, the idea may serve to read meaning, not only into another cow, but also into a horse or a buffalo. In course of time, however, as this first imperfect concept of the animal is used in interpreting cows and perhaps other animals, the first crude concept may in time, by comparison, develop into a relatively true, or logical, concept, applicable to only the actual members of the class. Now here, the child did not wait to generalize until such time as the several really essential characteristics were decided upon, but in each succeeding case applied his present knowledge to the particular thing presented. It was, in other words, by a series of regular selecting and relating processes, that his general notion was finally clarified.

B. In the School.—Practically the same conditions are noted in the child's study of particular examples in an inductive or conceptual lesson in the school, although the process is much more rapid on account of its being controlled by the teacher. In the lesson outlined above, the pupil finds a problem in the very first word *John*, and adjusts himself thereto in a more or less perfect way by an apperceptive process involving both a selecting and a relating of ideas. With this first more or less perfect notion as a working hypothesis, the pupil goes on to examine the next word. If he gains the true notion from the first example, he merely verifies this through the other particular examples. If his first notion is not correct, however, he is able to correct it by a further process of analysis and synthesis in connection with other examples. Throughout the formal stages, therefore, the pupil is merely applying his growing general knowledge in a selective, or analytic, way to the interpreting of several particular examples, until such time as a perfect general, or class, notion is obtained and verified. It is, indeed, on account of this immediate tendency of the mind to generalize, that care must be taken to present the children with typical examples. To make them examine a sufficient number of examples is to ensure the correcting of crude notions that may be formed by any of the pupils through their generalizing perhaps from a single particular.

Induction as a Learning Process

In like manner, in an inductive lesson, although the results of the process of the development of a general principle may for convenience be arranged logically under the above four heads, it is evident that the child could not wholly suspend his conclusions until a number of particular cases had been examined and compared. In the lesson on the rule for conversion of fractions to equivalent fractions with different denominators, the pupils could not possibly apperceive, or analyse, the examples as suggested under the head of selection, or analysis, without at the same time implicitly abstracting and generalizing. Also in the lesson below on the predicate adjective, the pupils could not note, in all the examples, all the features given under analysis and fail at the same time to abstract and generalize. The fact is that in such lessons, if the selection, or analysis, is completed in only one example, abstraction and generalization implicitly unfold themselves at the same time and constitute a relating, or synthetic, act of the mind. The fourfold arrangement of the matter, however, may let the teacher see more fully the children's mental attitude, and thus enable him to direct them intelligently through the apperceptive process. It will undoubtedly also impress on the teacher's mind the need of having the pupils compare particular cases until a correct notion is fully organized in experience.

TWO PROCESSES SIMILAR

Notwithstanding the distinction drawn by psychologists between conception as a process of gaining a general notion, and induction as a process of arriving at a general truth, it is evident from the above that the two processes have much in common. In the development of many lesson topics, in fact, the lesson may be viewed as involving both a conceptual and an inductive process. In the subject of grammar, for instance, a first lesson on the pronoun may be viewed as a conceptual lesson, since the child gains an idea of a class of words, as indicated by the new general term pronoun, this term representing the result of a conceptual process. It may equally be viewed as an inductive lesson, since the child gains from the lesson a general truth, or judgment, as expressed in his new definition—"A pronoun is a word that represents an object without naming it," the definition representing the result of an inductive process. This fact will be considered more fully, however, in Chapter XXVIII.

Further Examples of Inductive Lessons

As further illustrations of an inductive process, the following outlines of lessons might be noted. The processes are outlined according to the formal steps. The student-teacher should consider how the children are to approach each problem and to what extent they are likely to generalize as the various examples are being interpreted during the analytic stage.

1. THE SUBJECTIVE PREDICATE ADJECTIVE

Analysis, or selection:

Divide the following sentences into subject and predicate:

The man was old.
The weather turned cold.
The day grew stormy.
The boy became ill.
The concert proved successful.

What kind of man is referred to in the first sentence? What part of speech is "old"? What part of the sentence does it modify? In what part of the sentence does it stand? Could it be omitted? What then is its duty with reference to the verb? What are its two duties? (It completes the verb "was" and modifies the subject "man.")

Lead the pupils to deal similarly with "cold," "stormy," "ill," "successful."

Comparison, Abstraction, and Generalization, or Organization:

What two duties has each of these italicized words? Each is called a "Subjective Predicate Adjective." What is a Subjective Predicate Adjective? (A Subjective Predicate Adjective is an adjective that completes the verb and modifies the subject.)

2. CONDENSATION OF VAPOUR

Analysis, or selection:

The pupils should be asked to report observations they have made concerning some familiar occurrences like the following:

(1) Breathe upon a cold glass and upon a warm glass. What do you notice in each case? Where must the drops of water have come from? Can you see this water ordinarily? In what form must the water have been before it formed in drops on the cold glass?

(2) What have you often noticed on the window of the kitchen on cool days? From where did these drops of water come? Could you see the vapour in the air? How did the temperature of the window panes compare with the temperature of the room?

(3) When the water in a tea-kettle is boiling rapidly, what do you see between the mouth of the spout and the cloud of steam? What must have come through that clear space? Is the steam then at first visible or invisible?

The pupils should be further asked to report observations and make correct inferences concerning such things as:

(4) The deposit of moisture on the outside surface of a pitcher of ice-water on a warm summer day.

(5) The clouded condition of one's eye-glasses on coming from the cold outside air into a warm room.

Comparison, Abstraction, and Generalization, or Organization:

In all these cases you have reported what there has been in the air. Was this vapour visible or invisible? Under what condition did it become visible?

The pupils should be led to sum up their observations in some such way as the following:

Air often contains much water vapour. When this comes in contact with cooler bodies, it condenses into minute particles of water. In other words, the two conditions of condensation are (1) a considerable quantity of water vapour in the air, and (2) contact with cooler bodies.

It must be borne in mind that in a conceptual or an inductive lesson care is to be taken by the teacher to see that the particulars are sufficient in number and representative in character. As already pointed out, crude notions often arise through generalizing from too few particulars or from particulars that are not typical of the whole class. Induction can be most frequently employed in elementary school work in the subjects of grammar, arithmetic, and nature study.

Inductive-deductive lessons

Before we leave this division of general method, it should be noted that many lessons combine in a somewhat formal way two or more of the foregoing lesson types.

In many inductive lessons the step of application really involves a process of deduction. For example, after teaching the definition of a noun by a process of induction as outlined above, we may, in the same lesson, seek to have the pupil use his new knowledge in pointing out particular nouns in a set of given sentences. Here, however, the pupil is evidently called upon to discover the value of particular words by the use of the newly learned general principle. When, therefore, he discovers the grammatical value of the particular word "Provender" in the sentence "Provender is dear," the pupil's process of learning can be represented in the deductive form as follows:

> All naming words are nouns.
> *Provender* is a naming word.
> *Provender* is a noun.

Although in these exercises the real aim is not to have the pupil learn the value of the individual word, but to test his mastery of the general principle, such application undoubtedly corresponds with the deductive learning process previously outlined. Any inductive lesson, therefore, which includes the above type of application may rightly be described as an inductive-deductive lesson. A great many lessons in grammar and arithmetic are of this type.

CHAPTER XVI

THE LESSON UNIT

What Constitutes a Lesson Problem.—The foregoing analysis and description of the learning process has shown that the ordinary school lesson is designed to lead the pupil to build up, or organize, a new experience, or, as it is sometimes expressed, to gain control of a unit of valuable knowledge, presented as a single problem. From what has been learned concerning the relating activity of mind, however, it is evident that the teacher may face a difficulty when he is called upon to decide what extent of knowledge, or experience, is to be accepted as a knowledge unit. It was noted, for example, that many topics regularly treated in a single lesson fall into quite distinct sub-divisions, each of which represents to a certain extent a separate group of related ideas and, therefore, a single problem. On the other hand, many different lesson experiences, or topics, although taught as separate units, are seen to stand so closely related, that in the end they naturally organize themselves into a larger single unit of knowledge, representing a division, of the subject of study. From this it is evident that situations may arise, as in teaching the classes of sentences in grammar, in which the teacher must ask himself whether it will be possible to take up the whole topic with its important sub-divisions in a single lesson, or whether each sub-division should be treated in a single lesson.

How to Approach Associated Problems.—Even when it is realized that the related matter is too large for a single lesson, it must be decided whether it will be better to bring on each sub-division as a separate topic, and later let these sub-divisions synthesise into a new unity; or whether the larger topic should be taken up first in a general way, and the sub-divisions made topics of succeeding lessons. In the study of mood in grammar, for example, shall we introduce each mood separately, and finally have the child synthesise the separate facts; or shall we begin with a lesson on mood in general, and follow this with a study of the separate moods? In like manner, in the study of winds in geography, shall we study in order land and sea breezes, trade-winds, and monsoons, and have the child synthesise these facts at the end of the series; or shall we begin with a study of winds in general, and follow this with a more detailed study of the three classes of winds?

WHOLE TO PARTS

Advantages.—The second of these methods, which is often called the method of proceeding from whole to parts, should, whenever possible, be followed. For instance, in a study of such a lesson as *Dickens in the Camp*, the detailed study of the various stanzas should be preceded by an introductory lesson, bringing out the leading thought of the poem, and noting the sub-topics. When, in an introductory lesson, the pupil is able to gain control of a large topic, and see the relation to it of a given number of sub-topics, he is selecting and relating the parts of the whole topic by the normal analytic-synthetic method. Moreover, in the following lessons, he is much more likely to appreciate the relation of the various sub-topics to the central topic, and the inter-relations between these various sub-topics. For this reason, in such subjects as history, literature, geography, etc., pupils are often introduced to these large divisions, or complex lesson units, and given a vague knowledge of the whole topic, the detailed study of the parts being made in subsequent lessons.

Examples.—The following outlines will further illustrate how a series of lessons (numbered I, II, III, etc.) may thus proceed from a first study of the larger whole to a more detailed study of a number of subordinate parts.

THE ST. LAWRENCE RIVER SYSTEM

I. Topic.—The St. Lawrence River:

Position, size, extent of system, other characteristics. Importance—historical, commercial, industrial.

II. Sub-topic 1.—Importance historically:

Open mouth to Europe; Open door to continent; Cartier, Champlain. System of lakes and rivers large and small gave lines of communication, inviting discovery and subsequent development and settlement.

III. Sub-topic 2.—Importance commercially:

Large tracts of valuable land, timber, etc., made available. Highway—need of such between East and West. Difficulties to be overcome, canal, ships. Competition of railways, How? Classes of goods back and forth. Avenue to and from the wheat land.

IV. Sub-topic 3.—Importance industrially:

Great commercial centres—where located and why? Water powers, elevators, manufacturing of raw materials made available in the large areas; Immigration; Fishing.

STUDY OF BACTERIA

I. Topic.—Bacteria:

What they are; relations, comparisons; other plants in same class, or those of higher orders; size, shape; where found; conditions of growth; propagation; modes of distribution; etc.

II. Sub-topic 1.—Our interest in bacteria, arising out of the injury or good they do:

(*a*) Injury: Decay of fruits, trees, tissues, etc., diseases—diphtheria, typhoid, tuberculosis; how developed, conditions, favourable toxins.

(*b*) Benefits: In soil, cheese, butter, etc.; chemical action, building new compounds and breaking up other compounds.

III. Sub-topic 2.—Our interest in controlling them; the methods based on mode and conditions of growth, etc.:

(*a*) Prevention: Eliminating favourable conditions; low temperature, high temperatures, cleanliness; sewerage disposal; clean cow-stables, cellars, kitchens, etc.; antiseptics—carbolic, formalin, sugar for fruit, sealing up; quarantine, vaccination, antitoxin.

(*b*) Cultures,—alfalfa, cheese, butter, under control.

GEOGRAPHY OF EUROPE

I. Topic.—Europe:

What interest to us; why we study it; position, latitude, near water, boundaries, size; Surface features—highlands, lowlands, drainage rivers, coast-line, etc. Climate—temperature (means, Jan., July), wind, moisture.

II. Sub-topic 1.—Products (based on above conditions):

Vegetation, animal, mineral; vary over area according to physical climatic, and geological conditions; Kinds of products of each class, in each area, etc.

III. Sub-topic 2.—Occupations (based on Lesson II):

Study of operations and conditions favourable and unfavourable under which each product is produced, gathered, and manufactured. Industries, arising from work on the raw materials.

IV. Sub-topic 3.—Trade and Commerce (based on Lessons II and III):

Transportation, producers selling and manufacturers buying raw material, distributed to homes in country and city, to factories within the region itself, to regions beyond, across oceans, etc. Manufactured products sent out, exports and imports.

V. Sub-topic 4.—Civil advantages (based on Lessons I, III, and IV):

Conditions of living—homes, dress, work and pleasure; trades, education, government, social, religious, etc.

PARTS TO WHOLE

The method of whole to parts cannot be followed in all cases even where a number of lesson units may possess important points of inter-relation. Although, for instance, simple and compound addition and addition of fractions are only different phases of one process, no one would advocate the combining of these into such a unified lesson series. In Canadian History, also, although the conditions of the Quebec Act, the coming of the United Empire Loyalists, and the passing of the Constitutional Act, have definite points of inter-relation, it would nevertheless be unwise to attempt to evolve these out of a single complex lesson unit. In such cases, therefore, the synthesis of the various parts must be made as the lessons proceed. Moreover, it is well to ensure the complete organization of the elements by means of an outline review at the end of the lesson series. The student-teacher will meet an example of this process under the topical lesson in Chapter XVII.

PRECAUTIONS

It is evident from the above considerations, that certain precautions should be observed in deciding upon the particular subject-matter to be included in each lesson topic.

1. A just balance should be maintained between the difficulty of each lesson unit and the ability of the class. Matter that is too easy requires no effort in its mastery and hence is uninteresting. Matter that is too difficult discourages effort, and is, therefore, equally uninteresting. It should be sufficiently easy for every pupil to master, and sufficiently difficult to require real effort.

2. The amount of matter included should be carefully adjusted to the length of time taken for the lesson and to the attainments of the class. If too much is attempted, there will be insufficient time for adequate drill and review, and hence there will be lack of thoroughness. If too little is attempted, time will be wasted in needless repetition.

3. Each unit of instruction in any subject should, in general, grow out of the preceding unit taken in that subject, and be closely connected with it. It is in this way that a pupil's interest is aroused for the new problem and his knowledge becomes organized. Neglect in this regard results in the possession of disconnected and unsystematized facts.

Each lesson should contain one or more central facts around which the other facts are grouped. This permits easy organization of the material of the lesson, and ensures its retention by the pupils. Further, the pupils are by this means trained to discriminate between the essential and the non-essential.

CHAPTER XVII

LESSON TYPES

The Developing Lesson.—In the various lesson plans already considered, the aim has always appeared as an attempt to direct the learning process so that the pupil may both build up a new experience and also gain such control over it as will enable him to turn it to practical use. Because in all such lessons the teacher is supposed to direct the pupils through the four steps of the learning process in such a way that they discover for themselves some important new experience, or develop it out of their own present knowledge, the lessons are spoken of as developing lessons. Moreover, the two parts of the lesson in which the new experience is especially gained by the pupils, namely the selecting and relating processes, are often spoken of as a single step and called the step of *development,* the lesson then being treated under four heads: Problem, preparation, development, and application.

Auxiliary Lessons.—It is evident, however, that there may be lessons in which this direct attempt to have the pupils build up some wholly new experience through a regularly controlled learning process, will not appear as the chief purpose of the lesson. In the previous consideration of the deductive lesson, it was pointed out that this type may be used to give a further mastery of general rules previously learned, rather than a knowledge of particular examples. Such would be the case in an ordinary parsing and analysis lesson in grammar. Here the primary purpose is, evidently, not to give the pupils a grammatical knowledge of the particular words and sentences which are being parsed and analysed, but rather to give them better control of certain general rules of language which they have partially mastered in previous lessons. So also a lesson in writing may seek, not to teach the form of some new letter, but to give skill in writing a letter form which the pupils have already learned. In an exercise in addition of fractions, also, the aim is not so much to have the pupil know these particular questions, as to have him gain a more complete control of the previously learned rule. In other lessons the pupils may be left to secure new knowledge largely for themselves, and the recitation be devoted to testing whether they have been able to accomplish this successfully. In still other lessons the teacher may merely outline a certain topic or certain topics, preparatory to such independent study by the pupils.

The following outlines will explain and exemplify these auxiliary lesson types.

THE STUDY LESSON

Purpose of Study Lesson.—The purpose of the Study Lesson is the mastery by the pupils of a stated portion of the text-book. Ultimately, however it is the cultivation of the power of gleaning information from the printed page, of selecting essential features, and of arranging these in their proper relationships.

The main difficulty in connection with the study lesson is the adaptation of the matter to the interests of the pupils. This difficulty is sometimes due to their inability to interpret the language of the book, and to the difficulty of their distinguishing the salient features from the non-essential. The trouble in this regard is accentuated when they approach the lesson with an inadequate preparation of mind.

The study lesson falls naturally into two parts, the assignment and the seat work.

The Assignment.—The object of the assignment is to put the pupils in an attitude of inquiry toward the new matter. It corresponds to the conception of the problem and the step of preparation in the development lesson. The most successful assignment is one in which the interest of the pupils is aroused to such a pitch that they are anxious to read more about the subject. In general it will consist of a recall of those ideas, or a statement of those facts upon which the interpretation of the new matter depends. Most of the unsuccessful study lessons are due to insufficient care in the assignment. Often pupils are told to read so many pages of the book, without any preliminary preparation and without any idea of what facts they are to learn. Under such conditions, the result is usually a very slight interest in the lesson, and consequently an unsatisfactory grasp of it.

Examples of Assignment.—A few examples will serve to illustrate what is meant by an adequate assignment. When a new reading lesson is to be prepared, the assignment should include the pronunciation and meaning of the different words, and a general understanding of the passage to be read. For a new spelling lesson, the assignment should include the pronunciation and meaning of the words, and any special difficulties that may appear in them. In assigning a history lesson on, say, the Capture of Quebec, the teacher should discuss with the class the position of Quebec, the difficulties that would present themselves to a besieging army, the character and personal appearance of Wolfe (making him stand out as vividly as possible), and the position seized by the British army, illustrating as far as possible by maps and diagrams. Then the class will be in a mental attitude to read with interest the dramatic story of the taking of the fortress. If the pupils were about to study the geography of British Columbia, the teacher might, in the assignment, ask them to note from the map of Canada the position of the province and the direction of the mountain ranges; to infer the character and direction of the rivers and their value for navigation; to infer the nature of the climate, knowing the direction of the prevailing winds; to infer the character of the chief industries, knowing the physical features and climate. With these facts in mind the class will be able to read intelligently what the text-book says about British Columbia.

The Seat Work.—However good the assignment may be, there is always a danger that there will be much waste of time in connection with the seat work. The tendency to mind-wandering is always so great that the time devoted to the preparation of lessons at seats may to a large extent be lost, unless special precautions are taken in that regard. Unfortunately every lesson cannot be made so enthralling that the pupil's mind is kept upon it in spite of distractions. To prevent this possible waste of time, suggestions have already been made in another connection (page 67 above). These will bear repetition here. Questions upon the matter to be studied might be placed on the black-board and pupils asked to prepare answers for these. The difficulty with this plan is, that, unless the questions are carefully thought out by the teacher, the pupils may get from their reading only a few disconnected facts instead of organized knowledge. The pupils might be asked to prepare lists of questions for themselves, and the one who had the best list might be permitted to put his questions to the rest of the class. The difficulty here is that most pupils have a tendency to question about what is unimportant and to neglect the important. In the higher classes, the pupils might be required to make a topical outline of the lesson studied. This requires considerable analytic ability, and the results at first are likely to be disappointing. However, it is an ability worth striving for. The individual who can readily outline what he has read has mastered the art of reading.

Use of Study Lessons.—There is a danger that the study lesson may be used too much or too little. In an ungraded school containing many classes, the teacher may be tempted to rely solely upon the study lesson as a means of intellectual advancement. Used exclusively it becomes monotonous, and the pupils grow weary of the constant effort required. On the other hand, in the graded school, where a teacher has charge of only one class, there will be a tendency to depend entirely on the oral presentation of lessons, to the exclusion of the text-book altogether. The result is that pupils do not cultivate the power to obtain knowledge from books. The study lesson should alternate with the oral lesson, so that monotony may be avoided, and the pupils will reap the undoubted benefits of both methods.

THE RECITATION LESSON

Purpose of the Recitation Lesson.—The recitation lesson is the complement of the study lesson. Its purpose is to test the pupil's grasp of the facts he has read during the study period. Incidentally the teacher clears up difficulties and corrects misconceptions on the part of the pupil. The facts of the text-book may be amplified from the teacher's stock of information. Abstract facts may be illustrated in a concrete way. The important facts may be emphasized and the unimportant ones lightly passed over. The ultimate aim of the recitation lesson is to add something to the pupil's power of interpreting and organizing facts.

Precautions.—Some precautions are to be noted in connection with the recitation lesson. (1) Care must be exercised that the pupils are not reciting mere words that have no solid basis of ideas. Young children are particularly expert at verbalizing. (2) Care must also be taken that the pupils have not merely scrappy information, but have the ideas thoroughly organized. (3) The teacher must know the facts to be recited well enough to be independent of the text-book during the recitation. To conduct the lesson with an open book before him is a confession of weakness on the part of the teacher.

Conducting the recitation lesson

There are two methods of conducting the recitation lesson, namely, the question and answer method and the topical method.

A. The Question and Answer Method.—This is the easier method for the pupil, as he is called upon to answer only in a brief form detailed questions asked by the teacher. The onus of the analysis of the lesson rests largely upon the teacher. He must ask the questions in a proper sequence so that, if the answers of the pupils were written out, they would form a connected account of the matter. He must be able to detect from the pupils' answers whether they have real knowledge or are merely masquerading with words. To be able to question well is one of the most valuable accomplishments that a teacher can possess. The whole problem of the art of questioning will be considered in the next Chapter.

B. The Topical Method.—The topical recitation consists in the pupil's reporting the facts of the study lesson with a minimum of questioning on the part of the teacher. Two advantages are apparent: (1) It gives the pupil an excellent training in organizing his materials, and (2) it develops his language power. It is to be feared that the topical recitation is not so frequently used as its value warrants. The reason is probably that it is a difficult method to follow. Poor results are usually secured at first, teachers grow discouraged, they stop trying it, and thereafter put their whole faith in the question and answer recitation. This is unfortunate, for however good the latter may be, it is greatly inferior to the topical recitation in helping the pupil to institute relations among his facts, and in improving his power to use his mother-tongue effectively. Successful topical recitations can be secured only at the price of long, patient, and persistent effort. The teacher can gradually work towards them from detailed questions to questions requiring the combination of a few sentences in answer, and thence to the complete outline. In almost every lesson the pupils may be called upon to summarize some topic after it has been gone over by means of detailed questions. In such answers the pupils may reasonably be expected to state the facts in their proper connection and in good language form. In reviews, also, in such subjects as history and geography, the pupils should be frequently called upon to recite topically.

THE DRILL LESSON

Purpose of Drill Lesson.—The Drill Lesson involves the repetition of matter in the same form as it was originally learned, in order to fix it in the mind so firmly that its recall will eventually become automatic. In other words, the function of this type of lesson is habit-formation. It is necessary in those subjects that are more or less mechanical in nature, and that can be reduced to the plane of habit. The field of the drill lesson will, therefore, be largely restricted to spelling, writing, language, and the mechanical phases of art and arithmetic.

The Method.—As the purpose of the drill lesson is the formation of habit, the method will involve the application of the principles that lie at the basis of habit-formation. These are, (1) attention to the thing to be done so as to obtain a vivid picture or a clear understanding of it, and (2) repetition with attention. For instance, if the writing lesson is the formation of the capital E, the class will examine carefully a model form, note the parts of which it is composed, the relative size and position of the parts, how they are connected, etc. Then will follow the repetition of the form by the pupils, each time with careful attention to the method of making it, comparison with the model, and the noting of defects in their work. This will continue until the letter can be made correctly without attention, that is, until the method of making it has been reduced to a habit. If the lesson is on the spelling of difficult words, the first step will be to observe the pronunciation of each, the division into syllables, the difficult part of the word, and the order of the letters. Then the word will be repeated attentively until it can be spelled without effort. In a language lesson on the correct use, say, of "lie" and "lay," the pupils will first be called upon to observe the forms of each, "lie, lay, lain, lying," and "lay, laid, laying"—as used in sentences on the black-board, and the meaning of each group—"lie" meaning "to recline" and "lay" meaning "to place." The pupils will then repeat attentively the correct forms of the words in sentences, until they finally reach the stage when they unconsciously use the words correctly, or as habits of speech. The same principles apply in learning the addition and multiplication tables, and the tables of weights and measures in arithmetic; in the memorization of gems of poetry and prose; in the learning of dates, lists of events, and important provisions of acts in history; and in the memorization of lists of places and products in geography, where this is desirable. In all the cases mentioned, it must not be supposed that a single drill lesson will be sufficient for the fixing of the desired knowledge or skill. Before instant and unconscious reaction can be depended upon, repetition will be needed at intervals for some time.

Danger in Mere Repetition.—In connection with the repetition necessary in the second stage of the drill lesson, an important precaution should be noted. It is impossible for anybody to repeat anything *attentively* many times in succession unless there is some new element noted in each repetition. When there is no longer a new element, the repetition becomes mechanical, and hence comparatively useless so far as acquisition of knowledge or even habit is concerned. To ask a pupil who has difficulty with a combination in addition, or a product in multiplication, or the spelling of a word, to repeat it many times in succession, may be not only waste of time, but even worse, because a tendency toward mind-wandering may be encouraged. The practice of requiring pupils to write out new words, or words that have been mis-spelled in the dictation lesson, five, ten, or twenty times successively, cannot be too strongly condemned. The attention cannot possibly be concentrated upon the work beyond two or three repetitions, and the fact that pupils frequently make mistakes two or three words down the column and repeat this mistake to the end, is sufficient proof of the mechanical nature of the process. The little boy who had difficulty with the use of "went" and "gone," and was commanded by his teacher to write "I have gone" a hundred times on his slate, illustrates this principle exactly. He had been left to finish his task alone and, after writing "I have gone" faithfully forty or fifty times, grew tired of the monotony of the process. Turning the slate over, he wrote on the other side, "I have went home" and left it on the desk for the teacher's approval.

How to Overcome Dangers.—To avoid this difficulty, some device must be adopted to secure attention to each repetition until the knowledge is firmly fixed. For instance, instead of asking the pupil many times one after the other, what seven times six are, it would be better to introduce other combinations and come back frequently to seven times six. In that way the pupil would have to attend to it every time it came up. Similarly, in learning to spell a troublesome word like "separate," the best plan would be to mix it up with other words and come back to it often. Repetition is always necessary in the drill lesson, but it should always be *repetition with attention*.

THE REVIEW LESSON

Purpose of Review Lesson.—As the name implies, a review is a new view of old knowledge. While the drill lesson repeats the matter in the same form as it was originally learned, the review lesson repeats the matter from another standpoint or in new relations. The function of the review lesson is the organization of the material of a series of lessons into an inter-connected whole, and incidentally the fixing of these facts in the mind by the additional repetitions.

Kinds of Review.—Almost every lesson gives opportunities for incidental reviews. The step of preparation recalls old ideas in new connections, and may be properly considered a review. A lesson on the "gerund" in grammar would require a recall of the various relations in which a noun may stand, and the various ways in which a verb may be completed. It is quite probable that the pupils have never before brought these facts together in an organized way. Similarly, the step of expression affords opportunity for review. The solution of problems in simple interest confronts the pupils with new situations in which this principle can be applied. The reproduction of the matter of the history lesson requires the selection of the important facts from the mass of details given and the placing of these in their proper relationship to one another.

But besides the incidental reviews which form a part of nearly all lessons, there must be lessons which are purely reviews. Without these, the pupil, because of insufficient repetition, would rapidly forget the facts he had once learned or would never really know the facts at all, because he had not seen them in all their connections. There are two methods of conducting these reviews: (1) by means of the topical outline, (2) by means of the method of comparison.

The Topical Review

Purpose of Topical Outlines.—By this method the pupil gets a bird's-eye view of a whole field. In learning the matter originally, his attention was largely concentrated upon the individual facts, and it is quite probable that he has since lost sight of some of the threads of unity running through them. The topical outline will bring these into prominence. It will enable the pupil to keep in his mind the most important headings of a subject, the sub-headings, and the individual facts coming under these. Whatever may be said against the practice of memorizing topical outlines, it must be acknowledged that unless it is done the pupil's knowledge of the subject is likely to be very hazy, indefinite, and disconnected.

Illustrations from History.—As an illustration of the review lesson by means of the topical outline, take the history of the Hudson's Bay Company. If the pupil has followed the order of the text-book, he has probably learned this subject in pieces—a bit here, another some pages later, and still another a few chapters farther on. In the multiplicity of other events, he has probably missed the connections among the facts, and a topical review will be necessary to establish these. He may be required to go through his history text-book, reading all the parts relating to the Hudson's Bay Company. He will thus get a grasp of the relationships among the facts, and this will be made firmer if an outline such as the following is worked out with the assistance of the teacher.

THE HUDSON'S BAY COMPANY

I. Early History:

1. Groseilliers and Radisson interest Prince Rupert in possibilities of trade in North-Western Canada. Two vessels fitted out for Hudson's Bay. Report favourable.

2. Charter granted Hudson's Bay Company by Charles II, 1670.

3. Forts Nelson, Albany, Rupert, and Hayes attacked and captured by DeTroyes and D'Iberville, 1686. Restored by Treaty of Utrecht, 1713.

II. Nature of Fur-trade:

1. Furs gathered by Indians in winter.

2. Conveyed to forts in summer, after incredible difficulties.

3. Ceremonies on arrival of Indians at forts.

4. Articles exchanged for furs at first showy and worthless, but later more useful and valuable, for example, guns, hatchets, powder, shot, blankets, etc.

III. Rivals of Hudson's Bay Company:

1. Coureurs-de-bois.

2. Scottish traders—ranged from Michilimackinac to Saskatchewan. H.B. Co. built Cumberland House on Saskatchewan to compete for interior trade.

3. North-West Company, 1783-4—at first friendly to H.B. Co., but later bitter enemies.

IV. The Selkirk Settlement:

1. *Establishment.*—Lord Selkirk, a Scottish philanthropist, and a shareholder in the Hudson's Bay Co., purchased from the Company 70,000 square miles of land around Red River for Scotch col-

onies, 1811. About three hundred settlers came within three years. Miles Macdonell at head of the colony.

2. *Trouble with North-West Company.*—

(*a*) Suspicion of N.W. Co. that colony was established by H.B. Co. to compete for fur trade.

(*b*) Proclamation of Macdonell that food should not be taken out of settlement. Attack on colony by Metis Indians encouraged by N.W. Co. Withdrawal of colonists to Lake Winnipeg.

(*c*) Return with reinforcements under Semple. Skirmish at Seven Oaks, 1816. Semple with twenty others killed.

(*d*) Selkirk's descent upon Fort William. Arrest of several Nor'Westers. Colony at Red River restored.

(*e*) Nor'Westers acquitted of murder of Semple. Selkirk convicted and heavily fined for acts of violence. Selkirk withdrew from Canada in disappointment and disgust.

3. *Later Progress.*—

(*a*) Hardships of pioneer life like those of Ontario.

(*b*) A series of disasters—grasshoppers, floods.

(*c*) Prosperity finally came.

(*d*) Government at first administered by governor of H.B. Co., later assisted by Council of fourteen members.

V. Amalgamation of Rival Companies:

1. *Union.*—

After withdrawal of Selkirk, the H.B. Co. and the N.W. Co. united in 1821, under name of former.

2. *Subsequent Progress.*—

(*a*) Governor Sir George Simpson extended posts westward to Pacific.

(*b*) Through his energy Britain was able to retain possession of Western Canada in spite of aggression of United States and Russia.

VI. Relinquishment of Administrative Powers:

1. Canadian Government claimed that the rule of the Company hindered development of Western Canada because it was interested only in trade.

2. *Agreement with Canadian Government.*—

(*a*) Company sold Prince Rupert's Land and gave up its trade monopoly.

(*b*) In return.—

(i) Received £300,000.

(ii) Retained one twentieth of land south of the Saskatchewan.

(iii) Retained its posts and trading privileges.

3. Company still exists as a trading organization with many posts in the West and large stores in many cities.

VII. Services of H.B. Co. to Canada and the Empire:

1. Opened up a valuable trade in Western Canada.

2. Explored and opened up the West for settlement.

3. Retained for Britain the territory west of Rockies when it was in danger of falling into other hands.

The subjects of the Public and Separate School Course where topical reviews are most necessary are history and geography.

The Comparative Review

A thing always stands out most vividly in the mind when the relations of similarity and difference are perceived between it and other things. When we compare and contrast two things, certain features of each that would otherwise escape our attention are brought to light. We get a clearer idea of both the rabbit and the squirrel when we compare their various characteristics. Great Britain and Germany are each better understood geographically, when we set up comparisons between them; Pitt and Walpole stand out more clearly as statesmen when we compare and contrast them. One of the most effective forms of review is that in which the relations of likeness and difference are set up between subjects that have already been studied. For instance, the geographical features of Manitoba and British Columbia may be effectively reviewed by instituting comparisons between them in regard to (1) position and size, (2) physical features, (3) climate, (4) industries, (5) products, (6) commercial centres. The careers of Walpole and Pitt might be reviewed by comparing and contrasting them with regard to (1) circumstances under which each became Prime Minister, (2) domestic policy, (3) foreign policy, (4) circumstances surrounding the resignation of each, (5) personal character.

Whatever form the review lesson may take, the teacher should always keep in mind its two main purposes, namely, (1) the organization of knowledge which comes through the apprehension of new relationships, and (2) the deeper impression of facts on the mind which comes through attentive repetition.

CHAPTER XVIII

QUESTIONING

Importance.—As a teaching device, questioning must always occupy a place of the highest importance. While it may not be always true that good questioning is synonymous with good teaching, there can be no doubt that the good teacher must have, as one of his qualifications, the ability to question well. A good question is a problem to solve. A stimulating problem arouses and directs mental activity. Well-directed mental activity is the prime requisite of all learning and one of the ends which all effective teaching endeavours to realize. Questioning is one of the best means of securing that desirable activity of mind without which intellectual progress is impossible. The teacher who would master the technique of his art must study to attain skill in questioning.

QUALIFICATIONS OF THE GOOD QUESTIONER

A. Knowledge of Subject and of Mind.—The most obvious essentials are familiarity with the subject-matter and a knowledge of the mental processes of the child. Without the first, the questions will be pointless, haphazard, and unsystematic; without the second, they will be ill-adjusted to the interests and attainments of the pupils. A thorough knowledge of the facts of the lesson and a keen insight into the workings of the child mind are indispensable.

B. Analytic Ability.—As an accompaniment of the first of these qualifications, the good questioner must have analytic ability. The material of the lesson must be analysed into its elements and the relations of these must be clearly perceived if it is to be effectively presented to the pupils. The teacher must further have the power to discriminate between the important and the unimportant. The ability to seize upon the essential features and to give due prominence to these is one of the most valuable accomplishments a teacher can have.

C. Knowledge of Pupils' Experiences.—As an accompaniment of the second qualification, the good questioner must have a knowledge of the previous experience and of the capacities of the pupils. Good teaching consists largely in the skilful adjustment of the new to the old. The teacher must ascertain what the pupils already know, what their interests are, and what matter they may reasonably be expected to apprehend, if he is to have them assimilate properly the facts of the lesson. He must further show sympathy and tact in order to inspire the pupils to their best effort. He must be able to detect unerringly the symptoms of inattention, listlessness, and misbehaviour, and by a well-directed question to bring back the wandering attention to the subject in hand.

Faults in Questioning.—There are two serious weaknesses that many young teachers exhibit, namely, questioning when they ought to tell and telling when they ought to question. To tell pupils what they might easily discover for themselves is to deprive them of the joy of conquest and to miss an opportunity of exercising and strengthening their mental powers. On the other hand, to question upon matter which the pupils cannot reasonably be expected to know or discover is to discourage effort and encourage guessing. To know just when to question and when to tell requires considerable discrimination and insight on the part of the teacher.

PURPOSES OF QUESTIONING

Questioning has three main purposes, namely:

1. To determine the limits of the pupil's present knowledge in order that the teacher may have a definite basis upon which to build the new material;

2. To direct the pupil's thought along a prescribed channel to a definite end, to lead him to make discoveries and form conclusions on his own account;

3. To ascertain how far he has grasped the meaning of the new material that has been presented.

A. Preparatory.—The first of these purposes may be designated as preparatory. Here the teacher clears the ground for the presentation of the new matter by recalling the old related facts necessary to the interpretation of the new. In thus sounding the depths of the pupil's previous knowledge, the teacher should usually ask questions that demand fairly long answers instead of those which may be answered briefly. The onus of the recall should be placed largely upon the pupil. The teacher will do comparatively little talking; the pupil will do much.

B. Developing.—The second purpose may be described as developing. The pupil is led step by step to a conclusion. Each question grows naturally out of the preceding question, the responsibility for this logical connection falling upon the teacher. The pupil has before him a certain set of conditions, and he is asked to infer the logical result of such conditions. He forms inferences, makes new discoveries, sets up new relationships, and formulates definitions and laws. It should be noted that this form of questioning gives no entirely new information to the pupil. It merely classifies and organizes what is already in his mind in a more or less indistinct and nebulous form. New information cannot be questioned out of a pupil; it must be given to him directly.

C. Recapitulation.—The third purpose of questioning may be described as recapitulatory. The pupil is asked to reproduce what he has learned during the progress of the lesson. At convenient intervals during the presentation and at the close, he should be asked to summarize in a connected manner the main points already covered. Thus the teacher tests the pupil's comprehension of the facts of the lesson. The pupil, on his side, as a result of such reproduction, has the facts more clearly fixed in his mind. As in the first stage of the lesson, the answers should be of considerable length, logically connected, and expressed in good language. The responsibility for this is again thrown largely upon the pupil. He does most of the talking; the teacher does little.

How Employed in Lesson.—It will thus be recognized that questioning is employed for different purposes at the three different stages of the lesson. At the opening of the lesson it prepares the mind of the pupil for what is to follow. During the presentation it leads the pupil to form his own inferences. At the close of the lesson it tests his grasp of the facts and gives these greater clearness and fixity in his mind. The first and third might both be designated as *testing* purposes, and the second *training*.

SOCRATIC QUESTIONING

Its Characteristics.—Developing, or training, questions, are sometimes referred to as Socratic questions. The terms are, however, not altogether synonymous. The method of Socrates had two divisions, known as *irony* and *maieutics*. The former consisted in leading the pupil to express an opinion on some subject of current interest, an opinion that was apparently accepted by Socrates. Then, by a series of questions adroitly put, he drove his pupil into a contradiction or an absurd position, thus revealing the inadequacy of the answer. This phase of the Socratic method is rarely applicable with young children. Occasionally, in grammar or arithmetic, for instance, an incorrect answer may properly be followed up so as to lead the pupil into a contradiction, but it is usually not desirable to embarrass him unnecessarily. It is never agreeable to be covered with the confusion which such a situation usually brings about. The other phase of the Socratic method, the *maieutics*, consisted in leading the pupil, by a further series of questions, to formulate the correct opinion of which the first hastily-given answer was only a fragment. This coincides with the developing method and may sometimes be profitably employed with young children.

Example of Socratic Questioning.—As an example of Socratic questioning may be noted the following taken from Plato's *Minos*. Socrates has questioned his companion concerning the nature of Law and has received the answer, "Law is the decree of the city." To show his companion the inadequacy of this definition, Socrates engages with him in the following dialogue:

> *Socrates*: Justice and law, are highly honourable; injustice and lawlessness, highly dishonourable; the former preserves cities, the latter ruins them?
>
> *Pupil*: Yes, it does.
>
> *Socrates*: Well, then! we must consider law as something honourable; and seek after it, under the assumption that it is a good thing. You defined law to be the decree of the city: Are not some decrees good, others evil?
>
> *Pupil*: Unquestionably.
>
> *Socrates*: But we have already said that law is not evil?

Pupil: I admit it.

Socrates: It is incorrect therefore to answer, as you did broadly, that law is the decree of the city. An evil decree cannot be law.

Pupil: I see that it is incorrect.

Having shown his pupil the fallacy of his first definition, Socrates proceeds to teach him that only what is right is lawful. This part of the dialogue proceeds as follows:

Socrates: Those who know, must of necessity hold the same opinion with each other, on matters which they know: always and everywhere?

Pupil: Yes—always and everywhere.

Socrates: Physicians write respecting matters of health what they account to be true, and these writings of theirs are the medical laws?

Pupil: Certainly they are.

Socrates: The like is true respecting the laws of farming, the laws of gardening, the laws of cookery. All these are the writings of persons, knowing in each of the respective pursuits?

Pupil: Yes.

Socrates: In like manner, what are the laws respecting the government of a city? Are they not the writings of those who know how to govern—kings, statesmen, and men of superior excellence?

Pupil: Truly so.

Socrates: Knowing men like these will not write differently from each other about the same things, nor change what they have once written. If, then, we see some doing this, are we to declare them knowing or ignorant?

Pupil: Ignorant, undoubtedly.

Socrates: Whatever is right, therefore, we may pronounce to be lawful in medicine, gardening, or cookery; whatever is not right, not to be lawful but lawless. And the like in treatises respecting just and unjust, prescribing how the city is to be administered. That which is right, is the regal law; that which is not right, is not so, but only seems to be law in the eyes of the ignorant, being in truth lawless.

Pupil: Yes.

It will be seen from the above examples, that much of the Socratic questioning is really explanatory; the questions, though interrogative in form, being often rhetorical, and therefore assertive in value.

THE QUESTION

Characteristics of a Good Question.—Good questions should seize upon the important features and emphasize these. Unimportant details, though useful in giving vividness to a narrative and enabling the pupil to build up a clear picture of the scene or incident, may well be ignored in questioning. The teacher must see that the pupil grasps the essentials and must direct his questions towards the attainment of that end. The questions should be arranged in logical sequence, so that the answers, if written out in the order given, would form a connected account of the topic under discussion. Further, the questions should require the expression of a judgment on the part of the pupil. In the main they should not be answerable by a single word or a brief phrase. One of the greatest weaknesses in the answers of pupils is the tendency *to* extreme brevity. As a result, it is difficult to get pupils to give a connected and continuous narration, description, or exposition in any subject. The remedy for this defect is to ask questions which demand answers of considerable length, and to avoid those which require only a scrappy answer.

Form of the Question.—It should ever be borne in mind that the teacher's language influences the language habits of his pupils. Carelessly worded, poorly constructed questions are likely to result in answers having similar characteristics. On the other hand, correctness in the form of the questions asked, accuracy in the use of words, simple, straightforward statements of the thing wanted, will be reflected, dimly perhaps, in the form of the pupils' answers. Care must, therefore, be exercised as to the form in which questions are asked. They should be stripped of all superfluous introductory words, such as, "Who can tell?" "How many of you know?" etc. Such prefaces are not only useless and a waste of time, but they also put before pupils a bad model if we are to expect concise and direct statements from them. The questions should be so clear and definite in meaning as to admit of only one interpretation. Questions such as, "What happened after this?" "What did Cromwell become?" "What about the rivers of Germany?" "What might we say of this word?" are objectionable on the score of indefiniteness. Many correct answers might be given for each and the pupils can only guess at what is required. If the question cannot be so stated as to make what is desired unmistakable, the information had better be given outright. Questions should be brief and usually deal with only one point, except, perhaps in asking for summaries of what has been covered in the lesson. In the latter case it is frequently desirable to put a question involving several points in order to ensure definiteness, conciseness, and connectedness in the answer; for example, "For what is Alexander Mackenzie noted? State his great aim and describe his two most important undertakings connected therewith." But in dealing with matter taken up for the first time or involving original thought, this type of question, demanding as it does attention to several points, would put too great a demand upon the powers of young children. Under such conditions it is best to ask questions requiring only one point in answer.

THE ANSWER

Form of Answers.—The possibility of improving the pupil's language power through his answers has already been referred to. To secure the best results in this regard, the teacher should insist on answers that are grammatically correct and, usually, in complete sentences. It would be pedantic, however, to insist always upon the latter condition. For such questions as, "What British officer was killed at Queenston Heights?" or "What province lies west of Manitoba?" the natural answers are "General Brock," or "Saskatchewan." To require pupils to say, "The British officer killed at Queenston Heights was General Brock," or "The province west of Manitoba is Saskatchewan," would be to make the recitation unnatural and formal. When answers are a mere echo of the question, with some slight inversion or addition, they become exceedingly mechanical, and useless from the point of view of language training. While it is desirable to avoid, as far as possible, questions that admit of answers of a single word or short phrase, such questions are sometimes necessary and are not objectionable. Questions should not be thrown into the form of an elliptical statement in which the pupil merely fills a blank, for example, "The capital of Ontario is...?" "The first English parliament was called by...?" Nor should they be given in inverted form, as, "Montreal is situated where?" "The Great Charter was signed by what king?" Alternative questions such as, "Is this a noun or an adjective?" "Was Charles I willing or unwilling to sign the Petition of Right?" as well as those questions that are answerable by "Yes" or "No," require little thought to answer and should be avoided if possible. When they are used, the pupil should at once be required to give reasons for his answer. Neither the form of the question nor the teacher's tone of voice or manner should afford any inkling as to the answer expected.

Calling for Answers.—In order that the attention of the whole class may be maintained, the question should be proposed before the pupil who is to answer is indicated. No fixed order in calling upon the pupils should be adopted. If the pupils are never certain beforehand who is to be named to answer the question, they are more likely to be kept constantly on the alert. The questions should be carefully distributed among the class, the duller pupils being given rather more and easier questions than the brighter ones. One of the temptations that the teacher has to overcome is that of giving the clever and willing pupils the majority of the questions. The question should seldom be repeated unless the first wording is so unfortunate that the meaning is not clear and it is found necessary to recast it. To repeat questions habitually is to put a premium on inattention on the part of the pupils. A bad habit often noted among teachers is that of wording the question in several ways before any one is asked to answer it.

Methods of Dealing with Answers.—As has been already indicated in another connection, the answers of the pupils should be generally in complete sentences and frequently should be in the form of a continuous paragraph or series of paragraphs, especially in summaries and reviews. The continuous answer should be cultivated much more than it is, as a means of training pupils to organize their information and to express themselves in clear and connected discourse. On the other hand, however, children should be discouraged from giving more information than is demanded by the question. While it is desirable that the correctness of an answer should be indicated in some way, the teacher should guard against forming the habit of indicating every correct answer by a stereotyped word or phrase, such as, "Yes" or "That's right." Answers should seldom be repeated by the teacher, unless it is desirable to re-word them for purposes of emphasis. Repetition of answers encourages careless articulation on the part of the pupil answering and inattention on the part of the others. One of the worst habits a teacher can contract is the "gramophonic" repetition of pupils' answers. The answers given by the pupils should almost invariably be individual, not collective. Simultaneous answering makes a noisy class-room, cultivates a monotonous and measured method of speaking, and encourages the habit of relying on others. There are always a few leaders in the class that are willing to take the initiative in answering, and the others merely chime in with them. The method is not suitable for the expression of individual opinion, for all pupils must answer alike. There is, further, the possibility that absurd blunders may pass uncorrected, because in the general repetition the teacher cannot detect them.

LIMITATIONS

Though questioning is the most valuable of teaching devices, it is quite susceptible of being overworked. There is quite as much danger of using it too extensively as there is of using it too little. Frequently, teachers try to question from pupils what they could not be expected to know. Further, it is possible by too much questioning to cover up the point of the lesson rather than reveal it, and to mystify the pupils rather than clarify their ideas. These are the two main abuses of the device. After all, it should be remembered that, important as good questioning undoubtedly is, it is not the only thing in lesson technique. In teaching, as elsewhere, variety is the spice of life. Sympathy, sincerity, enthusiasm in the teacher will do more to secure mental activity in the pupils than mere excellence in questioning. The energetic, enthusiastic, sympathetic teacher may secure better results than the teacher whose ability in questioning is well-nigh perfect, but who lacks these other qualities. If, however, to these qualities he adds a high degree of efficiency in questioning, his success in teaching is so much the more assured.

PART III
EDUCATIONAL PSYCHOLOGY

CHAPTER XIX

CONSCIOUSNESS

Data of Psychology.—Throughout the earlier parts of the text, occasional reference has been made to various classes of mental states, and to psychology, as the science which treats of these mental states, under the assumption that such references would be understood in a general way by the student-teacher. At the outset of a study of psychology as the science of mind, however, it becomes necessary to inquire somewhat more fully into the nature of the data with which the science is to deal. Mind is usually defined either by contrasting it with the concrete world of matter, or by describing its activities. It is said, for instance, that mind is that which feels and knows, which hopes, fears, determines, etc. By some, indeed, mind is described as merely the sum of these states of knowing and feeling and willing. The practical man says, however, *I* know and feel so-and-so, and *my* wish is so-and-so. Here an evident distinction is drawn between the knower, or conscious self, and his conscious activities. While, however, we may agree with the practical man that there is a mind, or self, that knows and wills and feels; yet it is evident that the self, or knower, can know himself only through his conscious states. It must be understood, therefore, that mind in its ultimate sense cannot be studied directly, but only the conscious states, or conditions of mind. Thus psychology becomes a study of mental states, or states of consciousness; and it is, in fact, frequently described as the science of consciousness.

Nature of Consciousness.—Our previous study of the nature of experience has shown that various kinds of conscious states may arise in the mind, now the smell of burning cloth, now the sound of a ringing bell, now the feeling of bodily pain, now a remembered joy, now a future expectation or a resolution. Such a conscious state was seen, moreover, to represent on the part of the mind, not a mere passive impression coming from some external source, but an active attitude resulting in definite experience. It signifies, in other words, a power to react in a fixed way toward impressions, and direct our conduct in accordance with the resulting states of consciousness. Consciousness in the individual implies, therefore, that he is aware of phenomena as they are experienced, and is able to modify his behaviour accordingly.

Types of Consciousness.—Although allowable, from the standpoint of the learning process, to describe a conscious state as an attitude of awareness in which the individual grasps the significance of an experience in relation to his own needs; it must be recognized that not all consciousness manifests this meaningful quality, or this relation to a felt aim, or end. While lying, for instance, in a vague, half-awake state, although one is conscious, the mental condition is quite devoid of the meaningful quality referred to, and entirely lacks the feeling of reaction, or of mental effort. In this case there is no distinct reference to the needs of the self, and a lack of that focusing of attention necessary to give the consciousness a meaning and purpose in the life of the individual. All such passive, or effortless, states of consciousness, which make up those portions of mental existence in which no definite presentation seems to hold the attention, although falling within the sphere of the scientific psychologist, may nevertheless be left out of consideration in a study of educational psychology. Learning involves apperception, and apperception is always giving a meaning to new presentations by actively bringing old knowledge to bear upon them. For the educator, therefore, psychology may be limited to a study of the definite states of consciousness which arise through an apperceiving act of attention, that is, to our states of experience and the processes connected therewith. For this reason, psychology is by some appropriately enough defined as the science of experience.

Consciousness a Stream.—Although we describe the data of psychology as facts, or states, of consciousness, a moment's reflection will show that our conscious life is not made up of a number of mental states, or experiences, completely separated one from the other. Our consciousness is rather a unified whole, in which seemingly disconnected states blend into one continuous flow of conscious life. For this reason, consciousness is frequently compared to a stream, or river, moving onward in an unbroken course. This stream of consciousness appears as disjointed mental states, simply because the attention discriminates within this stream, and thus in a sense detaches different portions one from the other, or, as sometimes figuratively put, it creates successive waves on the stream of consciousness. A mental state, or experience, so-called, is such a discriminated portion of this stream of consciousness, and is, therefore, itself a process, the different processes blending in a continuous succession or relation to make up the unbroken flow of conscious life. For this reason psychology is frequently described as a study of conscious processes.

VALUE OF EDUCATIONAL PSYCHOLOGY

Within the school the child secures a control of experience only by passing through a process of mental reconstruction, or of changes in consciousness. Moreover, to bring about these mental changes, it is found necessary for the teacher's effort to conform as far as possible to the interests and tendencies of the child. So far, therefore, as the teacher's office is to direct and control the children's effort during the learning process, he must approach them primarily as mental, or conscious, beings. For this reason the educator should at least not violate the general principles governing all mental activity. By giving him an insight into the general principles underlying conscious processes, psychology should aid the teacher to control the learning process in the child.

Limitations of Educational Psychology

Psychology Cannot Give: A. Knowledge of Subject-matter.—It must not be assumed, however, that knowledge of psychology will necessarily imply a corresponding ability to teach. Psychology, for instance, cannot decide what should be taught to the child. This, as we have seen, is a problem of social experience, and must be decided by considering the types of experience which will add to the social efficiency of the individual, or which will enable him best to do his duty to himself and to others. All, therefore, that psychology can do here is to explain the process by which experience is acquired, leaving to social ethics the problem of deciding what knowledge is of most worth.

B. Love for Children.—Again, psychology will not necessarily furnish that largeness of heart and sympathy for childhood, without which no teacher can be successful. Indeed, it is felt by many that making children objects of psychological analysis will rather tend to destroy that more spiritual conception of their personality which should constitute the teacher's attitude toward his pupils. While this is no doubt true of the teacher who looks upon children merely as subjects for psychological analysis and experimentation, it is equally true that a knowledge of psychology will enable even the sympathetic teacher to realize more fully and deal more successfully with the difficulties of the pupil.

C. Acquaintance with the Individual Child.—Again, the teacher's problem in dealing with the mental attitude of the particular child cannot always be interpreted through general principles. The general principle would be supposed to have an application to every child in a large class. It is often found, however, that the character and disposition of the particular child demands, not general, but special treatment. Here, what is termed the knack of the sympathetic teacher is often more effective than the general principle of the psychologist. Admitting so much, however, it yet may be argued that a knowledge of psychology will not hinder, but rather assist the sympathetic teacher in dealing even with special cases.

METHODS OF PSYCHOLOGY

A. Introspection.—A unique characteristic of mind is its ability to turn attention inward and make an object of study of its own states, or processes. For instance, the mind is able to make its present sensation, its remembered state of anger, its idea of a triangle, etc., stand out in consciousness as a subject of study for conscious attention. On account of this ability to give attention to his own states of consciousness, man is said both to know and to know that he knows. This reflective method of studying our own mental states is known as the method of *Introspection*.

B. Objective Method.—Facts of mind may, however, be examined objectively. As previously noted, man, by his words, acts, and works, gives expression to his conscious states. These different forms of expression are accepted, therefore, as external indications of corresponding states of mind, and afford the psychologist certain data for developing his science. One of the most important of these objective methods is known as Child Study. Here, by the method of observing the acts and language of very young children, data are obtained concerning the native instincts of the child, concerning the genesis and development of the different mental processes, and the relation of these to physical development. A brief statement of the leading principles of Child Study will be found in Chapter XXXI.

C. Experimental Method.—A third method of studying mind is known as the *Experimental* method. Here, as in the case of the ordinary physical experimenter, the psychologist seeks to control certain mental processes by isolating them and regulating their action. This may be effectively done in the study of certain processes. For instance, by passing the two points of a pair of compasses over different parts of the body, the tactile sensibility of the skin may be compared at these different parts. By this means it may be shown that the tip of the finger can detect the two points when only one twelfth of an inch apart, while on the middle of the back they may require to be two and a half inches apart to give a double impression. The experimental method is often used in connection with the objective method in Child Study.

PHASES OF CONSCIOUSNESS

A. Knowledge.—Although, as previously stated, the stream of consciousness must at all times be looked upon as a unity, it will be found upon analysis to present three more or less distinct phases. A state of consciousness implies, in the first place, being aware of something as an object of attention. In other words, something is seized upon by consciousness as a presentation, and to the extent to which one is aware of this object of consciousness, he is said to recognize, or to know it. A state of consciousness is always, therefore, a state of knowledge, or of intelligence. Thus, whether we perceive this chair, imagine a mermaid, recall the looks of an absent friend, experience the toothache, judge the weight of this book, or become angry, our conscious state is a state of *knowledge.*

B. Feeling.—A conscious state is also a state of feeling. Every conscious state has its feeling side, since it is a personal state, or since the mind itself is affected toward its own state. Two men, for instance, may know equally well the taste of a particular food, but the taste may affect each one quite differently. To one the experience is pleasant, to the other it may be even painful. Two boys may know equally that a point has been scored by the visiting team, but the personal attitude of each toward the experience may be quite different. The one finds in it a quality of joy; the other a quality of sorrow. In the same way the mind always feels more or less pleased or displeased in its present state of consciousness. To speak of any particular experience as painful, joyous, sorrowful, etc., is, therefore, to refer to it as a state of *feeling.*

C. Will.—Consciousness is a state of effort, or will. It was especially pointed out above, that the purposeful consciousness always implies a straining or focusing of consciousness in order to attain a fuller control of the experience. This element of exertion manifest in consciousness may appear as a directing of attention, as the making of a choice, as determining upon a certain action, etc. This aspect of any conscious state is spoken of as a state of *will,* or volition.

In the unity of the conscious life, therefore, there are three attitudes from which consciousness may be viewed:

1. It is a state of Knowledge, or of Intelligence.

2. It is a state of Feeling.

3. It is a state of Will.

On account of this threefold aspect of mental states, consciousness has been represented in the following form:

The significance of comparing the threefold aspect of consciousness to the three sides of a triangle consists in the fact that if any side of a triangle is removed no triangle remains. In like manner, none of the three attributes of consciousness could be wanting without the conscious state ceasing to exist as such. No one, for instance, could feel the pressure of a tight shoe without at the same time knowing it, and fixing his attention upon it. Neither could a person at any particular time know that the shoe was pinching him unless he was also attending to and feeling the experience.

CHAPTER XX

MIND AND BODY

Relation of Mind to Bodily Organism.—Notwithstanding the antithesis which has been affirmed to exist between mind and matter, yet a very close relation exists between mind and the material organism known as the body. There are many ways in which this intimate connection manifests itself. Mental excitement is always accompanied with agitation of the body and a disturbance of such bodily processes as breathing, the beating of the heart, digestion, etc. Such mental processes as seeing, hearing, tasting, etc., are found also to depend upon the use of a bodily organ, as the eye, the ear, the tongue, without which it is quite impossible for the mind to come into relation with outside things. Moreover, disease or injury, especially to the organs of sense or to the brain, weakens or destroys mental power. The size of the brain, also, is found to bear a certain relation to mental capacity; the weight of the average brain being about 48 ounces, while the brain of an idiot often weighs only from 20 to 30 ounces.

THE NERVOUS SYSTEM

Divisions of Nervous System.—This intimate connection between mind and body is provided for through the existence of that part of the bodily organism known as the nervous system, and it is this part, together with its associated organs of sense, that chiefly interests the student of psychology. A study of the character and functions of the various parts of the nervous system, and of the nervous substance of which these parts are composed, belongs to physiology rather than to psychology. As the student-teacher is given a general knowledge of the structure of the nervous system in his study of physiology, a brief description will suffice for the present purpose. The nervous system consists of two parts, (1) the central part, or cerebro-spinal centre, and (2) an outer part—the spinal nerves. The central part, or cerebro-spinal centre, includes the spinal cord, passing upward through the vertebrae of the spinal column and the brain. The brain consists of three parts: The cerebrum, or great brain, consisting of two hemispheres, which, though connected, are divided in great part by a longitudinal fissure; the cerebellum, or little brain; and the medulla oblongata, or bulb. The spinal nerves consist of thirty-one pairs, which branch out from the spinal cord. Each pair of nerves contains a right and left member, distributed to the right and the left side of the body respectively. These nerves are of two kinds, sensory, or afferent, (in-carrying) nerves, which carry inward impressions from the outside world, and motor, or efferent, (out-carrying) nerves, which convey impulses outward to the muscles and cause them to contract. There are also twelve pairs of nerves connected with the eye, ear, nose, tongue, and face, which, instead of projecting from the spinal cord, proceed at once from the brain through openings in the cranium. These are, therefore, known as cerebral nerves. In their general character, however, they do not differ from the projection fibres.

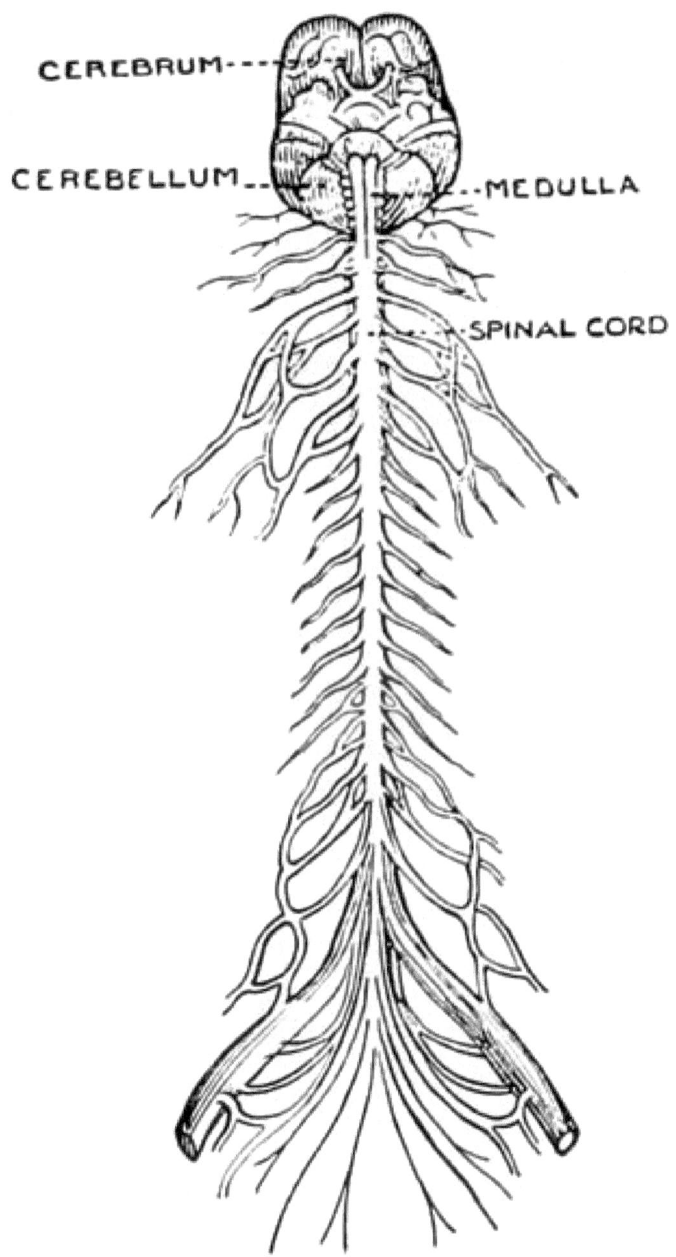

Brain and Spinal Cord

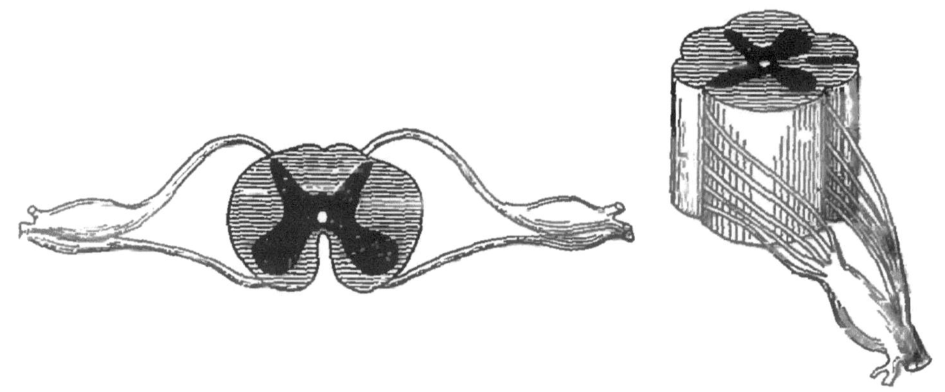

Pair of Spinal Nerves

Nervous Substance.—Nervous substance is divided into two kinds—grey, or cellular, substance and white, or fibrous, substance. The greater part of the grey matter is situated as a layer on the outside of the cerebrum, or great brain, where it forms a rind from one twelfth to one eighth of an inch in thickness, known as the cortex. It is also found on the surface of the cerebellum. Diffuse masses of grey matter are likewise met in the other parts of the brain, and extending downward through the centre of the spinal cord. The function of the grey matter is to form centres to which the nerve fibres tend and carry in stimulations, or from which they commence and carry out impulses.

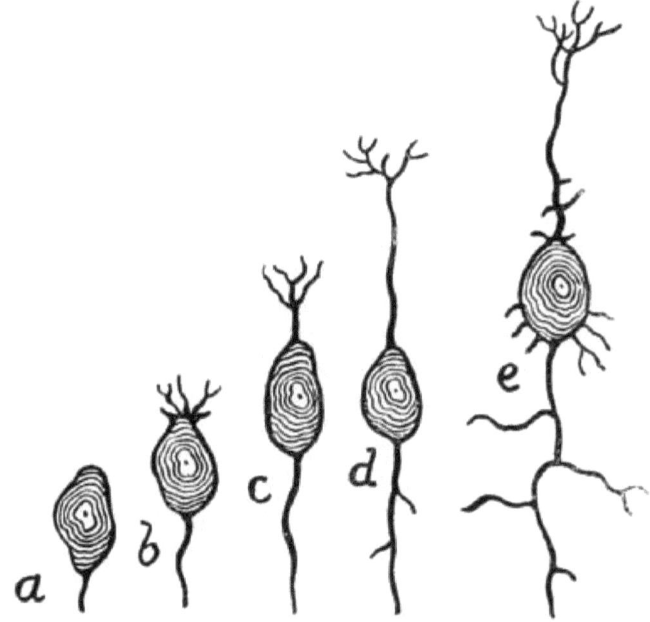

A Neuron in Stages of Development

The Neuron.—The centres of grey matter are composed of aggregations, or masses, of very small nerve cells called neurons. A neuron may range from $\frac{1}{300}$ to $\frac{1}{3000}$ of an inch in diameter, and there are several thousand millions of these cells in the nervous system. A developed neuron consists of a cell body with numerous prolongations in the form of white, thread-like fibres. The neuron with its outgoing fibres is the unit of the nervous system. Neurons are supposed to be of three classes, sensory to receive stimulations, motor to send out impulses to the muscles, and association to connect sensory and motor centres.

These neurons, as already noted, are collected into centres, and the outgoing fibres give connection to the cells, the number of connections for each neuron depending upon its outgoing fibres. Some of these connections are already established within the system at birth, while others, as we shall see more fully later, are formed whenever the organism is brought into action in our thinking and doing. To speak of such connections being formed between nerve centres by means of their outgoing fibres does not necessarily mean a direct connection, but may imply only that the fibres of one cell approach nearly enough to those of another to admit of a nervous impulse passing from the one cell to the other. This is often spoken of as the establishment of a path between the centres.

The Nerve Fibres.—The nerve fibres which transmit impressions to and from the centres of grey matter average about $\frac{1}{6000}$ of an inch in thickness, but are often of great length, some extending perhaps half the length of the body. Large numbers of these fibres unite into a sheath or single nerve. It is estimated that the number of fibres in a single nerve number in most cases several thousand, those in the nerve of sight being estimated at about one hundred thousand. The fibres in the white substance of the brain are estimated at several hundred million.

Classes of Fibres.—These fibres are supposed to be of four classes, as follows:

1. *Sensory Cerebral and Spinal Fibres*

These have already been referred to as spreading outward from the brain and spinal cord to different parts of the body. Their office is, therefore, to carry inward to the centres of grey matter impressions received from the outside world, thus setting up a connection between the various senses and the cortex of the brain.

2. *Motor Cerebral and Spinal Fibres*

These fibres connect the centres of grey matter directly with the muscles, and thus provide a means of communication between these muscles and the cortex of the brain.

3. *Association Fibres*

These connect one part of the cortex with another within the same hemisphere.

4. *Commissural Fibres*

These connect corresponding centres of the two hemispheres of the cerebrum.

Function of Parts.—Because the various cells are thus brought into relation, the whole nervous system combines into a single organism, which is able to receive impressions and provides conditions for the mind to interpret these impressions and, if necessary, react thereon. When, for instance, a stimulus is received by an end organ (the eye), it will be transmitted by a sensory nerve directly inward to a sensory centre, or cell, in the cortex of the brain. In such a case it may be interpreted by the mind and a line of action decided upon. Then by means of associating cells and fibres a motor centre may be stimulated and an impulse transmitted along an outgoing motor nerve to a muscle, whereupon the necessary motor reaction will take place. A pupil may, for instance, receive the impression of a word through the ear or through the eye and thereupon make a motor response by writing the word. The arrows in the accompanying figure indicate the course of the stimulus and the response in such cases.

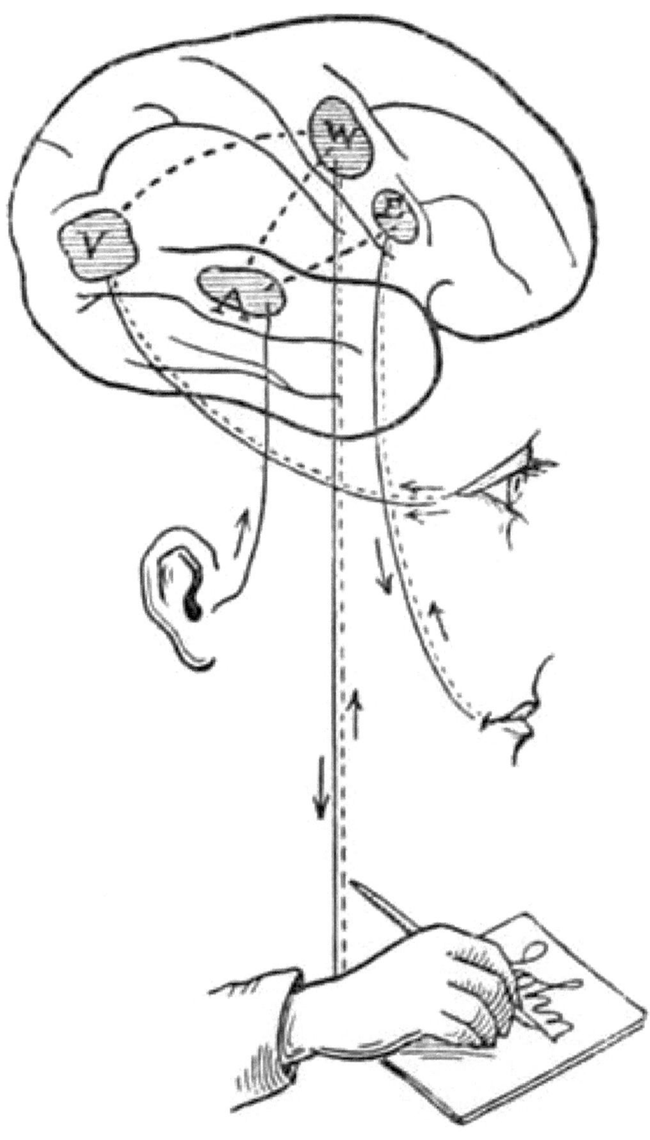

THE CORTEX

Cortex the Seat of Consciousness.—Experiments in connection with the different nerve cords and centres have demonstrated that intelligent consciousness depends upon the nerve centres situated in the cortex of the cerebrum. For instance, a sensory impulse may be carried inward to the cells of the spinal cord and upward to the cerebellum without any resulting consciousness. When, however, the stimulus reaches a higher centre in the cortex of the brain, the mind becomes conscious, or interprets the impression, and any resulting action will be controlled by consciousness, through impulses given to the motor nerves. It is for this reason that the cortex is called the seat of consciousness, and that mind is said to reside in the brain.

Localization of Function.—In addition, however, to placing the seat of consciousness in the cortex of the brain, psychologists also claim that different parts of the cortex are involved in different types of conscious activity. Sensations of sight, for instance, involve certain centres in the cortex, sensations of sound other centres, the movements of the organs of speech still other centres. Some go so far as to claim that each one of the higher intellectual processes, as memory, imagination, judgment, reasoning, love, anger, etc., involves neural activity in its own special section of the cortex. There seems no good evidence, however, to support this view. The fact seems rather that in all these higher processes, quite numerous centres of the cortex may be involved. The following figure indicates the main conclusions of the psychologists in reference to the localization of certain important functions in distinct areas of the cortex.

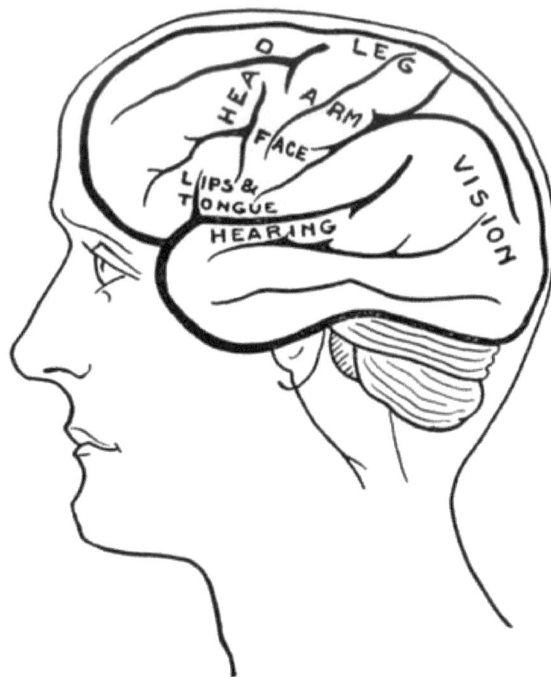

REFLEX ACTS

Nature of Reflex Action.—While a lower nerve centre is not a seat for purposeful consciousness, these centres may, in addition to serving as transmission points for cortical messages, perform a special function by immediately receiving sensory impressions and transmitting motor impulses. A person, for instance, whose mind is occupied with a problem, may move a limb to relieve a cramp, wink the eye, etc., without any conscious control of the action. In such a case the sensory impression was reported to a lower sensory centre, directly carried to a lower motor centre, and the motor impulse given to perform the movement. In the same way, after one has acquired the habit of walking, although it usually requires conscious effort to initiate the movements, yet the person may continue walking in an almost unconscious manner, his mind being fully occupied with other matters. Here, also, the complex actions involved in walking are controlled and regulated by lower centres situated in the cerebellum. In like manner a person will unconsciously close the eyelid under the stimulus of strong light. Here the impression caused by the light stimulus, upon reaching the medulla along an afferent nerve, is deflected to a motor nerve and, without any conscious control of the movements, the muscles of the eyelid receive the necessary impulse to close. Actions which are thus directed from a lower centre without conscious control, are usually spoken of as reflex acts. Acts directed by consciousness are, on the other hand, known as voluntary acts. The difference in the working of the nervous mechanism in consciously controlled and in reflex action may be illustrated by means of the accompanying figures.

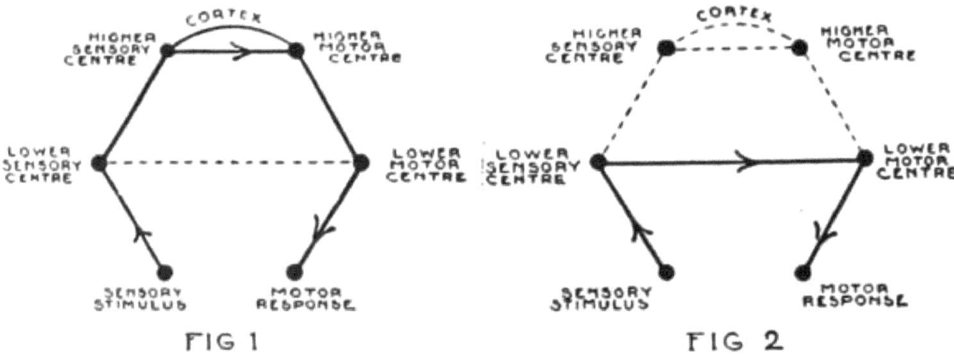

FIG 1 FIG 2

The heavy lines in Figure 1 on the opposite page show that the sensory-motor arc is made through the cortex, and that the mind is, therefore, conscious both of the sense stimulus and also of the resulting action. Figure 2 shows the same arc through a lower centre, in which case the mind is not directly attending to the impression or the resulting action.

Function of Consciousness.—The facts set forth above serve further to illustrate the purposeful character of consciousness as man interprets and adjusts himself to his surroundings. So long, for instance, as the individual walks onward without disturbance, his mind is free to dwell upon other matters, cortical activity not being necessary to control the process of walking. If, however, he steps upon anything which perhaps threatens him with a fall, the rhythmic interplay between sensory and motor activity going on in the lower centres is at once disturbed, and a message is flashed along the sensory nerve to the higher, or cortical, centres. This at once arouses consciousness, and the disturbing factor becomes an object of attention. Consciousness thus appears as a means of adaptation to the new and varying conditions with which the organism is confronted.

CHARACTERISTICS OF NERVOUS MATTER

A. Plasticity.—One striking characteristic of nervous matter is its plasticity. The nature of the connections within the nervous system have already been referred to. Mention has also been made of the fact that numerous connections are established within the nervous system as a result of movements taking place within the organism during life. In other words, the movements within the nervous system which accompany stimulations and responses bring about changes in the structure of the organism. The cause for these changes seems to be that the neurons which chance to work together during any experience form connections with one another by means of their outgrowing fibres. By this means, traces of past experiences are in a sense stored up within the organism, and it is for this reason that our experiences are said to be recorded within the nervous system.

B. Retentiveness.—A second characteristic of nervous matter is its retentive power. In other words, the modifications which accompany any experience, besides taking on the permanent character referred to above, pre-dispose the system to transmit impulses again through the same centres. Moreover, with each repetition of the nervous activity, there develops a still greater tendency for the movements to re-establish themselves. This power possessed by nervous tissue to establish certain modes of action carries with it also an increase in the ease and accuracy with which the movements are performed. For example, the impressions and impulses involved in the first attempts of the child to control the clasping of an object, are performed with effort and in an ineffective manner. The cause for this seems to be largely the absence of proper connections between the centres involved, as referred to above. This absence causes a certain resistance within the system to the nervous movements. When, however, the various centres involved in the movements establish the proper connections with one another, the act will be performed in a much more effective and easy manner. From this it is evident that the nervous system, as the result of former experiences, always retains a certain potential, or power, to repeat the act with greater ease, and thus improve conduct, or behaviour. This property of nervous matter will hereafter be referred to as its power of retention.

C. Energy.—Another quality of nervous matter is its energy. By this is meant that the cells are endowed with a certain potential, or power, which enables them to transmit impressions and impulses and overcome any resistance offered. Different explanations are given as to the nature of this energy, or force, with which nervous matter is endowed, but any study of these theories is unnecessary here.

D. Resistance.—A fourth characteristic to be noted regarding nervous matter is that a nervous impulse, or current, as it is transmitted through the system, encounters *resistance*, or consumes an amount of nervous energy. Moreover, when the nervous current, whether sensory or motor, involves the establishment of new connections between cells, as when one first learns combinations of numbers or the movements involved in forming a new letter, a relatively greater amount of resistance is met or, in other words, a greater amount of nervous energy is expended. On the other hand, when an impulse has been transmitted a number of times through a given arc, the resistance is greatly lessened, or less energy is expended; as indicated by the ease with which an habitual act is performed.

Education and Nervous Energy.—It is evident from the foregoing, that the forming of new ideas or of new modes of action tends to use up a large share of nervous energy. For this reason, the learning of new and difficult things should not be undertaken when the body is in a tired or exhausted condition; for the resistance which must be overcome, and the changes which must take place in the nervous tissue during the learning process, are not likely to be effectively accomplished under such conditions. Moreover, the energy thus lost must be restored through the blood, and therefore demands proper food, rest, and sleep on the part of the individual. It should be noted further that nervous tissue is more plastic during the early years of life. This renders it imperative, therefore, that knowledge and skill should be gained, as far as possible, during the plastic years. The person who wishes to become a great violinist must acquire skill to finger and handle the bow early in life. The person who desires to become a great linguist, if he allows his early years to pass without acquiring the necessary skill, cannot expect in middle life to train his vocal organs to articulate a number of different languages.

Cortical Habit.—In the light of what has been seen regarding the character and function of the nervous system, it will now be possible to understand more fully two important forms of adjustment already referred to. When nervous movements are transmitted to the cortex of the brain, they not only awaken consciousness, or make the individual aware of something, but the present impression also leaves certain permanent effects in the nervous tissue of the cortex itself. Since, however, cortical activity implies consciousness, the retention of such a tendency within the cortical centres will imply, not an habitual act in the ordinary sense, but a tendency on the part of a conscious experience to repeat itself. This at once implies an ability to retain and recall past experiences, or endows the individual with power of memory. Cortical habit, therefore, or the establishment of permanent connections within the cortical centres, with their accompanying dynamic tendency to repeat themselves, will furnish the physiological conditions for a revival of former experience in memory, or will enable the individual to turn the past to the service of the present.

Physical Habits.—The basis for the formation of physical habits appears also in this retentive power of nervous tissue. When the young boy, for instance, first mounts his new bicycle, he is unable, except with the most attentive effort and in a most laboured and awkward manner, either to keep his feet on the pedals, or make the handle-bars respond to the balancing of the wheel. In a short time, however, all these movements take place in an effective and graceful manner without any apparent attention being given to them. This efficiency is conditioned by the fact that all these movements have become habitual, or take place largely as reflex acts.

In school also, when the child learns to perform such an act as making the figure 2, the same changes take place. Here an impression must first proceed from the given copy to a sensory centre in the cortex. As yet, however, there is no vital connection established between the sensory centres and the motor centres which must direct the muscles in making the movement. As the movement is attempted, however, faint connections are set up between different centres. With each repetition the connection is made stronger, and the formation of the figure rendered less difficult. So long, however, as the connection is established within the cortex, the movement will not take place except under conscious direction. Ultimately, however, similar connections between sensory and motor neurons may be established in lower centres, whereupon the action will be performed as a reflex act, or without the intervention of a directing act of consciousness. This evidently takes place when a student, in working a problem, can form the figures, while his consciousness is fully occupied with the thought phases of the problem. Thus the neural condition of physical habit is the establishment of easy passages between sensory and motor nerves in centres lower than the cortex.

CHAPTER XXI

INSTINCT

Definition of Instinct.—In a foregoing section, it was seen that our bodily movements divide into different classes according to their source, or origin. Among them were noted certain inherited spontaneous, but useful, complex movements which follow, in a more or less uniform way, definite types of stimuli presented to the organism. Such an inherited tendency on the part of an organism to react in an effective manner, but without any definite purpose in view, whenever a particular stimulus presents itself, is known as instinct, and the resulting action is described as an instinctive act. As an example of purely instinctive action may be taken the maternal instinct of insects whose larvæ require live prey when they are born. To provide this the mother administers sufficient poison to a spider or a caterpillar to stupefy it, and then bears it to her nest. Placing the victim close to her eggs, she incloses the two together, thus providing food for her future offspring. This complex series of acts, so essential to the continuance of the species, and seemingly so full of purpose, is nevertheless conducted throughout without reference to past experience, and without any future end in view. Instinct may, therefore, be defined as the ability of an organism to react upon a particular situation so as to gain a desirable end, yet without any purpose in view or any previous training.

Characteristics of Instinct.—An instinctive act, it may be noted, is distinguished by certain well marked characteristics:

1. The action is not brought about by experience or guided by intelligence, but is a direct reaction on the part of the organism to definite stimulation.

2. Although not the result of reason, instinctive action is purposeful to the extent that it shows a predisposition on the part of the organism to react in an effective manner to a particular situation.

3. An instinctive movement is a response in which the whole organism is concerned. It is the discomfort of the whole organism, for instance, that causes the bird to migrate or the child to seek food. In this respect it differs from a mere reflex action such as the winking of the eye, breathing, coughing, etc., which involves only some particular part of the organism.

4. Although not a consciously purposed action, instinct nevertheless involves consciousness. In sucking, for instance, sensation accompanies both the discomfort of the organism giving rise to the movements and also the instinctive act itself. In this respect it differs from such automatic actions as breathing, the circulation of the blood, and the beating of the heart.

Origin of Instinct.—The various instinctive movements with which an organism is endowed, not being a result of experience or education, a question at once arises as to their source, or origin. Instinct has its origin in the fact that certain movements which have proved beneficial in the ancestral experience of the race have become established as permanent modes of reaction, and are transmitted to each succeeding generation. The explanation of this transmission of tendencies is, that beneficial movements are retained as permanent modifications of the nervous system of the animal, and are transmitted to the offspring as a *reactive tendency* toward definite stimuli. The partridge family, for instance, has preserved its offspring from the attacks of foxes, dogs, and other enemies only by the male taking flight and dragging itself along the ground, thus attracting the enemy away from the direction of the nest. The complex movements involved in such an act, becoming established as permanent motor connections within the system, are transmitted to the offspring as predispositions. Instinct would thus seem a physiological habit, or hereditary tendency, within the nervous system to react in a fixed manner under certain conditions. In many respects, however, instincts seem to depend more largely upon bodily development than upon nervous structure. While the babe will at first instinctively suck; yet as soon as teeth appear, the sucking at once gives way to the biting instinct. The sucking instinct then disappears so completely that only a process of education will re-establish it later. Birds also show no instinctive tendency to fly until their wings are developed, while the young of even the fiercest animals will flee from danger, until such time as their bodily organism is properly developed for attack. From this it would seem that instinctive action depends even more upon general bodily structure and development than upon fixed co-ordinations within the nervous system.

HUMAN INSTINCTS

On account of the apparently intelligent character of human actions, it is often stated that man is a creature largely devoid of instincts. The fact is, however, that he is endowed with a large number of impulsive or instinctive tendencies to act in definite ways, when in particular situations. Man has a tendency, under the proper conditions, to be fearful, bashful, angry, curious, sympathetic, grasping, etc. It is only, moreover, because experience finally gives man ideas of these instinctive movements, that they may in time be controlled by reason, and developed into orderly habits.

Classification of Human Instincts.—Various attempts have been made to classify human instincts. For educational purposes, perhaps the most satisfactory method is that which classifies them according to their relation to the direct welfare of the individual organism. Being inherited tendencies on the part of the organism to react in definite ways to definite stimuli, all instinctive acts should naturally tend to promote the good of the particular individual. Different instincts will be found to differ, however, in the degree in which they involve the immediate good of the individual organism. On this basis the various human instincts may be divided into the following classes:

1. *Individualistic Instincts.*—Some instincts gain their significance because

they tend solely to meet the needs of the individual. Examples of these would be the instincts involved in securing food, as biting, chewing, carrying objects to the mouth; such instinctive expressions as crying, smiling, and uttering articulate sounds; rhythmical bodily movements; bodily expression of fear, etc.

2. *Racial Instincts.*—These include such instinctive acts as make for the preservation of the species, as the sexual and parental instincts, jealousy, etc. The constructive instinct in man, also, may be considered parallel to the nesting instinct in birds and animals.

3. *Social Instincts.*—Among these are placed such instinctive tendencies as bashfulness, sympathy, the gregarious instinct, or love of companionship, anger, self-assertion, combativeness, etc.

4. *Instincts of Adjustment.*—Included among man's native tendencies are a number of complex responses which manifest themselves in his efforts to adjust himself to his surroundings. These may be called instinctive so far as concerns their mere impulsive tendency, which is no doubt inherited. In the operation of these so-called instincts, however, there is not seen that definite mode of response to a particular stimulus which is found in a pure instinct. Since, however, these are important human tendencies, and since they deal specifically with the child's attitude in adapting himself to his environment, they rank from an educational standpoint among the most important of human instincts. These include such tendencies as curiosity, imitation, play, constructiveness and acquisitiveness.

Human Instincts Modified by Experience.—Although instinctive acts are performed without forethought or conscious purpose, yet in man they may be modified by experience. This is true to a degree even in the case of the instincts of the lower animals. Young spiders, for instance, construct their webs in a manner inferior to that of their elders. In the case of birds, also, the first nest is usually inferior in structure to those of later date. In certain cases, indeed, if accounts are to be accepted, animals are able to vary considerably their instinctive movements according to the particular conditions. It is reported that a swallow had selected a place for her nest between two walls, the surfaces of which were so smooth that she could find no foundation for her nest. Thereupon she fixed a bit of clay to each wall, laid a piece of light wood upon the clay supports, and with the stick as a foundation proceeded to construct her nest. On the whole, however, there seems little variation in animal instincts. The fish will come a second time to take food off the hook, the moth will fly again into the flame, and the spider will again and again build his web over the opening, only to have it again and again torn away. But whatever may be the amount of variation within the instincts of the lower animals, in the case of man instinctive action is so modified by experience that his instincts soon develop into personal habits. The reason for this is quite evident. As previously pointed out, an instinctive act, though not originally purposeful, is in man accompanied with a consciousness of both the bodily discomfort and the resulting movements. Although, therefore, the child instinctively sucks, grasps at objects, or is convulsed with fear, these acts cannot take place without his gradually understanding their significance as states of experience. In this way he soon learns that the indiscriminate performance of an instinctive act may give quite different results, some being much more valuable to the individual than others. The young child, for instance, may instinctively bite whatever enters his mouth, but the older child has learned that this is not always desirable, and therefore exercises a voluntary control over the movement.

Instincts Differ in Value.—The fact that man's instinctive tendencies thus come within the range of experience, not only renders them amenable to reason, but also leaves the question of their ultimate outcome extremely indefinite. For this reason many instincts may appear in man in forms that seem undesirable. The instinct to seek food is a natural one, yet will be condemned when it causes the child to take fruit from the neighbour's garden. In like manner, the instinct to know his surroundings is natural to man, but will be condemned when it causes him to place his ear to the keyhole. The tendency to imitate is not in itself evil, yet the child must learn to weigh the value of what he imitates. One important reason, therefore, why the teacher should understand the native tendencies of the child is that he may direct their development into moral habits and suppress any tendencies which are socially undesirable.

Education of Instincts.—In dealing with the moral aspects of the child's instinctive tendencies, the educator must bear in mind that one tendency may come in conflict with another. The individualistic instinct of feeding or ownership may conflict with the social instinct of companionship; the instinct of egoism, with that of imitation; and the instinct of fear, with that of curiosity. To establish satisfactory moral habits on the basis of instinct, therefore, it is often possible to proceed by a method of substitution. The child who shows a tendency to destroy school furniture can best be cured by having constructive exercises. The boy who shows a natural tendency to destroy animal life may have the same arrested by being given the care of animals and thus having his sympathy developed. In other cases, the removal of stimuli, or conditions, for awaking the instinctive tendency will be found effective in checking the development of an undesirable instinct into a habit. The boy who shows a spirit of combativeness may be cured by having a generous and congenial boy as his chum. The pupil whose social tendencies are so strong that he cannot refrain from talking may be cured by isolation.

Instincts May Disappear.—In dealing with the instinctive tendencies of the child, it is important for the educator to remember that many of these are transitory in character and, if not utilized at the proper time, will perish for want of exercise. Even in the case of animals, natural instincts will not develop unless the opportunity for exercise is provided at the time. Birds shut up in a cage lose the instinct to fly; while ducks, after being kept a certain time from water, will not readily acquire the habit of swimming. In the same way, the child who is not given opportunity to associate with others will likely grow up a recluse. All work for a few years, and it will be impossible for Jack to learn later how to play. The girl who during her childhood has no opportunity to display any pride through neatness in dress will grow up untidy and careless as to her personal appearance. In like manner, it is only the child whose constructive tendency is early given an opportunity to express itself who is likely to develop into an expert workman; while one who has no opportunity to give expression to his æsthetic instinct in early life will not later develop into an artist.

Curiosity

Curiosity as Motive.—An important bearing of instinct upon the work of education is found in the fact that an instinctive tendency may add much to the force of the motive, or end, in any educative process. This is especially true in the case of such adaptive instincts as curiosity, imitation, and play. Curiosity is the inquisitive attitude, or appetite, of the mind which causes it to seek out what is strange in its surroundings and make it an object of attention. As an instinctive tendency, its significance consists in the fact that it leads the individual to interpret his surroundings. A creature devoid of curiosity, therefore, would not discover either the benefits to be derived from his surroundings or the dangers to be avoided. In addition to its direct practical value in leading the individual to study his environment in order to meet actual needs, curiosity often seeks a more theoretic end, appearing merely as a feeling of wonder or a thirst for knowledge.

Use and Abuse of Curiosity.—While curiosity is needful for the welfare of the individual, an inordinate development of this instinct is both intellectually and morally undesirable. Since curiosity directs attention to the novel in our surroundings, over-curiosity is likely to keep the mind wandering from one novelty to another, and thus interfere with the fixing of attention for a sufficient time to give definiteness to particular impressions. The virtue of curiosity is, therefore, to direct attention to the novel until it is made familiar. There is a type of curiosity, however, which craves for mere astonishment and not for understanding. It is such curiosity that causes children to pry into other people's belongings, and men into other people's affairs.

Sensuous and Apperceptive Curiosity.—Curiosity may be considered of two kinds also from the standpoint of its origin. In early life, curiosity must rest largely upon sense perception, being essentially an appetite of the senses to meet and interpret the objective surroundings. A bright light, a loud noise, a moving object, at once awakens curiosity. At this stage, curiosity serves as a counteracting influence to the instinct of fear, the one leading the child to use his senses upon his surroundings, and the other causing him to use them in a careful and judicious manner. As the child grows in experience, however, his curiosity limits itself more and more in accordance with the law of apperception. Here the object attracts attention not merely because of its sensuous properties, but because it suggests novel relations within the elements of past experience. The young child's curiosity, for instance, is aroused toward a strange plant simply because of its form and colour, that of the student of botany, because the plant presents features that do not relate themselves at once to his botanical experience. The first curiosity may be called objective, or sensuous, the second subjective, or apperceptive.

Relation of Two Types.—The distinction between sensuous and apperceptive curiosity is, of course, one of degree rather than one of kind. A novel object could not be an object of attention unless it bore some relation to the present mental content. The young child, however, seeks mainly to give meaning to novel sense impressions, and is not attracted to the more hidden relations in which objects may stand one to another. He is attracted, for instance, to the colour, scent, and general form of the flower, rather than to its structure. On the other hand, it is found that at a later stage curiosity is usually aroused toward a novel problem, to the extent to which the problem finds a setting in previous experience. This is seen in the fact that the young child takes no interest in having lessons grow out of each other in a connected manner, but must have his curiosity aroused to the present situation through its own intrinsic appeal. For this reason, young children are mainly interested in a lesson which deals with particular elements in a concrete manner, such as coloured blocks, bright pictures, and stories of action; while the older pupil seeks out the new problem because it stands in definite relation to what is already known.

Importance of Apperceptive Curiosity.—Since curiosity depends upon novelty, it is evident that sensuous should ultimately give place to apperceptive curiosity. Although objects first impress the senses with a degree of freshness and vigour, this freshness must disappear as the novelty of the impression wears off. When sensuous curiosity thus disappears, it is only by seeing in the world of sensuous objects other relations with their larger meaning, that healthy curiosity is likely to be maintained. Thus it is that the curiosity of the student is attracted to the more hidden qualities of objects, to the tracing of cause and effect, and to the discovery of scientific truth in general.

Novelty versus Variety.—While the familiar must lose something of its freshness through its very familiarity, it is to be noted that to remit any experience for a time will add something to the freshness of its revival. Persons and places, for instance, when revisited after a period of absence, gain something of the charm of novelty. Variety is, therefore, a means by which the effect of curiosity may be sustained, even after the original novelty has disappeared. This fact should be especially remembered in dealing with the studies of young children. Without being constantly fed upon the novel, the child may yet avoid monotony by having a measure of variety within a reasonable number of interests. It is in this way, in fact, that permanent centres of interest can best be established. To keep a child's attention continually upon one line of experiences would destroy both curiosity and interest. To keep him ever attending to the novel would prevent the building up of any centres of interest. By variety within a reasonable number of subjects, both depth of interest and reasonable variety in interests will be obtained. This is, therefore, another reason why the school curriculum should show a reasonable number of subjects and reasonable variety in the presentation of these subjects.

Imitation

Nature of Imitation.—In our study of the nervous system, attention was called to the close connection existing between sensory impulse and action. It may be noted further that, whenever the young child gains an idea of an action, he tends at once to express that idea in action. On account of this immediate connection between thought and expression, due to an inability to inhibit the motor discharge, a child, as soon as he is able to form ideas of the acts of others, must necessarily show a tendency to repeat, or reproduce, such acts. Granting that this immediate connection between sensory impulse and motor response is an inherited capacity, the tendency of the young child to imitate the acts of others may be classified as an instinct.

Imitation a Complex.—On closer examination, however, it will be found that imitation is really a complex of several tendencies. The nervous organism of the healthy young child is usually supercharged with nervous energy. This energy, like a swollen stream, seems ever striving to sweep away any resistance to the motor discharge of sensory impulses, and must necessarily reinforce the natural tendency to give immediate expression to ideas of action. Moreover, the social instincts of the child, his sympathy, etc., give him a special interest in human beings and in their acts. These tendencies, therefore, focus his attention upon human action, and cause his ideas of such acts to become more vivid and interesting. For this reason, observation of human acts is more likely to lead to motor expression. That the social instincts of the child reinforce the tendency to imitate is indicated by the fact that his early imitations are of human acts especially, as yawning, smiling, crying, etc. The same is further evidenced in that, at a later stage, when ordinary objects enter into his imitative acts, the imitation is largely symbolic, and objects are endowed with living attributes. Here blocks become men; sticks, horses, etc.

Kinds of. A. Spontaneous Imitation.—In its simplest form, imitation seems to follow directly upon the perception of a given act. As the child attends, now to the nod of the head, now to the shaking of the rattle, now to an uttered sound, he spontaneously reproduces these perceived acts. Because in such cases the imitative act follows directly upon the perception of the copy, without the intervention of any determination to imitate, it is termed spontaneous, or unconscious, imitation. It is by spontaneous imitation that the child gains so much knowledge of the world about him, and so much power over the movements of his own body. The occupations and language of the home, the operations of the workman, the movements and gestures of the older children in their games, all these are spontaneously reproduced through imitation. This enables the child to participate largely in the social life about him. It is for this reason that he should observe only good models of language and conduct during his early years.

B. Symbolic Imitation.—If we note the imitative acts of a child of from four to six years of age, we may find that a new factor is often entering into the process. At this stage the child, instead of merely copying the acts of others, further clothes objects and persons with fancied attributes through a process of imagination. By this means, the little child becomes a mother and the doll a baby; one boy becomes a teacher or captain, the others become pupils or soldiers. This form has already been referred to as symbolic imitation. Frequent use is made of this type of imitation in education, especially in the kindergarten. Through the gifts, plays, etc., of the kindergarten, the child in imagination exemplifies numberless relations and processes of the home and community life. The educative value of this type consists in the fact that the child, by acting out in a symbolic, or make-believe, way valuable social processes, though doing them only in an imaginative way, comes to know them better by the doing.

C. Voluntary Imitation.—As the child's increasing power of attention gives him larger control of his experiences, he becomes able, not only to distinguish between the idea of an action and its reproduction by imitation, but also to associate some further end, or purpose, with the imitative process. The little child imitates the language of his fellows spontaneously; the mimic, for the purpose of bringing out certain peculiarities in their speech. When first imitating his elder painting with a brush, the child imitates merely in a spontaneous or unconscious way the act of brushing. When later, however, he tries to secure the delicate touch of his art teacher, he will imitate the teacher's movements for the definite purpose of adding to his own skill. Because in this type the imitator first conceives in idea the particular act to be imitated, and then consciously strives to reproduce the act in like manner, it is classified as conscious, or voluntary, imitation.

Use of Voluntary Imitation.—Teachers differ widely concerning the educational value of voluntary imitation. It is evident, however, that in certain cases, as learning correct forms of speech, in physical and manual exercises, in conduct and manners, etc., good models for imitation count for more than rules and precepts. On the other hand, to endeavour to teach a child by imitation to read intelligently could only result in failure. In such a case, the pupil, by attempting to analyse out and set up as models the different features of the teachers reading, would have his attention directed from the thought of the sentence. But without grasping the meaning, the pupil cannot make his reading intelligent. In like manner, to have a child learn a rule in arithmetic by merely imitating the process from type examples worked by the teacher, would be worse than useless, since it would prevent independent thinking on the child's part. The purpose here is not to gain skill in a mechanical process, but to gain knowledge of an intelligent principle.

Play

Nature of Play Impulse.—Another tendency of early childhood utilized by the modern educator is the so-called instinct of play. According to some, the impulse to play represents merely the tendency of the surplus energy stored up within the nervous organism to express itself in physical action. According to this view, play would represent, not any inherited tendency, but a condition of the nervous organism. It is to be noted, however, that this activity spends itself largely in what seems instinctive tendencies. The boy, in playing hide-and-seek, in chasing, and the like, seems to express the hunting and fleeing instincts of his ancestors. Playing with the doll is evidently suggested and influenced by the parental instinct, while in all games, the activity is evidently determined largely by social instincts. Like imitation, therefore, play seems a complex, involving a number of instinctive tendencies.

Play versus Work.—An essential characteristic of the play impulse is its freedom. By this is meant that the acts are performed, not to gain some further end, but merely for the sake of the activity itself. The impulse to play, therefore, must find its initiative within the child, and must give expression merely to some inner tendency. So long, for example, as the boy shovels the sand or piles the stones merely to exercise his physical powers, or to satisfy an inner tendency to imitate the actions of others, the operation is one of play. When, on the other hand, these acts are performed in order to clean up the yard, or because they have been ordered to be done by a parent, the process is one of work, for the impulse to act now lies in something outside the act itself. To compel a child to play, therefore, would be to compel him to work.

Value of Play: A. Physical.—Play is one of the most effective means for promoting the physical development of the child. This result follows naturally from the free character of the play activity. Since the impulse to act is found in the activity itself, the child always has a strong motive for carrying on the activity. On the other hand, when somewhat similar activities are carried on as a task set by others, the end is too remote from the child's present interests and tendencies to supply him with an immediate motive for the activity. Play, therefore, causes the young child to express himself physically to a degree that tasks set by others can never do, and thus aids him largely in securing control of bodily movements.

B. Intellectual and Moral.—In play, however, the child not only secures physical development and a control of bodily movements, but also exercises and develops other tendencies and powers. Many plays and games, for instance, involve the use of the senses. Whether the young child is shaking his rattle, rolling the ball, pounding with the spoon, piling up blocks and knocking them over, or playing his regular guessing games in the kindergarten, he is constantly stimulating his senses, and giving his sensory nerves their needed development. As imitation and imagination, by their co-operation, later enable the child to symbolize his play, such games as keeping store, playing carpenter, farmer, baker, etc., both enlarge the child's knowledge of his surroundings, and also awaken his interest and sympathy toward these occupations. Other games, such as beans-in-the-bag, involve counting, and thus furnish the child incidental lessons in number under most interesting conditions. In games involving co-operation and competition, as the bowing game, the windmill, fill the gap, chase ball in ring, etc., the social tendencies of the child are developed, and such individual instincts as rivalry, emulation, and combativeness are brought under proper control.

PLAY IN EDUCATION

Assigning Play.—In adapting play to the formal education of the child, a difficulty seems at once to present itself. If the teacher endeavours to provide the child with games that possess an educative value, physical, intellectual, or moral, how can she give such games to the children, and at the same time avoid setting the game as a task? That such a result might follow is evident from our ordinary observation of young children. To the boy interested in a game of ball, the request to come and join his sister in playing housekeeping would, more than likely, be positive drudgery. May it not follow therefore, that a trade or guessing game given by the kindergarten director will fail to call forth the free activity of the child? One of the arguments of the advocates of the Montessori Method in favour of that system is, that the specially prepared apparatus of that system is itself suggestive of play exercises; and that, by having access to the apparatus, the child may choose the particular exercise which appeals to his free activity at the moment. This supposed superiority of the Montessori apparatus over the kindergarten games is, however, more apparent than real. What the skilful kindergarten teacher does is, through her knowledge of the interests and tendencies of the children, to suggest games that will be likely to appeal to their free activity, and at the same time have educative value along physical, intellectual, and moral lines. In this way, she does no more than children do among themselves, when one suggests a suitable game to his companions. In such a case, no one would argue, surely, that the leader is the only child to show free activity in the play.

Stages in Play.—In the selecting of games, plays, etc., it is to be noted that these may be divided into at least three classes, according as they appeal to children at different ages. The very young child prefers merely to play with somewhat simple objects that can make an appeal to his senses, as the rattle, the doll, the pail and shovel, hammer, crayon, etc. This preference depends, on the one hand, upon his early individualistic nature, which would object to share the play with another; and, on the other hand, upon the natural hunger of his senses for varied stimulations. At about five years of age, owing to the growth of the child's imagination, symbolism begins to enter largely into his games. At this age the children love to play church, school, soldier, scavenger man, hen and chickens, keeping store, etc. At from ten to twelve years of age, co-operative and competitive games are preferred; and with boys, those games especially which demand an amount of strength and skill. This preference is to be accounted for through the marked development of the social instincts at this age and, in the case of boys, through increase in strength and will power.

Limitations of Play.—Notwithstanding the value of play as an agent in education, it is evident that its application in the school-room is limited. Social efficiency demands that the child shall learn to appreciate the joy of work even more than the joy of play. Moreover, as noted in the early part of our work, the acquisition of race experience demands that its problems be presented to the child in definite and logical order. This can be accomplished only by having them presented to the pupil by an educative agent and therefore set as a problem or a task to be mastered. This, of course, does not deny that the teacher should strive to have the pupil express himself as freely as possible as he works at his school problem. It does necessitate, however, that the child should find in his lesson some conscious end, or aim, to be reached beyond the mere activity of the learning process. This in itself stamps the ordinary learning process of the school as more than mere play.

CHAPTER XXII

HABIT

Nature of Habit.—When an action, whether performed under the full direction, or control, of attention and with a sense of effort, or merely as an instinctive or impulsive act, comes by repetition to be performed with such ease that consciousness may be largely diverted from the act itself and given to other matters, the action is said to have become habitual. For example, if a person attempts a new manner of putting on a tie, it is first necessary for him to stand before a glass and follow attentively every movement. In a short time, however, he finds himself able to perform the act easily and skilfully both without the use of a glass and almost without conscious direction. Moreover if the person should chance in his first efforts to hold his arms and head in a certain way in order to watch the process more easily in the glass, it is found that when later he does the act even without the use of a glass, he must still hold his arms and head in this manner.

Basis of Habits.—The ability of the organism to habituate an action, or make it a reflex is found to depend upon certain properties of nervous matter which have already been considered.

These facts are:

1. Nervous matter is composed of countless numbers of individual cells brought into relation with one another through their outgoing fibres.

2. This tissue is so plastic that whenever it reacts upon an impression a permanent modification is made in its structure.

3. Not only are such modifications retained permanently, but they give a tendency to repeat the act in the same way; while every such repetition makes the structural modification stronger, and this renders further repetition of the act both easier and more effective.

4. The connections between the various nervous centres thus become so permanent that the action may run its course with a minimum of resistance within the nervous system.

5. In time the movements are so fixed within the system that connections are formed between sensory and motor centres at points lower than the cortex—that is, the stimulus and response become reflex.

An Example.—When a child strives to acquire the movements necessary in making a new capital letter, his eye receives an impression of the letter which passes along the sensory system to the cortex and, usually with much effort, finds an outlet in a motor attempt to form the letter. Thus a permanent trace, or course, is established in the nervous system, which will be somewhat more easily taken on a future occasion. After a number of repetitions, the child, by giving his attention fully to the act, is able to form the letter with relative ease. As these movements are repeated, however, the nervous system, as already noted, may shorten the circuit between the point of sensory impression and motor discharge by establishing associations in centres lower than those situated in the cortex. Whenever any act is repeated a great number of times, therefore, these lower associations are established with a resulting diminution of the impression upward through the cortex of the brain. This results also in a lessening of the amount of attention given the movement, until finally the act can be performed in a perfectly regular way with practically no conscious, or attentive, effort.

Habit and Consciousness.—While saying that such habitual action may be performed with facility in the absence of conscious direction, it must not be understood that conscious attention is necessarily entirely absent during the performance of an habitual act. In many of these acts, as for instance, lacing and tieing a shoe, signing one's name, etc., conscious effort usually gives the first impulse to perform the act. There may be cases, however, in which one finds himself engaged in some customary act without any seeming initial conscious suggestion. This would be noted, for instance, where a person starts for the customary clothes closet, perhaps to obtain something from a pocket, and suddenly finds himself hanging on a hook the coat he has unconsciously removed from his shoulders. Here the initial movement for removing the coat may have been suggested by the sight of the customary closet, or by the movement involved in opening the closet door, these impressions being closely co-ordinated through past experiences with those of removing the coat. When, also, a woman is sewing or kneading bread, although she seems to be able to give her attention fully to the conversation in which she may be engaged, yet no doubt a slight trace of conscious control is still exercised over the other movements. This is seen in the fact that, whenever the conversation becomes so absorbing that it takes a very strong hold on the attention, the habitual movements may cease without the person being at first aware that she has ceased working.

Habit and Nervous Action.—The general flow of the nervous energy during such processes as the above, in which there is an interchange between conscious and habitual control, may be illustrated by the following figures. In these figures the heavy lines indicate the process actually going on, while the broken lines indicate that although such nerve courses are established, they are not being brought into active operation in the particular case.

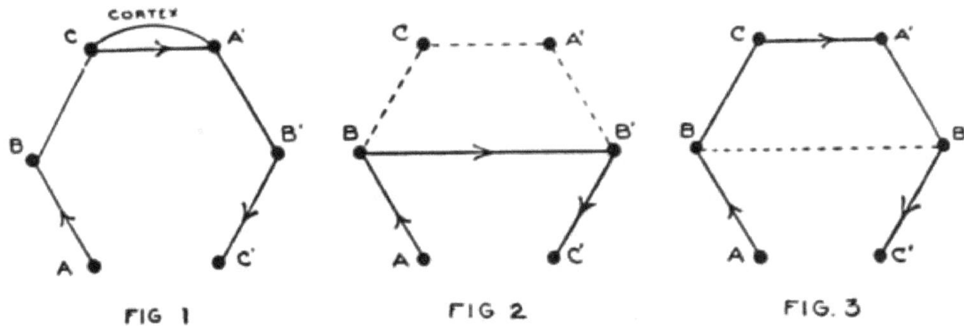

A. Sensory Stimulus	**A′ Higher Motor Centre**
B. Lower Sensory Centre	**B′ Lower Motor Centre**
C. Higher Sensory Centre	**C′ Motor Response**

The arrows in Figure 1 indicate the course of sensory stimulation and motor response during the first efforts to acquire skill in any movement. No connections are yet set up between lower centres and the acts are under conscious control.

The arrows in Figure 2 indicate the course of sensory stimulus and motor response in an ordinary habitual act, as when an expert fingers the piano keys or controls a bicycle while his mind is occupied with other matters.

The arrows in Figure 3 indicate how, even in performing what is ordinarily an habitual act, the mind may at any time assume control of the movement. This is illustrated in the case of a person who, when unconsciously directing his bicycle along the road, comes to a narrow plank over a culvert. Hereupon full attention may be given to the movements, that is, the acts may come under conscious control.

FORMATION OF HABITS

It is evident from the nature of the structure and properties of the nervous system, that man cannot possibly avoid the formation of habits. Any act once performed will not only leave an indelible trace within the nervous system, but will also set up in the system a tendency to repeat the act. It is this fact that always makes the first false step exceedingly dangerous. Moreover, every repetition further breaks down the present resistance and, therefore, in a sense further enslaves the individual to that mode of action. The word poorly articulated for the first time, the letter incorrectly formed, the impatient shrug of the shoulder—these set up their various tracks, create a tendency, and soon, through the establishment of lower connections, become unconscious habits. Thus it is that every one soon becomes a bundle of habits.

Precautions to be Taken.—A most important problem in relation to the life of the young child is that he should at the outset form right habits. This includes not only doing the right thing, but also doing it in the right way. For this he must have the right impression, make the right response, and continue this response until the proper paths are established in the nervous system, or, in other words, until practically all resistance within the system is overcome. It is here that teachers are often very lax in dealing with the pupil in his various forms of expressive work. They may indeed give the child the proper impression, for example, the correct form of the letter, the correct pronunciation of the new word, the correct position for the pen and the body, but too often they do not exercise the vigilance necessary to have the first responses develop into well-fixed habits. But it must be remembered that the child's first response is necessarily crude; for as already seen, there is always at first a certain resistance to the co-ordinated movements, on account of the tracks within the nervous system not yet being surely established. The result is that during the time this resistance is being overcome, there is constant danger of variations creeping into the child's responses. Unless, therefore, he is constantly watched during this practice period, his response may fall much below the model, or standard, set by the teacher. Take, for instance, the child's mode of forming a letter. At the outset he is given the correct forms for *g* and *m*, but on account of the resistance met in performing these movements he may, if left without proper supervision, soon fall into such movements as ƒ and *m*. The chief value of the Montessori sandpaper letters consists in the fact that they enable the child to continue a correct movement without variation until all resistance within the nervous organism has been overcome. Two facts should, therefore, be kept prominently in view by the teacher concerning the child's efforts to secure skill. First, the learner's early attempts must be necessarily crude, both through the resistance at first offered by the nervous system on account of the proper paths not being laid in the system, and also through the image of the movement not being clearly conceived. Secondly, there is constant danger of variations from the proper standard establishing themselves during this period of resistance.

VALUE OF HABITS

Habits Promote Efficiency.—But notwithstanding the dangers which seem to attend the formation of habits, it is only through this inevitable reduction of his more customary acts to unconscious habit that man attains to proficiency. Only by relieving conscious attention from the ordinary mechanical processes in any occupation, is the artist able to attend to the special features of the work. Unless, for instance, the scholar possesses as an unconscious habit the ability to hold the pen and form and join the various letters, he could never devote his attention to evolving the thoughts composing his essay. In like manner, without an habitual control of the chisel, the carver could not possibly give an absorbing attention to the delicate outlines of the particular model. It is only because the rider has habituated himself to the control of the handles, etc., that he can give his attention to the street traffic before him and guide the bicycle or automobile through the ever varying passages. The first condition of efficiency, therefore, in any pursuit, is to reduce any general movements involved in the process to unconscious habits, and thus leave the conscious judgment free to deal with the changeable features of the work.

Habit Conserves Energy.—Another advantage of habit is that it adds to the individual's capacity for work. When any movements are novel and require our full attention, a greater nervous resistance is met on account of the laying down of new paths in the nerve centres. Moreover longer nervous currents are produced through the cortex of the brain, because conscious attention is being called into play. These conditions necessarily consume a greater amount of nerve energy. The result is that man is able to continue for a longer time with less nervous exhaustion any series of activities after they have developed into habits. This can be seen by noting the ease with which one can perform any physical exercise after habituating himself to the movements, compared with the evident strain experienced when the exercise is first undertaken.

Makes the Disagreeable Easy.—Another, though more incidental, advantage of the formation of habits, is that occupations in themselves uninteresting or even distasteful may, through habit, be performed at least without mental revulsion. This results largely from the fact that the growth of habit decreases the resistance, and thus lessens or destroys the disagreeable feeling. Moreover, when such acts are reduced to mechanical habits, the mind is largely free to consider other things. In this way the individual, even in the midst of his drudgery, may enjoy the pleasures of memory or imagination. Although, therefore, in going through some customary act, one may still dislike the occupation, the fact that he can do much of it habitually, leaves him free to enjoy a certain amount of mental pleasure in other ways.

Aids Morality.—The formation of habits also has an important bearing on the moral life. By habituating ourselves to right forms of action, we no doubt make in a sense moral machines of ourselves, since the right action is the one that will meet the least nervous resistance, while the doing of the wrong action would necessitate the establishing of new co-ordinations in the nervous system. It is no doubt partly owing to this, that one whose habits are formed can so easily resist temptations; for to ask him to act other than in the old way is to ask him to make, not the easy, but the hard reaction. While this is true, however, it must not be supposed that in such cases the choice of the right thing involves only a question of customary nervous reaction. When we choose to do our duty, we make a conscious choice, and although earlier right action has set up certain nerve co-ordinations which render it now easy to choose the right, yet it must be remembered that *conscious judgment* is also involved. In such cases man does the right mainly because his judgment tells him that it is right. If, therefore, he is in a situation where he must act in a totally different way from what is customary, as when a quiet, peace-loving man sees a ruffian assaulting a helpless person, a moral man does not hesitate to change his habitual modes of physical action.

IMPROVEMENT OF HABITUAL REACTIONS

To Eliminate a Habit.—From what has been learned concerning the permanency of our habits, it is evident that only special effort will enable us to make any change in an habitual mode of reaction. In at least two cases, however, changes may be necessary. The fact that many of our early habits are formed either unconsciously, or in ignorance of their evil character, finds us, perhaps, as we come to years of discretion, in possession of certain habits from which we would gladly be freed. Such habits may range from relatively unimportant personal peculiarities to impolite and even immoral modes of conduct. In attempting to free ourselves from such acts, we must bear in mind what has been noted concerning the basis of retention. To repeat an act at frequent intervals is an important condition of retaining it as a habit. On the other hand, the absence of such repetition is almost sure, in due time, to obliterate the nervous tendency to repeat the act. To free one's self from an undesirable habit, therefore, the great essential is to avoid resolutely, for a reasonable time, any recurrence of the banned habit. While this can be accomplished only by conscious effort and watchfulness, yet each day passed without the repetition of the act weakens by so much the old nerve co-ordinations. To attempt to break an old habit, gradually, however, as some would prefer, can result only in still keeping the habitual tendency relatively strong.

To Modify a Habit.—At other times, however, we may desire not to eliminate an habitual co-ordination *in toto*, but rather to modify only certain phases of the reaction. In writing, for instance, a pupil may be holding his pen correctly and also using the proper muscular movements, but may have developed a habit of forming certain letters incorrectly, as *f* and *m*. In any attempt to correct such forms, a special difficulty is met in the fact that the incorrect movements are now closely co-ordinated with a number of correct movements, which must necessarily be retained while the other portions of the process are being modified. To effect such a modification, it is necessary for attention to focus itself upon the incorrect elements, and form a clear idea of the changes desired. With this idea as a conscious aim, the pupil must have abundant practice in writing the new forms, and avoid any recurrence of the old incorrect movements. This fact emphasizes the importance of attending to the beginning of any habit. In teaching writing, for instance, the teacher might first give attention only to the form of the letter and then later seek to have the child acquire the muscular movement. In the meantime, however, the child, while learning to form the letters, may have been allowed to acquire the finger movement, and to break this habit both teacher and pupil find much difficulty. By limiting the child to the use of a black-board or a large pencil and tablet, and having him make only relatively large letters while he is learning to form them, the teacher could have the pupil avoid this early formation of the habit of writing with the finger movement.

Limitations of Habit.—From what has here been learned concerning the formation of physical habits, it becomes evident that there are limitations to these as forms of reaction. Since any habit is largely an unconscious reaction to a particular situation, its value will be conditional upon the nature of the circumstances which call forth the reaction. These circumstances must occur quite often under almost identical conditions, otherwise the habit can have no value in directing our social conduct. On the contrary, it may seriously interfere with successful effort. For the player to habituate his hands to fingering the violin is very important, because this is a case where such constant conditions are to be met. For a salesman to habituate himself to one mode of presenting goods to his customers would be fatal, since both the character and the needs of the customers are so varied that no permanent form of approach could be effective in all cases. To habituate ourselves to some narrow automatic line of action and follow it even under varying circumstances, therefore, might prevent the mind from properly weighing these varying conditions, and thus deaden initiative. It is for this reason that experience is so valuable in directing life action. By the use of past experience, the mind is able to analyse each situation calling for reaction and, by noting any unusual circumstances it presents, may adapt even our habitual reactions to the particular conditions.

The relation of habit to interest and attention is treated in Chapter XXIV.

CHAPTER XXIII

ATTENTION

Nature of Attention.—In our study of the principles of general method, it was noted that the mind is able to set up and hold before itself as a problem any partially realized experience. From what has been said concerning nervous stimulation and the passing inward of sensuous impression, it might be thought that the mind is for the most part a somewhat passive recipient of conscious states as they chance to arise through the stimulations of the particular moment. Further consideration will show, however, that, at least after very early childhood, the mind usually exercises a strong selective control over what shall occupy consciousness at any particular time. In the case of a student striving to unravel the mazes of his mathematical problem, countless impressions of sight, sound, touch, etc., may be stimulating him from all sides, yet he refuses in a sense to attend to any of them. The singing of the maid, the chilliness of the room as the fire dies out, even the pain in the limb, all fail to make themselves known in consciousness, until such time as the successful solution causes the person to direct his attention from the work in hand. In like manner, the traveller at the busy station, when intent upon catching his train, is perhaps totally unconscious of the impressions being received from the passing throngs, the calling newsboys, the shunting engines, and the malodorous cattle cars. This ability of the mind to focus itself upon certain experiences to the exclusion of other possible experiences is known as *attention*.

Degree of Attention.—Mention has already been made of states of consciousness in which the mind seems in a passive state of reverie. Although the mind, even in such sub-conscious states, would seem to exercise some slight attention, it is yet evident that it does not exercise a definite selective control during such passive states of consciousness. Attention proper, on the other hand, may be described as a state in which the mind focuses itself upon some particular impression, and thus makes it stand out more clearly in consciousness as a definite experience. From this standpoint it may be assumed that, in a state of waking reverie, the attention is so scattered that no impression is made to stand out clearly in consciousness. On the other hand, as soon as the mind focuses itself on a certain impression, for example, the report of a gun, the relation of two angles, or the image of a centaur, this stands out so clearly that it occupies the whole foreground of consciousness, while all other impressions hide themselves in the background. This single focal state of consciousness is, therefore, pre-eminently a state of attention while the former state of reverie, on account of its diffuse character, may be said to be relatively devoid of attention.

Physical Illustrations of Attention.—To furnish a physical illustration of the working of attention, some writers describe the stream of our conscious life as presenting a series of waves, the successive waves representing the impressions or ideas upon which attention is focused at successive moments. When attention is in a diffuse state, consciousness is likened to a comparatively level stream. The focusing of attention upon particular impressions and thus making them stand out as distinct states of consciousness is said to break the surface of the stream into waves. This may be illustrated as follows:

Fig. 1—Consciousness in a state of passive reverie

Fig. 2—Active consciousness. Attention focussed on the definite experiences a, b, c, d, e, f, g.

By others, consciousness is described as a field of vision, in which the centre of vision represents the focal point of attention. For instance, if the student intent upon his problem in analysis does not notice the flickering light, the playing of the piano, or the smell of the burning meat breaking in upon him, it is because this problem occupies the centre of the attentive field. The other impressions, on the contrary, lie so far on the outside of the field that they fail to stand out in consciousness. This may be represented by the following diagram:

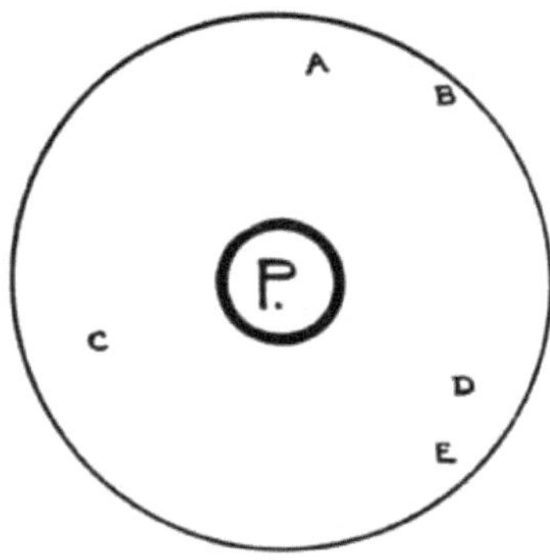

P represents the problem on which attention is fixed. A, B, C, D, E, represent impressions which, though stimulating the organism, do not attract definite attention.

It must be understood, however, that these are merely mechanical devices to illustrate the fact that when the mind selects, or attends to, any impression, this impression is made to stand out clearly as an object in consciousness; or, in other words, the particular impression becomes a clear-cut and definite experience.

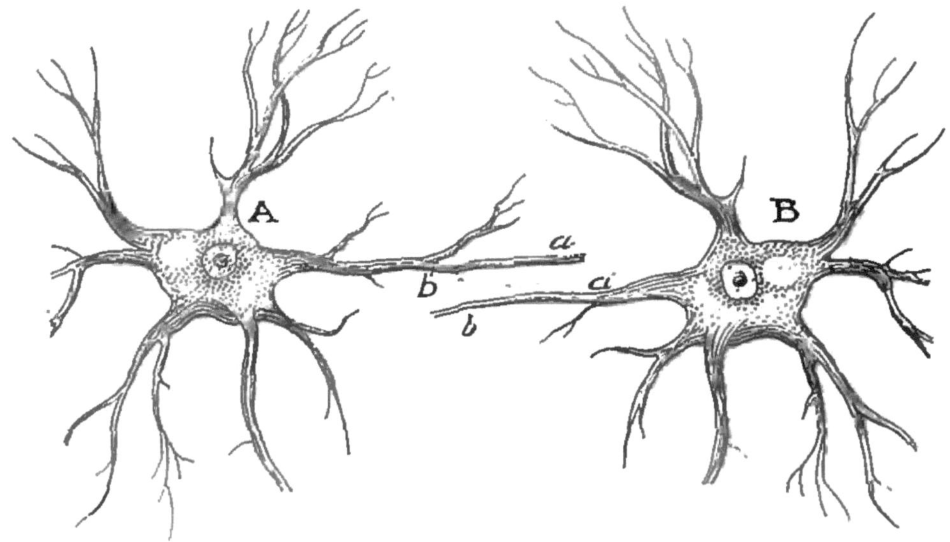

Probable adjusting of nerve ends during active attention

Neural Basis of Attention.—The neural conditions under which the mind exercises such active attention seem to be that during the attentive state the nervous energy concentrates itself upon the paths and centres involved in the particular experience, the resistance being decreased in the paths connecting the cells traversed by the impulse. Moreover, any nervous energy tending to escape in other channels is checked and the movements hindered, thus shutting off attention from other possible experiences. For instance, a person with little interest in horticulture might pass a flowering shrub, the colour, form, and scent making only a faint impression upon him. If, however, his companion should say, "What a lovely colour," his attention will direct itself to this quality, with the result that the colour stands out much more clearly in consciousness, and the other features practically escape his notice. Here the suggestion of the companion focuses attention upon the colour, this being accompanied with a lessening of the resistance between the centres involved in interpreting the colour sensations. At the same time resistance in the arcs involving form and smell is increased, and the energy diverted from these arcs into that of colour.

ATTENTION SELECTIVE

Attention and Interest.—At this point a question naturally arises why the mind, since it is continually subject to the influence of impressions from without and of reviving ideas from within, should select and focus attention upon certain of these to the exclusion of others. The answer usually given is that the mind feels in each case, at least vaguely, a personal interest in some change or adjustment to be wrought either in or through the impression which it makes an object of attention. When, for instance, the reader diverts his attention from the interesting story to the loud talking outside the window, he evidently desires to adjust his understanding more fully to the new and strange impression. So, also, when the spectator rivets his attention upon the flying ball, it is because he associates with this the interesting possibility of a change in the score. In like manner, the student in geometry fixes his attention upon the line joining the points of bisection of the sides, because he desires to change his present mental state of uncertainty as to its parallelism with the base into one of certainty. He further fixes his attention upon the qualities of certain bases and triangles, because through attending to these, he hopes to gain the desired experience concerning the parallelism of the two lines.

Attention and the Question.—The general conditions for determining the course of attention will be further understood by a reference to two facts already established in connection with general method. It has been seen that the question and answer method is usually a successful mode of conducting the learning process. The reason for this is that the question is a most effective means of directing a selective act of attention. For instance, in an elementary science lesson on the candle flame, although the child, if left to himself, might observe the flame, he would not, in all probability, notice particularly the luminous part. Or again, if a dry glass is simply held over the flame and then removed by the demonstrator, although the pupil may have watched the experiment in a general way, it is doubtful whether he would notice particularly the moisture deposited upon the glass. A question from the demonstrator, however, awakens interest, causes the mind to focus in a special direction, and banishes from consciousness features which might otherwise occupy attention. This is because the question suggests a problem, and thus awakens an expectant or unsatisfied state of mind, which is likely to be satisfied only by attending to what the question suggests as an object of attention.

Attention and Motive.—It has already been noted that any process of learning is likely to be more effective when the child realizes a distinct problem, or aim, in the lesson, or feels a need for going through the learning process. The cause of this is that the aim, by awaking curiosity, etc., is an effective means of securing attention. When, for example, the pupil, in learning that $3 \times 4 = 12$, begins with the problem of finding out how many threes are contained in his twelve blocks, his curiosity can be satisfied only by grasping certain significant relations. In approaching the lesson, therefore, with such an actual problem before him, the child feels a desire to change, or alter, his present mental relation to the problem. In other words, he wishes to gain something involved in the problem which he does not now know or is not yet able to do. His desire to bring about this change or to reach this end not only holds his attention upon the problem, but also adjusts it to whatever ideas are likely to assist in solving the problem. When, therefore, pupils approach a lesson with an interesting problem in mind, the teacher finds it much easier to centre their attention upon those factors which make for the acquisition of the new experience.

INVOLUNTARY ATTENTION

Nature of Involuntary Attention.—Attention is met in its simplest form when the mind spontaneously focuses itself upon any strong stimulus received through the senses, as a flashing light, a loud crash, a bitter taste, or a violent pressure. As already noted, the significance of this type of attention lies in the fact that the mind seeks to adjust itself intelligently to a new condition in its surroundings which has been suggested to it through the violent stimulus. The ability to attend to such stimuli is evidently an inherited capacity, and is possessed by animals as well as by children. It is also the only form of attention exercised by very young children, and for some time the child seems to have little choice but to attend to the ever varying stimuli, the attention being drawn now to a bright light, now to a loud voice, according to the violence of the impressions. On account of the apparent lack of control over the direction of attention, this type is spoken of as spontaneous, or involuntary, attention.

Place and Value.—It is only, however, during his very early years that man lacks a reasonable control even over relatively strong stimulations. As noted above, the mind acquires an ability to concentrate itself upon a single problem in the midst of relatively violent stimulations. Moreover, in the midst of various strong stimulations, it is able to select the one which it desires, to the exclusion of all others. At a relatively early age, for instance, the youth is able, in his games, to focus his attention upon the ball, and pays little attention to the shouts and movements of the spectators. On the other hand, however, it is also true that man never loses this characteristic of attending in an involuntary, or reflex, way to any strong stimulus. Indeed, without the possession of this hereditary tendency, it is hard to see how he could escape any dangers with which his body might be threatened while his attention is strongly engaged an another problem.

Educational Precautions.—That young children naturally tend to give their attention to strong stimuli, is a matter of considerable moment to the primary teacher. It is for this cause, among others, that reasonable quiet and order should prevail in the class-room during the recitation. When the pupil is endeavouring to fix his attention upon a selected problem, say the relation of the square foot to the square yard, any undue stimulation of his senses from the school-room environment could not fail to distract his attention from the problem before him. For the same reason, the external conditions should be such as are not likely to furnish unusual stimulations, as will be the case if the class-room is on a busy street and must be ventilated by means of open windows. Finally, in the use of illustrative materials, the teacher should see that the concrete matter will not stimulate the child unduly in ways foreign to the lesson topic. For example, in teaching a nature lesson on the crow, the teacher would find great difficulty in keeping the children's attention on the various topics of the lesson, if he had before the class a live crow that kept cawing throughout the whole lesson period. Nor would it seem a very effective method of attracting attention to the problem of a lesson, if the teacher were continually shouting and waving his arms at the pupils.

NON-VOLUNTARY ATTENTION

Nature of Non-voluntary Attention.—On account of the part played by interest in the focusing of attention, it is possible to distinguish a second type of spontaneous attention in which the mind seems directly attracted to an object of thought because of a natural satisfaction gained from contemplating the subject. The lover, apparently without any determination, and without any external stimulus to suggest the topic, finds his attention ever centring itself upon the image of his fair lady. The young lad, also, without any apparent cause, turns his thoughts constantly to his favourite game. Here the impulse to attend is evidently from within, rather than from without, and arises from the interest that the mind has in the particular experience. This type of attention is especially manifest when trains of ideas pass through the mind without any apparent end in view, one idea suggesting another in accordance with the prevailing mood. The mind, in a half passive state, thinks of last evening, then of the house of a friend, then of the persons met there, then of the game played, etc. In the same way the attention of the student turns without effort to his favourite school subject, and its various aspects may pass in view before him without any effort or determination on his part. Because in this type of attention the different thoughts stand out in consciousness without any apparent choice, or selection, on the part of the mind, it is described as non-voluntary attention.

VOLUNTARY ATTENTION

Nature of Voluntary Attention.—The most important form of attention, however, is that in which the mind focuses itself upon an idea, not as a result of outside stimulation, but with some further purpose in view. For instance, when a person enters a room in which a strange object seems to be giving out musical notes automatically, he may at first give spontaneous attention to the sounds coming from the instrument. When, however, he approaches the object later with a desire to discover the nature of its mechanism, his attention is focused upon the object with a more remote aim, or end, in view, to discover where the music comes from. So also, when the lad mentioned in Chapter II fixed his attention on the lost coin, he set this object before his attention with a further end in view—how to regain it. Because the person here *determines* to attend to, or think about, a certain problem, in order that he may reach a certain consciously set end, this form of attention is described as voluntary, or active, attention.

Near and Remote Ends.—It is to be noted, however, that the interesting end toward which the mind strives in voluntary attention may be relatively near or remote. A child examining an automatic toy does it for the sake of discovering what is in the toy itself; an adult in order to see whether it is likely to interest his child. A student gives attention to the problem of the length of the hypotenuse because he is interested in the mathematical problem itself, the contractor because he desires to know how much material will be necessary for the roof of the building. One child may apply himself to mastering a reading lesson because the subject itself is interesting to him, another because he desires to take home a perfect report at the end of the week, and a third because a sense of obligation tells him that teacher and parents will expect him to study it.

How we Attend to a Problem.—Since voluntary attention implies mental movement directed to the attainment of some end, the mind does not simply keep itself focused on the particular problem. For instance, in attempting to solve the problem that the exterior angle of a triangle equals the sum of the two interior and opposite angles, no progress toward the attainment of the end in view could be made by merely holding before the mind the idea of their equality. It is, in fact, impossible for the attention to be held for any length of time on a single topic. This will be readily seen if one tries to hold his attention continuously upon, say, the tip of a pencil. When this is attempted, other ideas constantly crowd out the selected idea. The only sense, therefore, in which one holds his attention upon the problem in an act of voluntary attention is, that his attention passes forward and back between the problem and ideas felt to be associated with it. Voluntary attention is, therefore, a mental process in which the mind shifts from one idea to another in attaining to a desired end, or problem. In this shifting, or movement, of voluntary attention, however, two significant features manifest themselves. First, in working forward and back from the problem as a controlling centre, attention brings into consciousness ideas more or less relevant to the problem. Secondly, it selects and adjusts to the problem those that actually make for its solution, and banishes from consciousness whatever is felt to be foreign to obtaining the desired end.

Example of Controlled Attention.—To exemplify a process of voluntary attention we may notice the action of the mind in solving such a problem as:

> Two trains started at the same moment from Toronto and Hamilton respectively, one going at the rate of thirty miles an hour and the other at the rate of forty miles an hour. Supposing the distance between Toronto and Hamilton to be forty miles, in how many minutes will the trains meet?

Here the pupil must first fix his attention upon the problem—the number of minutes before the trains will meet. This at once forms both a centre and a standard for measuring other related ideas. In this way his attention passes to the respective rates of the two trains, thirty and forty miles per hour. Then perhaps he fixes attention on the thought that one goes a mile in two minutes and the other a mile in 1½ minutes. But as he recognizes that this is leading him away from the problem, resistance is offered to the flow of attention in this direction, and he passes to the thought that in a *minute* the former goes ½ mile and the later ⅔ of a mile. From this he passes to the thought that in one minute they together go 1⅙ miles. Hereupon perhaps the idea comes to his mind to see how many miles they would go in an hour. This, however, is soon felt to be foreign to the problem, and resistance being set up in this direction, the attention turns to consider in what time the two together cover 40 miles. Now by dividing 40 miles by 1⅙, he obtains the number 34²⁄₇ and is satisfied that his answer is 34²⁄₇ minutes. The process by which the attention here selected and adjusted the proper ideas to the problem might be illustrated by the following Figure:

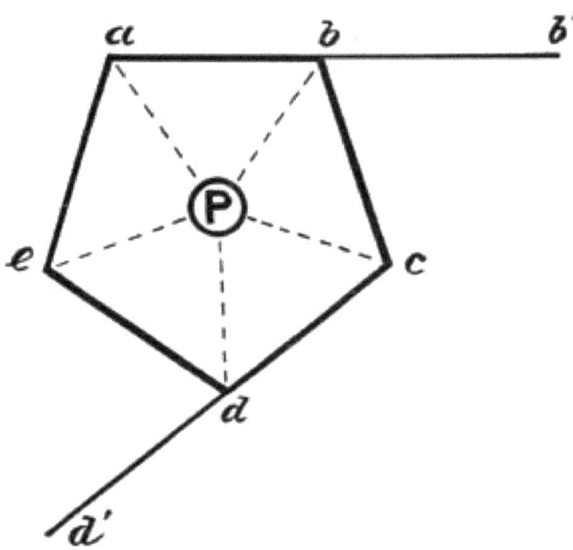

Here "P" represents the problem; a, b, c, d, and e, ideas accepted as relevant to the problem; and b′, d′ ideas suggested by b and d, but rejected as not adjustable to the problem.

Factors in Process.—The above facts demonstrate, however, that the mind can take this attitude toward any problem only if it has a certain store of old knowledge relative to it. Two important conditions of voluntary attention are therefore, first, that the mind should have the necessary ideas, or knowledge, with which to attend and, secondly, that it would select and adjust these to the purpose in view. Here the intimate connection of voluntary attention to the normal learning process is apparent. The step of preparation, for instance, is merely putting the mind in the proper attitude to attend voluntarily to an end in view, namely the lesson problem; while the so-called analytic-synthetic process of learning involves the selecting and adjusting movements of voluntary attention.

Spontaneous and Voluntary Attention Distinguished.—In describing voluntary attention as an active form of attention, psychologists assume that since the mind here wills, or resolves, to attend, in order to gain a certain end in view; therefore voluntary attention must imply a much greater degree of effort, or strain, than other types. That such is always the case, however, is at times not very apparent. If one may judge by the straining of eye or ear, the poise of the body, the holding of the breath, etc., when a person gives involuntary attention to any sudden impression, as a strange noise at night, it is evident that the difference of effort, or strain, in attending to this and some selected problem may not, during the time it continues, be very marked.

It is of course true that in voluntary attention the mind must choose its own object of attention as an end, or aim, while in the involuntary type the problem seems thrust upon us. This certainly does imply a deliberate choice in the former, and to that extent may be said to involve an effort not found in the latter. In like manner, when seeking to attain the end which has been set up, the mind must select the related ideas which will solve its problem. This in turn may demand the grasping of a number of complex relations. To say, however, that all striving to attain an end is lacking in a case of involuntary attention would evidently be fallacious. When the mind is startled by a strange noise, the mind evidently does go out, though in a less formal way, to interpret a problem involuntarily thrust upon it. When, for instance, we receive the violent impression, the mind may be said to ask itself, "What strange impression is this?" and to that extent, even here, faces a selected problem. The distinguishing feature of voluntary attention, therefore, is the presence of a consciously conceived end, or aim, upon which the mind deliberately sets its attention as something to be thought *about*.

ATTENTION IN EDUCATION

Voluntary Attention and Learning.—From what has been seen, it is evident that, when a pupil in his school approaches any particular problem, the learning process will represent a process of voluntary attention. This form of attention is, therefore, one of special significance to the teacher, since a knowledge of the process will cast additional light upon the learning process. The first condition of voluntary attention is the power to select some idea as an end, or problem, for attention. It was seen, however, that the focusing of attention upon any problem depends upon some form of desirable change to be effected in and through the set problem. For instance, unless the recovery of the coin is conceived as producing a desirable change, it would not become a deliberately set problem for attention. It is essential, therefore, that the end which the child is to choose as an object of attention should be one conceived as demanding a desired change, or adjustment. For instance, to ask a child to focus his attention upon two pieces of wood merely as pieces of wood is not likely to call forth an active effort of attention. To direct his attention to them to find out how many times the one is contained in the other, on the other hand, focuses his attention more strongly upon them; since the end to be reached will awaken his curiosity and set an interesting problem.

Non-voluntary Attention in Education.—On account of the ease with which attention seems to centre itself upon its object in non-voluntary attention, it is sometimes erroneously claimed that this is the type of attention to be aimed at in the educative process, especially with young children. Such a view is, however, a fallacious one, and results from a false notion of the real character of both non-voluntary and voluntary attention. In a clear example of non-voluntary attention, the mind dwells upon the ideas merely on account of their inherent attractiveness, and passes from one idea to its associated idea without any purposeful end in view. This at once shows its ineffectiveness as a process of learning. When the young lover's thoughts revert in a non-voluntary way to the fair one, he perhaps passes into a state of mere reminiscence, or at best of idle fancy. Even the student whose thoughts run on in a purposeless manner over his favourite subject, will merely revive old associations, or at best make a chance discovery of some new knowledge. In the same way, the child who delights in musical sounds may be satisfied to drum the piano by the hour, but this is likely to give little real advance, unless definite problems are set up and their attainment striven for in a purposeful way.

Voluntary Attention and Interest.—A corollary of the fallacy mentioned above is the assumption that voluntary attention necessarily implies some conflict with the mind's present desire or interest. It is sometimes said, for instance, that in voluntary attention, we compel our mind to attend, while our interest would naturally direct our attention elsewhere. But without a desire to effect some change in or through the problem being attended to, the mind would not voluntarily make it an object of attention. The misconception as to the relation of voluntary attention to interest is seen in an illustration often given as an example of non-voluntary attention. It is said, rightly enough, that if a child is reading an interesting story, and is just at the point where the plot is about to unravel itself, there will be difficulty in diverting his attention to other matters. This, it is claimed, furnishes a good example of the power of non-voluntary attention. But quite the opposite may be the case. When called upon, say by his parent, to lay aside the book and attend to some other problem, the child, it is true, shows a desire to continue reading. But this may be because he has a definite aim of his own in view—to find out the fate of his hero. This is a strongly felt need on his part, and his mind refuses to be satisfied until, by further attention to the problem before him, he has attained to this end. The only element of truth in the illustration is that the child's attention is strongly reinforced through the intense feeling tone associated with the selected, or determined, aim—the fate of his hero. The fact is, therefore, that a process of voluntary attention may have associated with its problem as strong an interest as is found in the non-voluntary type.

Voluntary Attention Depends on Problem.—It is evident from the foregoing that the characteristic of voluntary attention is not the absence or the presence of any special degree of interest, but rather the conception of some end, or purpose, to be reached in and through the attentive process. In other words, voluntary attention is a state of mind in which the mental movements are not drifting without a chart, but are seeking to reach a set haven. A person who is greatly interested in automobiles, for instance, on seeing a new machine, may allow his attention to run now to this part of the machine, now to that, as each attracts him in turn. Here no fixed purpose is being served by the attentive process, and attention may pass from part to part in a non-voluntary way, the person's general interest in automobiles being sufficient to keep the attention upon the subject. Suddenly, however, he may notice something apparently new in the mechanism of the machine, and a desire arises to understand its significance. This at once becomes an end to which the mind desires to attain, and voluntary attention proceeds to direct the mental movements toward its attainment. To suppose, however, that the interest, manifest in the former mental movements, is now absent, would evidently be fallacious. The difference lies in this, that at first the attention seemed fixed on the object through a general interest only, and drifted from point to point in a purposeless way, while in the second case an interesting end, or purpose, controlled the mental movements, and therefore made each movement significant in relation to the whole conscious process.

Attention and Knowledge.—Mention has already been made of the relation of attention to interest. It should be noted, further, that the difference in our attention under different circumstances is largely dependent upon our knowledge. The stonecutter, as he passes the fine mansion, gives attention to the fretted cornice; the glazier, to the beautiful windows; the gardener, to the well-kept lawn and beds. Even the present content of the mind has its influence upon attention. The student on his way to school, if busy with his spelling lesson, is attracted to the words and letters on posters and signs. If he is reviewing his botany, he notes especially the weeds along the walk; if carrying to his art teacher, with a feeling of pride, the finished landscape drawing, his attention goes out to the shade and colour of field and sky. That such a connection must exist between knowledge and attention is apparent from what has been already noted concerning the working of the law of apperception.

Physical Conditions of Attention.—From what was learned above regarding the relation of nervous energy to active attention, it is evident that the ability to attend to a problem at any given time will depend in part upon the physical condition of the organism. If, therefore, the nervous energy is lowered through fatigue or sickness, the attention will be weakened. For this reason the teaching of subjects, such as arithmetic, grammar, etc., which present difficult problems, and therefore make large demands upon the attention of the scholars, should not be undertaken when the pupils' energy is likely to be at a minimum. Similarly, unsatisfactory conditions in the school-room, such as poor ventilation, uncomfortable seats, excessive heat or cold, all tend to lower the nervous energy and thus prevent a proper concentration of attention upon the regular school work.

Precautions Relating to Voluntary Attention.—Although voluntary attention is evidently the form of attention possessing real educational value, certain precautions would seem necessary concerning its use. With very young children the aim for attending should evidently not be too remote. In other words, the problem should involve matter in which the children have a direct interest. For this reason it is sometimes said that young children should set their own problems. This is of course a paradox so far as the regular school work is concerned, though it does apply to the pre-school period, and also justifies the claim that with young children the lesson problem should be closely connected with some vital interest. It would be useless, for instance, to try to interest young children in the British North America Act by telling them that the knowledge will be useful when they come to write on their entrance examinations. The story of Sir Isaac Brock, on the other hand, wins attention for itself through the child's patriotism and love of story. Again, the problem demanding attention should not, in the case of young children, be too long or complex. For example, a young child might easily attend to the separate problems of finding out, (1) how many marbles he must have to give four to James and three to William; (2) how many times seven can be taken from twenty-eight; (3) how many marbles James would have if he received four marbles four times; and (4) how many James would have if he received three marbles three times. But if given the problem "to divide twenty-eight marbles between James and William, giving James four every time he gives William three," the problem may be too complex for his present power of attention. A young child has not the control over his knowledge necessary to continue any long process of selecting attention. A relatively short period of attention to any problem, therefore, exhausts the nervous energy in the centres connected with a particular set of experiences. It is for this reason that the lessons in primary classes should be short and varied. One of the objections, therefore, to a narrow curriculum is that attention would not obtain needed variety, and that a narrowness in interest and application may result. On the other hand, it is well to note that the child must in time learn to concentrate his attention for longer periods and upon topics possessing only remote, or indirect, interest.

CHAPTER XXIV

THE FEELING OF INTEREST

Nature of Feeling.—Feeling has already been described (Chapter XIX) as the pleasurable or painful side of any state of consciousness. We may recall how it was there found that any conscious state, or experience, for instance, being conscious of the prick of a pin, of success at an examination, or of the loss of a friend, is not merely a state of knowledge, or awareness, but is also a state of feeling. It is a state of feeling because it *affects* us, that is, because being a state of *our* consciousness, it appeals to us pleasurably or painfully in a way that it can to no one else.

Neural Conditions of Feeling.—It has been seen that every conscious state, or experience, has its affective, or feeling, tone, and also that every experience involves the transmission of nervous energy through a number of connected brain cells. On this basis it is thought that the feeling side of any conscious state is conditioned by the degree of the resistance encountered as the nervous energy is transmitted. If the centres involved in the experience are not yet properly organized, or if the stimulation is strong, the resistance is greater and the feeling more intense. A new movement of the limbs in physical training, for example, may at first prove intensely painful, because the centres involved in the exercise are not yet organized. So also, because a very bright light stimulates the nerves violently, it causes a painful feeling. That morphine deadens pain is to be explained on the assumption that it decreases nervous energy, and thus lessens the resistance being encountered between the nervous centres affected at the time.

Feeling and Habit.—That the intensity of a feeling is conditioned by the amount of the resistance seems evident, if we note the relation of feeling to habit. The first time the nurse-in-training attends a wounded patient, the experience is marked by intense feeling. After a number of such experiences, however, this feeling becomes much less. In like manner, the child who at first finds the physical exercise painful, as he becomes accustomed to the movements, finds the pain becoming less and less intense. In such cases it is evident that practice, by organizing the centres involved in the experience, decreases the resistance between them, and thus gradually decreases the intensity of the feeling. When finally the act becomes habitual, the nervous impulse traverses only lower centres, and therefore all feeling and indeed all consciousness will disappear, as happens in the habitual movements of the limbs in walking and of the arms during walking.

CLASSES OF FEELINGS

Sensuous Feeling.—As already noted, while feelings vary in intensity according to the strength of the resistance, they also differ in kind according to the arcs traversed by the impulse. Experiencing a burn on the hand would involve nervous impulses, or currents, other than those involved in hearing of the death of a friend. The one experience also differs in feeling from the other. Our feeling states are thus able to be divided into certain important classes with more or less distinct characteristics for each. In one class are placed those feelings which accompany sensory impulses. The sensations arising from the stimulations of the sense organs, as a sweet or bitter taste, a strong smell, the touch of a hot, sharp, rough, or smooth object, etc., all present an affective, or feeling, side. So also feeling enters into the general or organic sensations arising from the conditions of the bodily organs; as breathing, the circulation of the blood, digestion, the tension of the muscles, hunger, thirst, etc. The feeling which thus enters as a factor into any sensation is known as sensuous feeling.

Ideal Feeling.—Other feelings enter into our ideas and thoughts. The perception or imagination of an accident is accompanied with a painful feeling, the memory or anticipation of success with a feeling of joy, the thought of some particular person with a thrill of love. Such feelings are known as ideal feelings. When a child tears his flesh on a nail, he experiences sensuous feeling, when he shrinks away, as he perceives the teeth of a snarling dog, he experiences an ideal feeling, known as the emotion of fear.

Interest.—A third type of feeling especially accompanies an active process of attention. In our study of attention, it was seen that any process of attention is accompanied by a concentration of nervous energy upon the paths or centres involved in the experience, thus organizing the paths more completely and thereby decreasing the resistance. The impulse to attend to any experience is, therefore, accompanied with a desirable feeling, because a new adjustment between nerve centres is taking place and resistance being overcome. This affective, or feeling, tone which accompanies a process of attention is known as the feeling of interest.

Interest and Attention.—In discussions upon educational method, it is usually affirmed that the attention will focus upon a problem to the extent to which the mind is interested. While this statement may be accepted in ordinary language, it is not psychologically true that I first become interested in a strange presentation, and then attend to it afterwards. In such a case it is no more true to say that I attend because I am interested, than to say that I am interested because I attend. In other words, interest and attention are not successive but simultaneous, or, as sometimes stated, they are back and front of the same mental state. This becomes evident by noting the nervous conditions which must accompany interest and attention. When one is attending to any strange phenomenon, say a botanist to the structure of a rare plant, it is evident that there are not only new groupings of ideas in the mind, but also new adjustments being set up between the brain centres. This implies in turn a lessening of resistance between the cells, and therefore the presence of the feeling tone known as interest.

Interest, Attention, and Habit.—Since the impulse to attend to a presentation is conditioned by a process of adjustment, or organization, between brain centres, it is evident that, while the novel presentations call forth interest and attention, repetition, by habituating the nervous arcs, will tend to deaden interest and attention. For this reason the story, first heard with interest and attention, becomes stale by too much repetition. The new toy fails to interest the child after the novelty has worn off. It must be noted, however, that while repetition usually lessens interest, yet when any set of experiences are repeated many times, instead of lessening interest the repetition may develop a new interest known as the interest of custom. Thus it is that by repeating the experience the man is finally compelled to visit his club every evening, and the boy to play his favourite game every day. This secondary interest of custom arises because repetition has finally established such strong associations within the nervous system that they now have become a part of our nature and are thus able to make a new demand upon interest and attention.

INTEREST IN EDUCATION

Uses of Term: A. Subjective; B. Objective.—That the educator describes interest as something that causes the mind to give attention to what is before it, when in fact interest and attention are psychologically merely two sides of a single process, is accounted for by the fact that the term "interest" may be used with two quite different meanings. Psychologically, interest is evidently a feeling state, that is, it represents a phase of consciousness. My *interest* in football, for instance, represents the *feeling* of worth which accompanies attention to such experiences. In this sense interest and attention are but two sides of the single experience, interest representing the feeling, and attention the effort side of the experience. As thus applied, the term interest is said to be used subjectively. More, often, however, the term is applied rather to the thing toward which the mind directs its attention, the object being said to possess interest for the person. In this sense the rattle is said to have interest for the babe; baseball, for the young boy; and the latest fashions, for the young lady. Since the interest is here assumed to reside in the object, it seems reasonable to say that our attention is attracted through interest, that is, through an interesting presentation. As thus applied, the term interest is said to be used objectively.

Types of Objective Interest.—The interest which various objects and occupations thus possess for the mind may be of two somewhat different types. In some cases the object possesses a direct, or intrinsic, interest for the mind. The young child, for instance, is spontaneously attracted to bright colours, the boy to stories of adventure, and the sentimental youth or maiden to the romance. In the case of any such direct interests, however, the feeling with which the mind contemplates the object may transfer itself at least partly to other objects associated more or less closely with the direct object of interest. It is thus that the child becomes interested in the cup from which his food is taken, and the lover in the lap dog which his fair one fondles. As opposed to the *direct interest* which an object may have for the mind, this transferred type is known as *indirect interest.*

Importance of Transference of Interest.—The ability of the mind thus to transfer its interests to associated objects is often of great pedagogical value. Abstract forms of knowledge become more interesting to young children through being associated with something possessing natural interest. A pupil who seems to take little interest in arithmetic may take great delight in manual training. By associating various mathematical problems with his constructive exercises, the teacher can frequently cause the pupil to transfer in some degree his primary interest in manual training to the associated work in arithmetic. In the same way the child in the primary grade may take more delight in the alphabet when he is able to make the letters in sand or by stick-laying. It may be said, in fact, that much of man's effort is a result of indirect interest. What is called doing a thing from a sense of duty is often a case of applying ourselves to a certain thing because we are interested in avoiding the disapproval of others. The child also often applies himself to his tasks, not so much because he takes a direct interest in them, but because he wishes to gain the approval and avoid the censure of teacher and parents.

Native and Acquired Interest.—Interest may also be distinguished on the basis of its origin. As noted above, certain impressions seem to demand a spontaneous interest from the individual. For this cause the child finds his attention going out immediately to bright colours, to objects which give pleasure, such as candy, etc., or to that which causes personal pain. On the other hand, objects and occupations which at first seem devoid of interest may, after a certain amount of experience has been gained, become important centres of interest. A young child may at first show no interest in insects unless it be a feeling of revulsion. Through the visit of an entomologist to his home, however, he may gain some knowledge of insects. This knowledge, by arousing an apperceptive tendency in the direction of insect study, gradually develops in him a new interest which lasts throughout his whole life. It is in this way that the various school subjects widen the narrow interests of the child. By giving him an insight into various phases of his social environment, the school curriculum awakens in him different centres of interest, and thus causes him to become in the truest sense a part of the social life about him. This fact is one of the strongest arguments, also, against a narrow public school course of study in a society which is itself a complex of diversified interests.

Interest versus Interests.—On account of the evident connection of interest and attention, the teacher may easily err in dealing with the young pupil. It is allowable, as pointed out above, that the teacher should take advantage of any native interest to secure the attention and effort of the child in his school work. This does not mean, however, that children are to be given only problems in which they are naturally interested. It must be remembered, as seen in a former paragraph, that, according to the interest of custom, any line of school work, when intelligently followed, may soon build up a centre of interest for itself. For this reason a proper study of arithmetic should develop an interest in arithmetic; a study of history, an interest in history; and a study of geography, an interest in geography. The saying that school work should follow a child's interest might, therefore, be better expressed by saying that the child's interests should follow the school work. It is only, in fact, as any one becomes directly interested in his pursuits, that the highest achievement can be reached. It is not the workman who is always looking forward to pay-day, who develops into an artist, or the teacher who is waiting for the summer holiday, who is a real inspiration to her pupils. In like manner, it is only as the child forms centres of interest in connection with his school work, that his life and character are likely to be affected permanently thereby.

Development of Interests

Development of Interests.—The problem for the educator is, therefore, not so much to follow the interest of the child, as it is to develop in him permanent centres of interest. For this reason the following facts concerning the origin and development of interests should be understood by the practical educator. First among these is the fact that certain instinctive tendencies of early childhood may be made a starting-point for the development of permanent valuable interest. The young child has a tendency to collect or an instinct of ownership, which may be taken advantage of in directing him to make collections of insects, plants, coins, stamps, and thus prove of permanent educative value. His constructive tendencies, or desire to do with what comes into his hand, as well as his imitative instincts, may be turned to account in building up an interest in various occupations. His social instinct, also, provides a means for developing permanent emotional interests as sympathy, etc. In like manner, the character of the child's surroundings tends to create in him various centres of interest. The young child, for instance, who is surrounded with beautiful objects, is almost sure to develop an interest in works of art, while the child who is early provided with fable and story will develop an interest in history.

When to Develop Interests.—It is to be noted further concerning many of these forms of interest, that youth is the special period for their development. The child who does not, during his early years, have an opportunity to develop his social tendencies, is not likely later in life to acquire an interest in his fellow-men. In the same manner, if youth is spent in surroundings void of æsthetic elements, manhood will be lacking in artistic interests. It is in youth also that our intellectual interests, such as love of reading, of the study of nature, of mathematics, must be laid.

Interests Must be Limited.—While emphasizing the importance of establishing a wide range of interests when educating a child, the teacher must remember that there is danger in a child acquiring too wide a range. This can result only in a dissipation of effort over many fields. While this prevents narrowness of vision and gives versatility of disposition, it may prevent the attainment of efficiency in any department, and make of the youth the proverbial "Jack-of-all-trades."

A study of the feeling of interest has been made at this stage on account of its close connection with the problem of attention, and in fact with the whole learning process. An examination of the other classes of feeling will be made at a later stage in the course.

CHAPTER XXV

SENSE PERCEPTION

Sensation and Perception Distinguished.—Sensation and perception are two terms applied usually without much distinction of meaning to our recognition of the world of objects. When, for instance, a man draws near to a stove, he may say that it gives him a *sensation* of heat, or perhaps that he *perceives* it to be hot. In psychology, however, the term sensation has been used in two somewhat different meanings. By some the term is used to signify a state of consciousness conditioned merely upon the stimulation of a sense organ, as the eye, ear, etc., by its appropriate stimulus. To others, however, sensation signifies rather a mental image experienced by the mind as it reacts upon and interprets any sensory impression. Perception, on the other hand, signifies the recognition of an external object as presented to the mind here and now.

Sensation Implies Externality.—When, however, a sensory image, such as smooth, yellow, cold, etc., arises in consciousness as a result of the mind reacting when an external stimulus is applied to some sense organ, it is evident that, at least after very early infancy, one never has the image without at once referring it to some external cause. If, for instance, a person is but half awake and receives a sound sensation, he does not ask himself, "What mental state is *this*?" but rather, "What is *that*?" This shows an evident tendency to refer our sensations at once to an external cause, or indicates that our sensations always carry with them an implicit reference to an external object. Leaving, therefore, to the scientific psychologist to consider whether it is possible to have a pure sensation, we shall treat sensation as the recognition of a quality which is at least vaguely referred to an external object. In other words, sensation is a medium by which we are brought into relation with real things existing independently of our sensations.

Perception Involves Sensation Element.—Moreover, an object is perceived as present here and now only because it is revealed to us through one or more of the senses. When, for instance, I reach out my hand in the dark room and receive a sensation of touch, I perceive the table as present before me. When I receive a sensation of sound as I pass by the church, I perceive that the organ is being played. When I receive a colour sensation from the store window, I say that I perceive oranges. Perception, therefore, involves the referring of the sensuous state, or image, to an external thing, while in adult life sensation is never accepted by our attention as satisfactory unless it is referred to something we regard as immediately presenting itself to us by means of the sensation. It is on account of this evident interrelation of the two that we speak of a process of sense perception.

Perception an Acquired Power.—On the other hand, however, investigation will show that this power to recognize explicitly the existence of an external object through the presentation of a sensation, was not at first possessed by the mind. The ability thus to perceive objects represents, therefore, an acquirement on the part of the individual. If a person, although receiving merely sensations of colour and light, is able to say, "Yonder is an orange," he is evidently interpreting, or giving meaning to, the present sensations largely through past experience; for the images of colour and light are accepted by the mind as an indication of the presence of an external thing from which could be derived other images of taste, smell, etc., all of which go to make up the idea "orange." An ordinary act of perception, therefore, must involve not merely sensation, but also an interpretation of sensation through past experience. It is, in fact, because the recognition of an external object involves this conscious interpretation of the sensuous impressions, that people often suffer delusion. When the traveller passing by a lone graveyard interprets the tall and slender shrub laden with white blossoms as a swaying ghost, the misconception does not arise from any fault of mere vision, but from the type of former knowledge which the other surroundings of the moment call up, these evidently giving the mind a certain bias in its interpretation of the sensuous, or colour, impressions.

Perception in Adult Life.—In our study of general method, sense perception was referred to as the most common mode of acquiring particular knowledge. A description of the development of this power to perceive objects through the senses should, therefore, prove of pedagogical value. But to understand how an individual acquires the ability to perceive objects, it is well to notice first what takes place in an ordinary adult act of perception, as for instance, when a man receives and interprets a colour stimulus and says that he perceives an orange. If we analyse the person's idea of an orange we find that it is made up of a number of different quality images—colour, taste, smell, touch, etc., organized into a single experience, or idea, and accepted as a mental representation of an object existing in space. When, therefore, the person referred to above says that he perceives an orange, what really happens is that he accepts the immediate colour and light sensation as a sign of the whole group of qualities which make up his notion of the external object, orange, the other qualities essential to the notion coming back from past experience to unite with the presented qualities. Owing to this fact, any ordinary act of perception is said to contain both presentative and representative elements. In the above example, for instance, the colour would be spoken of as a presentative element, because it is immediately presented to the mind in sensuous terms, or through the senses. Anything beyond this which goes to make up the individual's notion orange, and is revived from past experience, is spoken of as representative. For the same reason, the sensuous elements involved in an ordinary act of perception are often spoken of as immediate, and the others as mediate elements of knowledge.

GENESIS OF PERCEPTION

Genesis of Perception.—To trace the development of this ability to mingle both presentative and representative elements of knowledge into a mental representation, or idea, of an external object, it is necessary to recall what has been noted regarding the relation of the nervous system to our conscious acts. When the young child first comes in contact with the world of strange objects with which he is surrounded, the impressions he receives therefrom will not at first have either the definite quality or the relation to an external thing which they later secure. As a being, however, whose first tendencies are those of movement, he grasps, bites, strokes, smells, etc., and thus goes out to meet whatever his surroundings thrust upon him. Gradually he finds himself expand to take in the existence of a something external to himself, and is finally able, as the necessary paths are laid down in his nervous system, to differentiate various quality images one from the other; as, touch, weight, temperature, light, sound, etc. This will at once involve, however, a corresponding relating, or synthetic, attitude of mind, in which different quality images, when experienced together as qualities of some vaguely felt thing, will be organized into a more or less definite knowledge, or idea, of that object, as illustrated in the figure below. As the child in time gains the ability to *attend* to the sensuous presentations which come to him, and to discriminate one sensation from another, he discovers in the vaguely known thing the images of touch, colour, taste, smell, etc., and finally associates them into the idea of a better known object, orange.

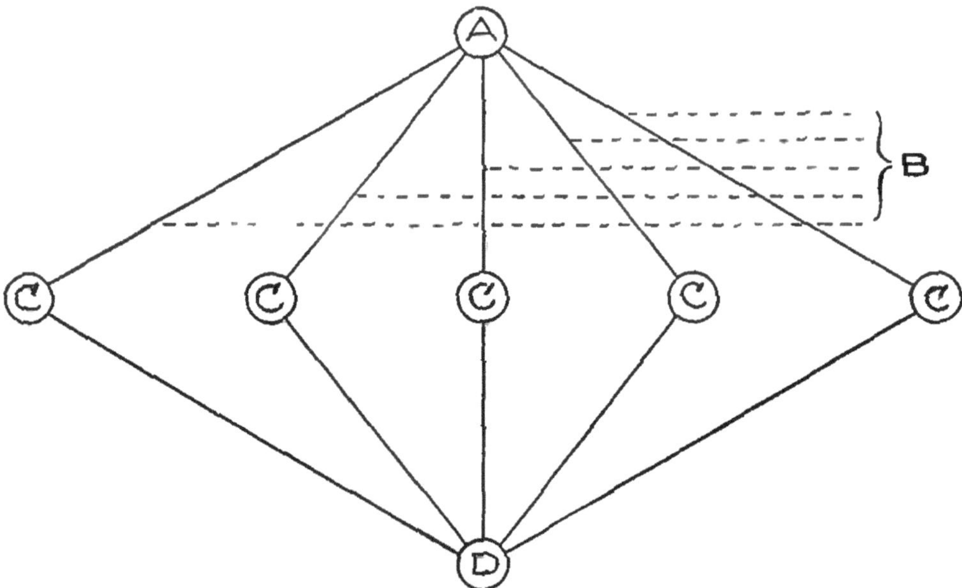

A. Unknown thing. B. Sensory stimuli. C. Sensory images. D. Idea of object.

Control of Sensory Image as Sign.—Since the various sense impressions are carried to the higher centres of the brain, they will not only be interpreted as sensory images and organized into a knowledge of external objects, but, owing to the retentive power of the nervous tissue, will also be subject to recall. As the child thus gains more and more the ability to organize and relate various sensory images into mental representations, or ideas, of external objects, he soon acquires such control over these organized groups, that when any particular sensation image out of a group is presented to the mind, it will be sufficient to call up the other qualities, or will be accepted as a sign of the presence of the object. When this stage of perceptual power is reached, an odour coming from the oven enables a person to perceive that a certain kind of meat is within, or a noise proceeding from the tower is sufficient to make known the presence of a bell. To possess the ability thus to refer one's sensations to an external object is to be able to perceive objects.

Fulness of Perception Based on Sensation.—From the foregoing account of the development of our perception of the external world, it becomes evident that our immediate knowledge, or idea, of an individual object will consist only of the images our senses have been able to discover either in that or other similar objects. To the person born without the sense of sight, for instance, the flower-bed can never be known as an object of tints and colours. To the person born deaf, the violin cannot really be known as a *musical* instrument. Moreover, only the person whose senses distinguish adequately variations in colour, sound, form, etc., is able to perceive fully the objects which present themselves to his senses. Even when the physical senses seem equally perfect, one man, through greater power of discrimination, perceives in the world of objects much that totally escapes the observation of another. The result is that few of us enter as fully as we might into the rich world of sights, sounds, etc., with which we are surrounded, because we fail to gain the abundant images that we might through certain of our senses.

FACTORS INVOLVED IN SENSATION

Passing to a consideration of the senses as organs through which the mind is made aware of the concrete world, it is to be noted that a number of factors precede the image, or mental interpretation, of the impression. When, for instance, the mind becomes cognizant of a musical note, an analysis of the whole process reveals the following factors:

1. The concrete object, as the vibrating string of a violin.

2. Sound waves proceeding from the vibrating object to the sense organ.

3. The organ of sense—the ear.

4. The nerves—cells and fibres involved in receiving and conveying the sense stimulus.

5. The interpreting cells.

6. The reacting mind, which interprets the impression as an image of sound.

The different factors are somewhat arbitrarily illustrated in the accompanying diagram, the arrows indicating the physical stimulation and the conscious response:

Of the six factors involved in the sensation, 1 and 2 are purely physical and belong to the science of acoustics; 3, 4, and 5 are physiological; 6 is conscious, or psychological. It is because they always involve the immediate presence of some physical object, that the sensation elements involved in ordinary perception are spoken of as immediate, or presentative, elements of knowledge.

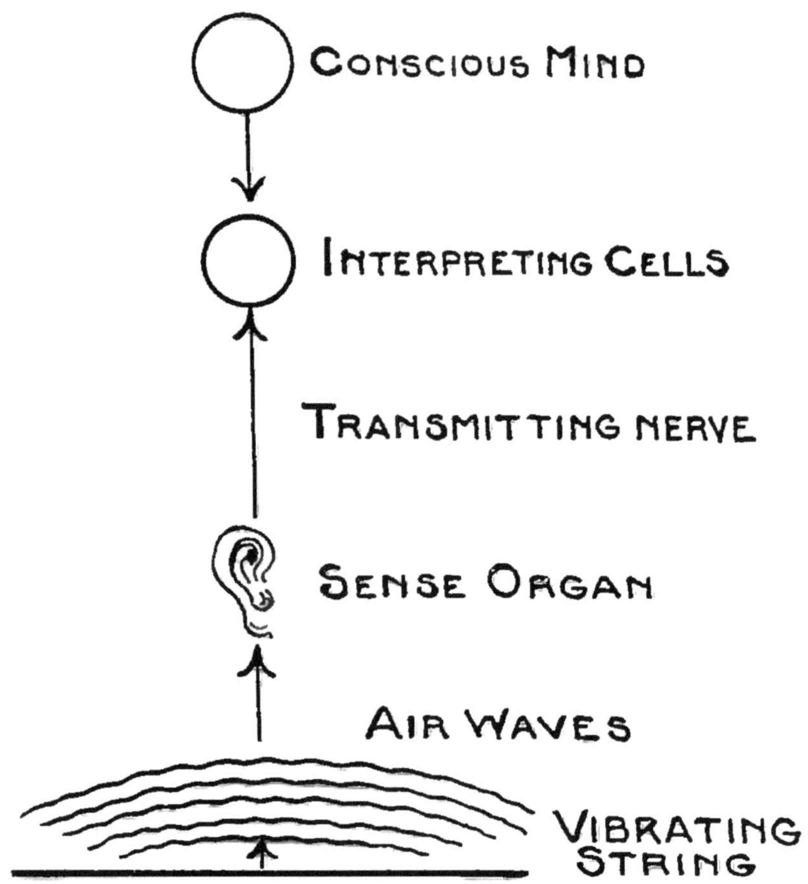

CLASSIFICATION OF SENSATIONS

Our various sensations are usually divided into three classes as follows:

1. Sensations of the special senses, including: sight, sound, touch (including temperature), taste, and smell.

2. Motor, or muscular, sensations.

3. Organic sensations.

Sensations of the Special Senses.—As a study of the five special senses has been made by the student-teacher under the heading of physiology, no attempt will be made to explain the structure of these organs. It must be noted, however, that not all senses are equally capable of distinguishing differences in quality. For example, it seems quite beyond our power to recall the tastes and odours of the various dishes of which we may have partaken at a banquet, while on the other hand we may recall distinctly the visual appearance of the room and the table. It is worthy of note, also, that in the case of smell, animals are usually much more discriminative than man. Certain of our senses are, therefore, much more intellectual than others. By this is meant that for purposes of distinguishing the objects themselves, and for providing the mind with available images as materials for further thought, our senses are by no means equally effective. Under this heading the special senses are classified as follows:

Higher Intellectual Senses: sight, hearing, touch.

Lower Intellectual Senses: taste and smell.

Muscular Sensations.—Under motor, or muscular, sensations are included the feelings which accompany consciousness of muscular exertion, or movement. In distinction from the other sense organs, the muscles are stimulated by having nervous energy pass outward over the motor nerves to the muscles. As the muscles are thus stimulated to movement, sensory nerves in turn convey inward from the muscles sensory impressions resulting from these movements. The important sensations connected with muscular action are those of strain, force, and resistance, as in lifting or pushing. By means of these motor sensations, joined with the sense of touch, the individual is able to distinguish especially weight, position, and change of position. In connection with the muscular sense, may be recalled that portion of the Montessori apparatus known as the weight tablets. These wooden tablets, it will be noted, are designed to educate the muscular sense to distinguish slight differences in weight. The muscular sense is chiefly important, however, in that delicate distinctions of pressure, movement, and resistance must be made in many forms of manual expression. The interrelation between sensory impression and motor impulse within the nervous system, as illustrated in the figures on page 122, is already understood by the reader. For an adequate conscious control of movements, especially when one is engaged in delicate handwork, as painting, modelling, wood-work, etc., there must be an ability to perceive slight differences in strain, pressure, and movement. Moreover, the most effective means for developing the muscular sense is through the expressive exercises referred to above.

Organic Sensations.—The organic sensations are those states of consciousness that arise in connection with the processes going on within the organism, as circulation of the blood, digestion; breathing, or respiration; hunger; thirst; etc. The significance of these sensations lies in the fact that they reveal to consciousness any disturbances in connection with the vital processes, and thus enable the individual to provide for the preservation of the organism.

EDUCATION OF THE SENSES

Importance.—When it is considered that our general knowledge must be based on a knowledge of individuals, it becomes apparent that children should, through sense observation, learn as fully as possible the various qualities of the concrete world. Only on this basis can they build their more general and abstract forms of knowledge. For this reason the child in his study of objects should, so far as safety permits, bring all of his senses to bear upon them and distinguish as clearly as possible all their properties. By this means only can he really know the attributes of the objects constituting his environment. Moreover, without such a full knowledge of the various properties and qualities of concrete objects, he is not in a position to turn them fully to his own service. It is by distinguishing the feeling of the flour, that the cook discovers whether it is suited for bread-making or pastry. It is by noting the texture of the wood, that the artisan can decide its suitability for the work in hand. In fine, it was only by noting the properties of various natural objects that man discovered their social uses.

How to be Effected.—One of the chief defects of primary education in the past has been a tendency to overlook the importance of giving the child an opportunity to exercise his senses in discovering the properties of the objects constituting his environment. The introduction of the kindergarten, objective methods of teaching, nature study, school gardening, and constructive occupations have done much, however, to remedy this defect. One of the chief claims in favour of the so-called Montessori Method is that it provides especially for an education of the senses. In doing this, however, it makes use of arbitrarily prepared materials instead of the ordinary objects constituting the child's natural environment. The one advantage in this is that it enables the teacher to grade the stimulations and thus exercise the child in making series of discriminations, for instance, a series of colours, sounds, weights, sizes, etc. Notwithstanding this advantage, however, it seems more pedagogical that the child should receive this needful exercise of the senses by being brought into contact with the actual objects constituting his environment, as is done in nature study, constructive exercises, art, etc.

Dangers of Neglecting the Senses.—The former neglect of an adequate exercise of the senses during the early education of the child was evidently unpedagogical for various reasons. As already noted, other forms of acquiring knowledge, such as constructive imagination, induction, and deduction, must rest primarily upon the acquisitions of sense perception. Moreover, it is during the early years of life that the plasticity and retentive power of the nervous system will enable the various sense impressions to be recorded for the future use of the mind. Further, the senses themselves during these early years show what may be termed a hunger for contact with the world of concrete objects, and a corresponding distaste for more abstract types of experience.

Learning Through all the Senses.—In recognizing that the process of sense perception constitutes a learning process, or is one of the modes by which man enters into new experience, the teacher should further understand that the same object may be interpreted through different senses. For example, when a child studies a new bird, he may note its form and colour through the eye, he may recognize the feeling and the outline through muscular and touch sensations, he may discover its song through the ear, and may give muscular expression to its form in painting or modelling. In the same way, in learning a figure or letter, he may see its form through the eye, hear its sound through the ear, make the sound and trace the form by calling various muscles into play, and thus secure a number of muscular sensations relative to the figure or letter. Since all these various experiences will be co-ordinated and retained within the nervous system, the child will not only know the object better, but will also be able to recall more easily any items of knowledge concerning it, on account of the larger number of connections established within the nervous system. One chief fact to be kept in mind by the teacher, therefore, in using the method of sense perception, is to have the pupil study the object through as many different senses as possible, and especially through those senses in which his power of discrimination and recall seems greatest.

Use of Different Images in Teaching.—The importance to the teacher of an intimate knowledge of different types of imagery and of a further acquaintance with the more prevailing images of particular pupils, is evident in various ways. In the first place, different school subjects may appeal more especially to different types of imagery. Thus a study of plants especially involves visual, or sight, images; a study of birds, visual and auditory images; oral reading and music, auditory images; physical training, motor images; constructive work, visual, tactile, and motor images; a knowledge of weights and measures, tactile and motor images. On account of a native difference in forming images, also, one pupil may best learn through the eye, another through the ear, a third through the muscles, etc. In learning the spelling of words, for example, one pupil may require especially to visualize the word, another to hear the letters repeated in their order, and a third to articulate the letters by the movement of the organs of speech, or to trace them in writing. In choosing illustrations, also, the teacher will find that one pupil best appreciates a visual illustration, a second an auditory illustration, etc. Some young pupils, for instance, might best appreciate a pathetic situation through an appeal to such sensory images as hunger and thirst.

An Illustration.—The wide difference in people's ability to interpret sensuous impressions is well exemplified in the case of sound stimuli. Every one whose ear is physically perfect seems able to interpret a sound so far as its mere quality and quantity are concerned. In the case of musical notes, however, the very greatest difference is found in the ability of different individuals to distinguish pitch. So also the distinguishing of distance and direction in relation to sound is an acquired ability, in which different people will greatly differ. Finally, to interpret the external relations involved in the sound, that is, whether the cry is that of an insect or a bird, or, if it is the former, from what kind of bird the sound is proceeding, this evidently is a phase of sense interpretation in which individuals differ very greatly. Yet an adequate development of the sense of hearing might be supposed to give the individual an ability to interpret his surroundings in all these ways.

Power of Sense Perception Limited: A. By Interest.—It should be noted, however, that so far as our actual life needs are concerned, there is no large demand for an all-round ability to interpret sensuous impressions. For practical purposes, men are interested in different objects in quite different ways. One is interested in the colour of a certain wood, another in its smoothness, a third in its ability to withstand strain, while a fourth may even be interested in more hidden relations, not visible to the ordinary sense. This will justify one in ignoring entirely qualities in the object which are of the utmost importance to others. From such a practical standpoint, it is evidently a decided gain that a person is not compelled to see everything in an object which its sensuous attributes might permit one to discover in it. In the case of the man with the so-called untrained sense, therefore, it is questionable whether the failure to see, hear, etc., is in many cases so much a lack of ability to use the particular sense, as it is a lack of practical interest in this phase of the objective world. In such processes as induction and deduction, also, it is often the external relations of objects rather than their sensory qualities that chiefly interest us. Indeed, it is sometimes claimed that an excessive amount of mere training in sense discrimination might interfere with a proper development of the higher mental processes.

B. By Knowledge.—From what has been discovered regarding the learning process, it is evident that the development of any sense, as sight, sound, touch, etc., is not brought about merely by exercising the particular organ. It has been learned, for instance, that the person who is able to observe readily the plant and animal life as he walks through the forest, possesses this skill, not because his physical eye, but because his mind, has been prepared to see these objects. In other words, it is because his knowledge is active along such lines that his eye beholds these particular things. The chief reason, therefore, why the exercise of any sense organ develops a power to perceive through that sense, is that the exercise tends to develop in the individual the knowledge and interest which will cause the mind to react easily and effectively on that particular class of impressions. A sense may be considered trained, therefore, to the extent to which the mind acquires knowledge of, and interest in, the objective elements.

CHAPTER XXVI

MEMORY AND APPERCEPTION

Nature of Memory.—Mention has been made of the retentive power of the nervous system, and of a consequent tendency for mental images to revive, or *re-present,* themselves in consciousness. It must now be noted that such a re-presentation of former experiences is frequently accompanied with a distinct recognition that the present image or images have a definite reference to past time. In other words, the present mental fact is able to be placed in the midst of other events believed to make up some portion of our past experience. Such an ideal revival of a past experience, together with a recognition of the fact that it formerly occurred within our experience, is known as an act of memory.

Neural Conditions of Memory.—When any experience is thus reproduced, and recognized as a reproduction of a previous experience, there is physiologically a transmission of nervous energy through the same brain centres as were involved in the original experience. The mental reproduction of any image is conditioned, therefore, by the physical reproduction of a nervous impulse through a formerly established path. That this is possible is owing to the susceptibility of nervous tissue to take on habit, or to retain as permanent modifications, all impressions received. From this it is evident that when we say we retain certain facts in our mind, the statement is not in a sense true; for there is no knowledge stored up in consciousness as so many ideas. The statement is true, therefore, only in the sense that the mind is able to bring into consciousness a former experience by reinstating the necessary nervous impulses through the proper nervous arcs. What is actually retained, however, is the tendency to reinstate nervous movements through the same paths as were involved in the original experience. Although, therefore, retention is usually treated as a factor in memory, its basis is, in reality, physiological.

DISTINGUISHED

Memory Distinguished from Apperception.—The distinguishing characteristics of memory as a re-presentation in the mind of a former experience is evidently the mental attitude known as recognition. Memory, in other words, always implies a belief that the present mental state really represents a fact, or event, which formed a part of our past experience. In the apperceptive process as seen in an ordinary process of learning, on the other hand, although it seems to involve a re-presentation of former mental images in consciousness, this distinct reference of the revived imagery to past time is evidently wanting. When, for instance, the mind interprets a strange object as a pear-shaped, thin-rinded, many-seeded fruit, all these interpreting ideas are, in a sense, revivals of past experience; yet none carry with them any distinct reference to past time. In like manner, when I look at an object of a certain form and colour and say that it is a sweet apple, it is evidently owing to past experience that I can declare that particular object to be sweet. It is quite clear, however, that in such a case there is no distinct reference of the revived image of sweetness to any definite occurrence in one's former experience. Such an apperceptive revival, or re-presentation of past experience, because it includes merely a representation of mental images, but fails to relate them to the past, cannot be classed as an act of memory.

But Involves Apperceptive Process.—While, however, the mere revival of old knowledge in the apperceptive process does not constitute an act of memory, memory is itself only a special phase of the apperceptive process. When I think of a particular anecdote to-day, and say I remember having the same experience on Sunday evening last, the present mental images cannot be the very same images as were then experienced. The former images belonged to the past, while those at present in consciousness are a new creation, although dependent, as we have seen, upon certain physiological conditions established in the past. In an act of memory, therefore, the new presentation, like all new presentations, must be interpreted in terms of past experience, or by an apperceiving act of attention. Whenever in this apperceptive act there is, in addition to the interpretation, a further feeling, or sense, of familiarity, the presentation is accepted by the mind as a reproduction from past experience, or is recognized as belonging to the past. When, on the way down the street, for instance, impressions are received from a passing form, and a resulting act of apperceiving attention, besides reading meaning into them, awakens a sense of familiarity, the face is recognized as one seen on a former occasion. Memory, therefore, is a special mode of the apperceptive process of learning, and includes, in addition to the interpreting of the new through the old, a belief that there is an identity between the old and the new.

FACTORS OF MEMORY

In a complete example of memory the following factors may be noted:

1. The original presentation—as the first perception of an object or scene, the reading of a new story, the hearing of a particular voice, etc.

2. Retention—this involves the permanent changes wrought in the nervous tissue as a result of the presentation or learning process and, as mentioned above, is really physiological.

3. Recall—this implies the re-establishment of the nervous movements involved in the original experiences and an accompanying revival of the mental imagery.

4. Recognition—under this heading is included the sense of familiarity experienced in consciousness, and the consequent belief that the present experience actually occurred at some certain time as an element in our past experience.

CONDITIONS OF MEMORY

A. Physical Conditions.—One of the first conditions for an effective recollection of any particular experience will be, evidently, the strength of the co-ordinations set up in the nervous system during the learning process. The permanent changes brought about in the nervous tissue as a result of conscious experience is often spoken of as the physical basis of memory. The first consideration, therefore, relative to the memorizing of knowledge is to decide the conditions favourable to establishing such nervous paths during the learning process. First among these may be mentioned the condition of the nervous tissue itself. As already seen, the more plastic and active the condition of this tissue, the more susceptible it is to receive and retain impressions. For this reason anything studied when the body is tired and the mind exhausted is not likely to be remembered. It is for the same reason, also, that knowledge acquired in youth is much more likely to be remembered than things learned late in life. The intensity and the clearness of the presentation also cause it to make a stronger impression upon the system and thus render its retention more permanent. This demands in turn that attention should be strongly focused upon the presentations during any learning process. By adding to the clearness and intensity of any impressions, attention adds to the likelihood of their retention. The evident cause of the scholar's ability to learn even relatively late in life is the fact that he brings a much greater concentration of attention to the process than is usually found in others. Repetition also, since it tends to break down any resistance to the paths which are being established in the nervous system during the learning process, is a distinct aid to retention. For this reason any knowledge acquired should be revived at intervals. This is especially true of the school knowledge being acquired by young children, and their acquisitions must be occasionally reviewed and used in various ways, if the knowledge is to become a permanent possession. A special application of the law of repetition may be noted in the fact that we remember better any topic learned, say, in four half-hours put upon it at different intervals, than we should by spending the whole two hours upon it at one time.

Another condition favourable to recall is the recency of the original experience. Anything is more easily recalled, the more recently it has been learned. The physiological cause for this seems to be that the nervous co-ordinations being recent, they are much more likely to re-establish themselves, not having yet been effaced or weakened through the lapse of time.

B. Mental Conditions.—It must be noted, however, that although there is evidently the above neural concomitant of recall, yet it is not the nervous system, but the mind, that actually recalls and remembers. The real condition of recall, therefore, is mental, and depends largely upon the number of associations formed between the ideas themselves in the original presentation. According to the law of association, different ideas arise in the mind in virtue of certain connections existing between the ideas themselves. It would be quite foreign to our present purpose to examine the theories held among philosophic psychologists regarding the principle of the association of ideas. It is evident, however, that ideas often come to our minds in consequence of the presence in consciousness of a prior idea.

When we see the name "Queenston Heights," it suggests to us Sir Isaac Brock; when we see a certain house, it calls to mind the pleasant evening spent there; and when we hear the strains of solemn music, it brings to mind the memories of the dead. Equally evident is the fact that anything experienced in isolation is much harder to remember than one experienced in such a way that it may enter into a larger train of ideas. If, for instance, any one is told to call up in half an hour telephone 3827, it is more than likely that the number will be forgotten, if the person goes on with other work and depends only on the mere impression to recall the number at the proper time. This would be the case also in spite of the most vivid presentation of the number by the one giving the order or the repetition of it by the person himself. If, however, the person says, even in a casual way, "Call up 1867," and the person addressed associates the number with the Confederation of the Dominion, there is practically no possibility of the number going out of his mind. An important mental condition for recall, therefore, is that ideas should be learned in as large associations, or groups, as possible. It is for the above reason that the logical and orderly presentation of the topics in any subject and their thorough understanding by the pupil give more complete control over the subject-matter. When each lesson is taught as a disconnected item of knowledge, there seems nothing to which the ideas are anchored, and recall is relatively difficult. When, on the other hand, points of connection are established between succeeding lessons, and the pupil understands these, one topic suggests another, and the mind finds it relatively easy to recall any particular part of the related ideas.

TYPES OF RECALL

A. Involuntary.—In connection with the working of the principle of association, it is interesting to note that practically two types of recall manifest themselves. As a result of their suggestive tendency, the ideas before consciousness at any particular time have a tendency to revive old experiences which the mind may recognize as such. Here there is no effort on the part of the voluntary attention to recall the experience from the past, the operation of the law of association being, as it were, sufficient to thrust the revived image into the centre of the field of consciousness, as when the sight of a train recalls a recent trip.

B. Voluntary.—At times the mind may set out with the deliberate aim, or purpose, of reviving some forgotten experience. This is because attention is at the time engaged upon a definite problem, as when the student writing on his examination paper strives to recall the conditions of the Constitutional Act. This type is known as voluntary memory. Such a voluntary attempt at recall is, however, of the same character as the involuntary type in that both involve association. What the mind really strives for is to start a train of ideas which shall suggest the illusive ideas involved in the desired answer. Such a process of recall might be illustrated as follows:

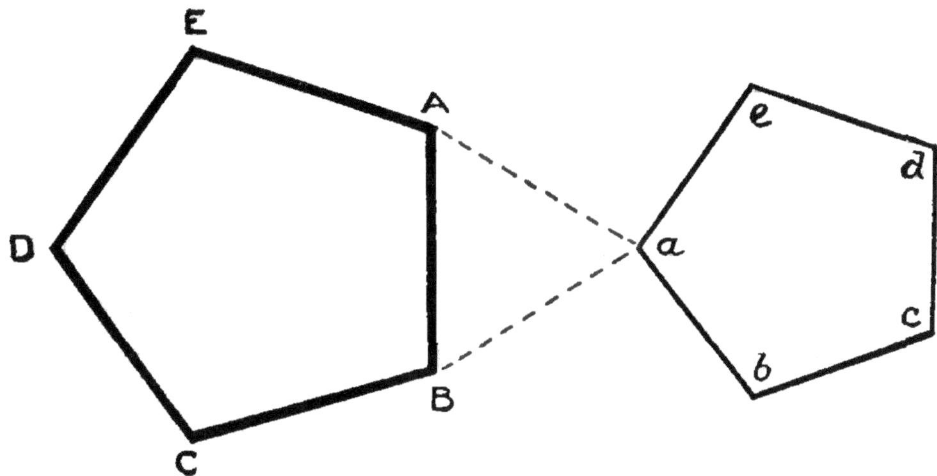

Here a, b, c, d, e represent the forgotten series of ideas to be recalled. A, B, C, D, E represent other better known ideas, some of which are associated with the desired ones. By having the mind course over the better known facts—A, B, C, D, E, attention may finally focus upon the relation A, a, B, and thus start up the necessary revival of a, b, c, d, e.

Attention May Hinder Memory.—While active attention is thus able under proper conditions to reinforce memory, yet occasionally attention seems detrimental to memory. That such is the case will become evident from the preceding figure. If the experience a, b, c, d, e, is directly associated only with A, B, but the mind believes the association to centre in C, D, E, attention is certain to keep focused upon the sub-group—C, D, E. At an examination in history, for example, we may desire to recall the circumstances associated with the topic, "The Grand Remonstrance," and feel vaguely that this is connected with a revolutionary movement. This may cause us, however, to fix attention, not upon the civil war, but upon the revolution of 1688. In this case, instead of forcing a nervous impulse into the proper centres, attention is in reality diverting it into other channels. When, a few minutes later, we have perhaps ceased our effort to remember, the impulse seems of itself to stimulate the proper centres, and the necessary facts come to us apparently without any attentive effort.

LOCALIZATION OF TIME

It has been pointed out that in an act of memory there must be a recognition of the present experience as one which has occurred in a series of past events. The definite reference of a memory image to a past series is sometimes spoken of as localization. The degree to which a memory image is localized in the past differs greatly, however, in different cases. Your recollection of some interesting personal event in your past school history may be very definitely located as to time, image after image reinstating themselves in memory in the order of their actual occurrence. Such a similar series of events must have taken place when, by means of handling a number of objects, you learned different number and quantity relations or, by drawing certain figures, discovered certain geometrical relations. At the present time, however, although you remember clearly the general relations, you are utterly unable to recall the more incidental facts connected with their original presentation, or even localize the remembered knowledge at all definitely in past time. Nothing, in fact, remains as a permanent possession except the general, or scientific, truth involved in the experience.

CLASSIFICATION OF MEMORIES

A. Mechanical.—The above facts would indicate that in many cases the mind would find it more effective to omit from conscious recall what may appear irrelevant in the original presentation, and fix attention upon only the essential features. From this standpoint, two somewhat different types of memory are to be found among individuals. With many people, it seems as if a past experience must be revived in every detail. If such a one sets out to report a simple experience, such as seeing a policeman arrest a man on the street, he must bring in every collateral circumstance, no matter how foreign to the incident. He must mention, for example, that he himself had on a new straw hat, that his companion was smoking a cigar, was accompanied by his dog, and was talking about his crops, at the time they observed the arrest. This type is known as a mechanical memory. Very good examples of such will be seen in the persons of "Farmer Philip" in Tennyson's *Brook* and the "landlady" in Shakespeare's *King Henry IV*.

B. Logical.—In another type of memory, the mind does not thus associate into the memory experience every little detail of the original experience. The outstanding facts, especially those which are bound by some logical sequence, are the only ones which enter into permanent association. Such a type of mind, therefore, in recalling the past, selects out of the mass of experiences the incidents which will constitute a logical revival, and leaves out the trivial and incidental. This type is usually spoken of as a logical memory. This type of memory would, in the above incident, recall only the essential facts connected with the arrest, as the cause, the incidents, and the result.

MEMORY IN EDUCATION

Value of Memory.—It is evident that without the ability to reinstate past experiences in our conscious life, such experiences could not serve as intelligent guides for our present conduct. Each day, in fact, we should begin life anew so far as concerns intelligent adaptation, our acquired aptitude being at best only physical. It will be understood, therefore, why the ability to recall past experiences is accepted as an essential factor in the educative process. It will be noted, indeed, in our study of the history of education, that, at certain periods, the whole problem of education seemed to be to memorize knowledge so thoroughly that it might readily be reinstated in consciousness. Modern education, however, has thrown emphasis upon two additional facts regarding knowledge. These are, first, that the ability to use past knowledge, and not the mere ability to recall it, is the mark of a truly educated man. The second fact is that, when any experience is clearly understood at the time of its presentation, the problem of remembering it will largely take care of itself. For these reasons, modern education emphasizes clearness of presentation and ability to apply, rather than the mere memorizing of knowledge. It is a question, however, whether the modern educator may not often be too negligent concerning the direct problem of the ability to recall knowledge. For this reason, the student-teacher may profitably make himself acquainted with the main conditions of retention and recall.

The Training of Memory.—An important problem for the educator is to ascertain whether it is possible to develop in the pupil a general power of memory. In other words, will the memorizing of any set of facts strengthen the mind to remember more easily any other facts whatsoever? From what has been noted regarding memory, it is evident that, leaving out of consideration the physical condition of the organism, the most important conditions for memory at the time are attention to, and a thorough understanding of, the facts to be remembered. From this it must appear that a person's ability to remember any facts depends primarily, not upon the mere amount of memorizing he has done in the past, but upon the extent to which his interests and old knowledge cause him to attend to, understand, and associate the facts to be remembered. There seems no justification, therefore, for the method of the teacher who expected to strengthen the memories of her pupils for their school work by having them walk quickly past the store windows and then attempt to recall at school what they had seen. In such cases the boys are found to remember certain objects, because their interests and knowledge enable them to notice these more distinctly at the time of the presentation. The girls, on the other hand, remember other objects, because their interests and knowledge cause them to apprehend these rather than the others.

APPERCEPTION

Apperception a Law of Learning.—In the study of the lesson process, Chapter III, attention was called to the fact that the interpretation which the mind places upon any presentation depends in large measure upon the mind's present content and interest. It is an essential characteristic of mind that it always attempts to give meaning to any new impression, no matter how strange that impression may be. This end is reached, however, only as the mind is able to apply to the presentation certain elements of former experience. Even in earliest infancy, impressions do not come to the organism as total strangers; for the organism is already endowed with instinctive tendencies to react in a definite manner to certain stimuli. As these reactions continue to repeat themselves, however, permanent modifications, as previously noted, are established in the nervous system, including both sensory and motor adjustments. Since, moreover, these sensory and motor adjustments give rise to ideas, they result in corresponding associations of mental imagery. As these neural and mental elements are thus organized into more and more complex masses, the recurrence of any element within an associated mass is able to reinstate the other elements. The result is that when a certain sensation is received, as, for instance, a sound stimulus, it reinstates sensory impressions and motor reactions together with their associated mental images, thus enabling the mind to assert that a dog is barking in the distance. In such a case, the present impression is evidently joined with, and interpreted through, what has already formed a part of our experience. What is true of this particular case is true of all cases. New presentations are always met and interpreted by some complex experiences with which they have something in common, otherwise the stimuli could not be attended to at all. This ability of the mind to interpret new presentations in terms of old knowledge on account of some connection they bear to that content, is known as *apperception*. In other words, apperception is the law of the mind to attend to such elements in a new presentation as possess some degree of *familiarity* with the already assimilated experience, although there may be no distinct recognition of this familiarity.

Conditions of Apperception

A. Present Knowledge.—Since the mind can apperceive only that for which it is prepared through former experience, the interpretation of the same presentations will be likely to differ greatly in different individuals. The book lying before him is to the young child a place in which to find pictures, to the ignorant man a source of mysterious information, and to the scholar a symbolic representation of certain mathematical knowledge. In the same manner, the object outside the window is a noxious weed to the farmer, a flower to the naturalist, and a medicinal plant to the physician or the druggist. From this it is clear that the interpretation of the impressions must differ according to the character of our present knowledge. In other words, the more important the aspects read into any presentation, the more valuable will be the present experience. Although when the child apperceives a stick as a horse, and the mechanic apperceives it as a lever, each interpretation is valuable within its own sphere, yet there is evidently a marked difference in the ultimate significance of the two interpretations. Education is especially valuable, in fact, in that it so adds to the experience of the child that he may more fully apperceive his surroundings.

B. Present Interests and Needs.—But apperception is not solely dependent upon present knowledge. The interests and needs of the individual reflect themselves largely in his apperceptive tendencies. While the boy sees a tent in the folded paper, the girl is more likely to find in it a screen. To the little boy the lath is a horse, to the older boy it becomes a sword. Feelings and interest, therefore, as well as knowledge, dominate the apperceptive process. Nor should this fact be overlooked by the teacher. The study of a poem would be very incomplete and unsatisfactory if it stopped with the apprehension of the ideas. There must be emotional appreciation as well; otherwise the study will result in entire indifference to it. In introducing, for instance, the sonnet, "Mysterious Night" (page 394, *Ontario Reader, Book IV*), the teacher might ask: "Why can we not see the stars during the day?" The answer to this question would put the pupils in the proper intellectual attitude to interpret the ideas of the poem, but that is not enough. A recall of such an experience as his contemplation of the starry sky on a clear night will put the pupil in a suitable emotional attitude. He is a rare pupil who has not at some time gazed in wonder at the immense number and magnificence of the stars, or who has not thought with awe and reverence of the infinite power of the Creator of "such countless orbs." A recall of these feelings of wonder, awe, and reverence will place the pupil in a suitable mood for the emotional appreciation of the poem. It is in the teaching of literature that the importance of a proper feeling attitude on the part of the pupil is particularly great. Without it the pupil is coldly indifferent toward literature and will never cultivate an enthusiasm for it.

Factors in Apperception

Retention and Recall.—The facts already noted make it plain that apperception involves two important factors. First, apperception implies retention and recall. Unless our various experiences left behind them the permanent effects already noted in describing the retentive power of the nervous organism and the consequent possibility of recall, there could be no adjustment to new impressions on the basis of earlier experiences.

Attention.—Secondly, apperception involves attention. Since to apperceive is to bring the results of earlier experience to bear actively upon the new impression, it must involve a reactive, or attentive, state of consciousness; for, as noted in our study of the learning process, it is only by selecting elements out of former experience that the new impression is given definite meaning in consciousness. For the child to apperceive the strange object as a "bug-in-a-basket," demands from him therefore a process of attention in which the ideas "bug" and "basket" are selected from former experience and read into the new impression, thereby giving it a meaning in consciousness. A reference to any of the lesson topics previously considered will provide further examples of these apperceptive factors.

CHAPTER XXVII

IMAGINATION

Nature of.—In our study of the various modes of acquiring individual notions, attention was called to the fact that knowledge of a particular object may be gained through a process of imagination. Like memory, imagination is a process of re-presentation, though differing from it in certain important regards.

1. Although imagination depends on past experiences for its images, these images are used to build up ideal representations of objects without any reference to past time.

2. In imagination the associated elements of past experience may be completely dissociated. Thus a bird may be imagined without wings, or a stone column without weight.

3. The dissociated elements may be re-combined in various ways to represent objects never actually experienced, as a man with wings, or a horse with a man's head.

Imagination is thus an apperceptive process by which we construct a mental representation of an object without any necessary reference to its actual existence in time.

Product of Imagination, Particular.—It is to be noted that in a process of imagination the mind always constructs in idea a representation of a *particular* object or individual. For instance, the ideal picture of the house I imagine situated on the hill before me is that of a particular house, possessing definite qualities as to height, size, colour, etc. In like manner, the future visit to Toronto, as it is being run over ideally, is constructed of particular persons, places, and events. So also when reading such a stanza as:

> The milk-white blossoms of the thorn
> Are waving o'er the pool,
> Moved by the wind that breathes along,
> So sweetly and so cool;

if the mind is able to combine into a definite outline of a particular situation the various elements depicted, then the mental process of the reader is one of imagination. It is not true, of course, that the particular elements which enter into such an ideal representation are always equally vivid. Yet one test of a person's power of imagination is the definiteness with which the mind makes an ideal representation stand out in consciousness as a distinct individual.

TYPES OF IMAGINATION

Passive

A. Passive.—In dissociating the elements of past experience and combining them into new particular forms, the mind may proceed in two quite different ways. In some cases the mind seemingly allows itself to drift without purpose and almost without sense, building up fantastic representations of imaginary objects or events. This happens especially in our periods of day-dreaming. Here various images, evidently drawn from past experience, come before consciousness in a spontaneous way and enter into most unusual forms of combination, with little regard even to probability. In these moods the timid lad becomes a strong hero, and his rustic Audrey, a fair lady, for whose sake he is ever performing untold feats of valour. Here the ideas, instead of being selected and combined for a definite purpose through an act of voluntary attention, are suggested one after the other by the mere law of association. Because in such fantastic products of the imagination the various images appear in consciousness and combine themselves without any apparent control or purpose, the process is known as passive imagination, or phantasy. Such a type, it is evident, will have little significance as an actual process of learning.

Active

B. Active, or Constructive.—Opposed to the above type is that form of imagination in which the mind proceeds to build up a particular ideal representation with some definite purpose, or end, in view. A student, for example, who has never seen an aeroplane and has no direct knowledge of the course to be traversed, may be called upon in his composition work to describe an imaginary voyage through the air from Toronto to Winnipeg. In such an act of imagination, the selecting of elements to enter into the ideal picture must be chosen with an eye to their suitability to the end in view. When also a child is called upon in school to form an ideal representation of some object of which he has had no direct experience, as for instance, a mental picture of a volcano, he must in the same way, under the guidance of the teacher, select and combine elements of his actual experience which are adapted to the building up of a correct mental representation of an actual volcano. This type of imagination is known as active, or constructive, imagination.

Factors in Constructive Imagination.—In such a purposeful, or active, process of imagination the following factors may be noticed:

1. The purpose, end, or problem calling for the exercise of the imagination.

2. A selective act of attention, in which the fitness or unfitness of elements of past experience, or their adaptability to the ideal creation, is realized.

3. A relating, or synthetic, activity combining the selected elements into a new ideal representation.

USES OF IMAGINATION

Imagination in Education.—One important application of imagination in school work is found in connection with the various forms of constructive occupation. In such exercises, it is possible to have the child first build up ideally the picture of a particular object and then have him produce it through actual expression. For example, a class which has been taught certain principles of cutting may be called upon to conceive an original design for some object, say a valentine. Here the child, before proceeding to produce the actual object, must select from his knowledge of valentines certain elements and interpret them in relation to his principles of cutting. This ideal representation of the intended object is, therefore, a process of active, or constructive, imagination. In composition, also, the various events and situations depicted may be ideal creations to which the child gives expression in language. In geography and nature study likewise, constant use must be made of the imagination in gaining a knowledge of objects which have never come within the actual experience of the child. In science there is a further appeal to the child's imagination. When, for instance, he studies such topics as the law of gravity, chemical affinity, etc., the imagination must fill in much that falls outside the sphere of actual observation. In history and literature, also, the student can enter into the life and action of the various scenes and events only by building up ideal representations of what is depicted through the words of the author.

Imagination in Practical Life.—In addition to the large use of constructive imagination in school work, this process will be found equally important in the after affairs of life. It is by use of the imagination that the workman is able to see the changes we desire made in the decoration of the room or in the shape of the flower-beds. It is by the use of imagination, also, that the general is able to outline the plan of campaign that shall lead his army to victory. Without imagination, therefore, the mind could not set up those practical aims toward the attainment of which most of life's effort is directed. In the dominion of conduct, also, imagination has its important part to play. It is by viewing in his imagination the effect of the one course of action as compared with the other, that man finally decides what constitutes the proper line of conduct. Even when indifferent as to his moral conduct, man pictures to himself what his friends may say and think of certain lines of action. For the enjoyment of life, also, the exercise of imagination has a place. It is by filling up the present with ideals and hopeful anticipations for the future, that much of the monotony of our work-a-day hours is relieved.

Development of Imagination.—A prime condition of a creative imagination is evidently the possession of an abundance of mental materials which may be dissociated and re-combined into new mental products. These materials, of course, consist of the images and ideas retained by the mind from former experiences. One important result, therefore, of providing the young child with a rich store of images of sight, sound, touch, movement, etc., is that it provides his developing imagination with necessary materials. But the mere possession of abundant materials in the form of past images will not in itself develop the imagination. Here, as elsewhere, it is only by exercising imagination that ability to imagine can be developed. Opportunity for such an exercise of the imagination, moreover, may be given the child in various ways. As already noted, a chief function of play is that it stimulates the child to use his imagination in reconstructing the objects about him and clothing them with many fancied attributes. In supplementary reading and story work, also, the imagination is actively exercised in constructing the ideal situations, as they are being presented in words by the book or the teacher. Nature study, likewise, by bringing before the child the secret processes of nature, as noting, for instance, the life history of the butterfly, the germination of seeds, etc., will call upon him to use his imagination in various ways. On the other hand, to deprive a young child of all such opportunities will usually result in preventing a proper development of the imagination.

CHAPTER XXVIII

THINKING

Nature of Thinking.—In the study of general method, as well as in that of the foregoing mental processes, it has been taken for granted that our minds are capable of identifying different objects on the basis of some common feature or features. This tendency of the mind to identify objects and group individual things into classes, depends upon its capacity to detect similarity and difference, or to make comparisons. When the mind, in identifying objects, events, qualities, etc., discovers certain relations between its various states, the process is especially known as that of thinking. In its technical sense, therefore, thought implies a more or less explicit apprehension of relation.

Thinking Involved in all Conscious States.—It is evident, however, that every mental process must involve thinking, or a grasping of relations. When, by my merely touching an object, my mind perceives it is an apple, this act of perception, as already seen, takes place because elements of former experience come back as associated factors. This implies, evidently, that the mind is here relating elements of its past experience with the present touch sensation. Perception of external objects, therefore, implies a grasping of relations. In the same way, if, in having an experience to-day, one recognizes it as identical with a former experience, he is equally grasping a relation. Every act of memory, therefore, implies thinking. Thus in all forms of knowledge the mind is apprehending relations; for no experience could have meaning for the mind except as it is discriminated from other experiences. In treating thinking as a distinct mental process, however, it is assumed that the objects of sense perception, memory, etc., are known as such, and that the mind here deals more directly with the relations in which ideas stand one to another. As a mental process, thinking appears in three somewhat distinct forms, known as conception, judgment, and reasoning.

CONCEPTION

The Abstract Notion.—It was seen that at least in adult life, the perception of any object, as this particular orange, horse, cow, etc., really includes a number of distinct images of quality synthesised into the unity of a particular idea or experience. Because of this union of a number of different sensible qualities in the notion of a single individual, the mind may limit its attention upon a particular quality, or characteristic, possessed by an object, and make this a distinct problem of attention. Thus the mind is able to form such notions as length, roundness, sweetness, heaviness, four-footedness, etc. When such an attribute is thought of as something distinct from the object, the mental image is especially known as an abstract idea, or notion, and the process as one of abstraction.

The Class Notion.—One or more of such abstracted qualities may, moreover, be recognized as common to an indefinite number of objects. For instance, in addition to its ability to abstract from the perception of a dog, the abstract notions four-footedness, hairy, barking, etc., the mind further gives them a general character by thinking of them as qualities common to an indefinite number of other possible individuals, namely, the class four-footed, hairy, barking objects. Because the idea representing the quality or qualities is here accepted by the mind as a means of identifying a number of objects, the idea is spoken of as a class notion, and the process as one of classification, or generalization. Thus it appears that, through its ability to detect sameness and difference, or discover relations, the mind is able to form two somewhat different notions. By mentally abstracting any quality and regarding it as something distinct from the object, it obtains an abstract notion, as sweetness, bravery, hardness, etc.; by synthesising and symbolizing the images of certain qualities recognized in objects, it obtains a general, or class, notion by which it may represent an indefinite number of individual things as, triangle, horse, desert, etc. Thus abstract notions are supposed to represent qualities; class notions, things. Because of its reference to a number of objects, the class notion is spoken of especially as a general notion, and the process of forming the notion as one of generalization. These two types of notions are technically known as concepts, and the process of their formation as one of conception.

Formal Analysis of Process.—At this point may be recalled what was stated in Chapter XV concerning the development of a class notion. Mention was there made of the theory that in the formation of such concepts, or class notions, as cow, dog, desk, chair, adjective, etc., the mind must proceed through certain set stages as follows:

1. Comparison: The examination of a certain number of particular individuals in order to discover points of similarity and difference.
2. Abstraction: The distinguishing of certain characteristics common to the objects.
3. Generalization: The mental unification, or synthesis, of these common characteristics noted in different individuals into a class notion represented by a name, or general term.

But Conception is Involved in Perception.—From what has been seen, however, it is evident that the development of our concepts does not proceed in any such formal way. If the mind perceives an individual object with any degree of clearness, it must recognize the object as possessing certain qualities. If, therefore, the child can perceive such an object as a dog, it implies that he recognizes it, say, as a hairy, four-footed creature. To recognize these qualities, however, signifies that the mind is able to think of them as something apart from the object, and the child thus has in a sense a general notion even while perceiving the particular dog. Whenever he passes to the perception of another dog, he undoubtedly interprets this with the general ideas already obtained from this earlier percept of a dog. To say, therefore, that to gain a concept he compares the qualities found in several individual things is not strictly true, for if his first percept becomes a type by which he interprets other dogs, his first experience is already a concept. What happens is that as this concept is used to interpret other individuals, the person becomes more conscious of the fact that his early experience is applicable to an indefinite number of objects. So also, when an adult first perceives an individual thing, say the fruit of the guava, he must apprehend certain qualities in relation to the individual thing. Thereupon his idea of this particular object becomes in itself a copy for identifying other objects, or a symbol by which similar future impressions may be given meaning. In this sense the individual idea, or percept, will serve to identify other particular experiences. Such being the case, this early concept of the guava has evidently required no abstraction of qualities beyond apprehending them while perceiving the one example of the fruit. This, however, is but to say that the perception of the guava really implied conception.

Comparison of Individuals Necessary for Correct Concepts.—It is, of course, true that the correctness of the idea as a class symbol can be verified only as we apply it in interpreting a number of such individual things. As the person meets a further number of individuals, he may even discover the presence of qualities not previously recognized. A child, for instance, may have a notion of the class triangle long before he discovers that all triangles have the property of containing two right angles. When this happens, he will later modify his first concept by synthesising into it the newly discovered quality. Moreover, if certain features supposed to be common are later found to be accidental, if, for instance, a child's concept of the class fish includes the quality *always living in water*, his meeting with a flying fish will not result in an utterly new concept, but rather in a modification of the present one. Thus the young child, who on seeing the Chinese diplomat, wished to know where he had his laundry, was not without a class concept, although that concept was imperfect in at least one respect.

Concept and Term.—A point often discussed in connection with conception is whether a general notion can be formed without language. By some it is argued that no concept could exist in the mind without the name, or general term. It was seen, however, that our first perception of any object becomes a sort of standard by which other similar experiences are intercepted, and is, therefore, general in character. From this it is evident that a rudimentary type of conception exists prior to language. In the case of the young child, as he gains a mental image of his father, the experience evidently serves as a centre for interpreting other similar individuals. We may notice that as soon as he gains control of language, other men are called by the term papa. This does not imply an actual confusion in identity, but his use of the term shows that the child interprets the new object through a crude concept denoted by the word papa. It is more than probable, moreover, that this crude concept developed as he became able to recognize his father, and had been used in interpreting other men before he obtained the term, papa. On the other hand, it is certain that the term, or class name, is necessary to give the notion a definite place in consciousness.

Factors Involved in Concept

It will appear from the foregoing that a concept presents the following factors for consideration:

1. The essential quality or qualities found in the individual things, and supposed to be abstracted sooner or later from the individuals.

2. The concept itself, the mental image or idea representative of the abstracted quality; or the unification of a number of abstracted qualities, when the general notion implies a synthesis of different qualities.

3. The general term, or name.

4. The objects themselves, which the mind can organize into a class, because they are identified as possessing common characteristics. When, however, a single abstracted quality is taken as a symbol of a class of objects, for example, when the quality bitterness becomes the symbol for the class of bitter things, there can be no real distinction between the abstracted quality and the class concept. In other words, to fix attention upon the quality bitterness as a quality distinct from the object in which it is found, is at the same time to give it a general character, recognizing it as something which may be found in a number of objects—the class bitter things. Here the abstract term is in a sense a general notion representative of a whole class of objects which agree in the possession of the quality.

Intension of Concepts.—Certain of our general notions are, however, much more complex than others. When a single attribute such as four-footedness is generalized to represent the class four-footed objects, the notion itself is relatively simple. In other words, a single property is representative of the objects, and in apprehending the members of the class all other properties they chance to possess may be left out of account. In many cases, however, the class notion will evidently be much more complex. The notion dog, for instance, in addition to implying the characteristic four-footedness, may include such qualities as hairy, barking, watchful, fearless, etc. This greater or less degree of complexity of a general notion is spoken of as its intensity. The notion dog, for instance, is more intensive than the notion four-footed animals; the notion lawyer, than the notion man.

Extension of Concepts.—It is to be noted further that as a notion increases in intension it becomes limited to a smaller class of objects. From this standpoint, notions are said to differ in extension. The class lawyer, for instance, is not so extensive as the class man; nor the class dog, as the class four-footed objects. It will appear from the above that an abstract notion viewed as a sign of a class of objects is distinguished by its extension, while a class notion, so far as it implies a synthesis of several abstracted qualities, is marked rather by its intension.

Aims of conceptual lessons

So far as school lessons aim to establish and develop correct class notions in the minds of the pupils, three somewhat distinct types of work may be noted:

1. TO DEFINE CLASSES

In some lessons no attempt is made to develop an utterly new class notion, or concept; the pupils in fact may already know the class of objects in a general way and be acquainted with many of their characteristics. The object of the lesson is, therefore, to render the concept more scientific by having it include the qualities which essentially mark it as a class and especially separate it from other co-ordinate classes. In studying the grasshopper; for instance, in entomology, the purpose is not to give the child a notion of the insect in the ordinary sense of the term. This the pupil may already have. The purpose is rather to enable him to decide just what general characteristics distinguish this from other insects. The lesson may, therefore, leave out of consideration features which are common to all grasshoppers, simply because they do not enter into a scientific differentiation of the class.

2. TO ENLARGE A CONCEPT

In many lessons the aim seems to be chiefly to enlarge certain concepts by adding to their intensiveness. The pupil, for instance, has a scientific concept of a triangle, that is, one which enables him to distinguish a triangle from any other geometrical figure. He may, however, be led to see further that the three angles of every triangle equal two right angles. This is really having him discover a further attribute in relation to triangles, although this knowledge is not essential to the concept as a symbol of the members of the class. In the same way, in grammar the pupil is taught certain attributes common to verbs, as mood and tense, although these are not essential attributes from the standpoint of distinguishing the verb as a special class of words.

3. TO BUILD UP NEW CONCEPTS

A. Presentation of Unknown Individuals.—In many lessons the chief object seems to be, however, to build up a new concept in the mind of the child. This would be the case when the pupil is presented with a totally unknown object, say a platypus, and called upon to examine its characteristics. In such lessons two important facts should be noticed. First, the child finds seemingly little difficulty in accepting a single individual as a type of a class, and is able to carry away from the lesson a fairly scientific class notion through a study of the one individual. In this regard the pupil but illustrates what has been said of the ability of the child to use his early percepts as standards to interpret other individuals. The pupil is able the more easily to form this accurate notion, because he no doubt has already a store of abstract notions with which to interpret the presentation, and also because his interest and attention is directed into the proper channels by the teacher.

B. Division of Known Classes.—A second common mode of developing new concepts in school work is in breaking up larger classes into co-ordinate sub-classes. This, of course, involves the developing of new concepts to cover these sub-classes. In such cases, however, the new notions are merely modified forms of the higher class notion. When, for example, the pupil gains general notions representative of the classes, proper noun and common noun, the new terms merely add something to the intension of the more extensive term noun. This will be evident by considering the difference between the notions noun and proper noun. Both agree in possessing the attribute *used to name*. The latter is more intensive, however, because it signifies *used to name a particular object*. Although in such cases the lesson seems in a sense to develop new general notions, they represent merely an adding to the intension of a notion already possessed by the child.

Use of the Term.—A further problem regarding the process of conception concerns the question of the significance of a name. When a person uses such a term as dog, whale, hepatica, guava, etc., to name a certain object, what is the exact sense, or meaning, in which the name is to be applied? A class name, when applied scientifically to an object, is evidently supposed to denote the presence in it of certain essential characteristics which belong to the class. It is clear, however, that the ordinary man rarely uses these names with any scientific precision. A man can point to an object and say that it is a horse, and yet be ignorant of many of the essential features of a horse. In such cases, therefore, the use of the name merely shows that the person considers the object to belong to a certain class, but is no guarantee that he is thinking of the essential qualities of the class. It might be said, therefore, that a class term is used for two somewhat different purposes, either to denote the object merely, or to signify scientifically the attributes possessed by the object. It is in the second respect that danger of error in reasoning arises. So far as a name represents the attributes of a class, it will signify for us just those attributes which we associate with that class. So long, therefore, as the word fish means to us an animal living in the water, we will include in the class the whale, which really does not belong to the class, and perhaps exclude from the class the flying fish, although it is scientifically a member of the class.

The definition

It has been noted that, when man discovers common characteristics in a number of objects, he tends on this basis to unite such objects into a class. It is to be noted in addition, however, that in the same manner he is also able, by examining the characteristics of a large class of objects, to divide these into smaller sub-classes. Although, for example, we may place all three-sided figures into one class and call them triangles, we are further able to divide these into three sub-classes owing to certain differences that may be noted among them. Thus an important fact regarding classification is that while a class may possess some common quality or qualities, yet its members may be further divided into sub-classes and each of these smaller classes distinguished from the others by points of difference. Owing to this fact, there are two important elements entering into a scientific knowledge of any class, first, to know of what larger class it forms a part, and secondly, to know what characteristics distinguish it from the other classes which go with it to make up this larger class. To know the class equilateral triangle, for instance, we must know, first, that it belongs to the larger class triangle, and secondly, that it differs from other classes of triangles by having its three sides equal. For this reason a person is able to know a class scientifically without knowing all of its common characteristics. For instance, the large class of objects known as words is subdivided into smaller classes known as parts of speech. Taking one of these classes, the verb, we find that all verbs agree in possessing at least three common characteristics, they have power to assert, to denote manner, and to express time. To distinguish the verb, however, it is necessary to note only that it is a word used to assert, since this is the only characteristic which distinguishes it from the other classes of words. When, therefore, we describe any class of objects by first naming the larger class to which it belongs, and then stating the characteristics which distinguish it from the other co-ordinate classes, we are said to give a definition of the class, or to define it. The statement, "A trimeter is a verse of three measures," is a definition because it gives, first, the larger class (verse) to which the trimeters belong, and secondly, the difference (of three measures) which distinguishes the trimeter from all other verses. The statement, "A binomial is an algebraic expression consisting of two terms," is a definition, because it gives, first, the larger class (algebraic expression) to which binomials belong, and secondly, the difference (consisting of two terms) which distinguishes binomials from other algebraic expressions.

JUDGMENT

Nature of Judgment.—A second form, or mode, of thinking is known as judgment. Our different concepts were seen to vary in their intension, or meaning, according to the number of attributes suggested by each. My notion *triangle* may denote the attributes three-sided and three-angled; my notion *isosceles triangle* will in that case include at least these two qualities plus equality of two of the sides. This indicates that various relations exist between our ideas and may be apprehended by the mind. When a relation between two concepts is distinctly apprehended in thought, or, in other words, when there is a mental assertion of a union between two ideas, or objects of thought, the process is known as *judgment*. Judgment may be defined, therefore, as the apprehension, or mental affirmation, of a relation between two ideas. If the idea, or concept, *heaviness* enters as a mental element into my idea *stone*, then the mind is able to affirm a relation between these concepts in the form, "Stone is heavy." In like manner when the mind asserts, "Glass is transparent" or "Horses are animals," there is a distinct apprehension of a relation between the concepts involved.

Judgment Distinguished from Statement.—It should be noted that judgment is the mental apprehension of a relation between ideas. When this relation is expressed in actual words, it is spoken of as a proposition, or a predication. A proposition is, therefore, the statement of a judgment. The proposition is composed of two terms and the copula, one term constituting the subject of the proposition and the other the predicate. Although a judgment may often be expressed in some other form, it can usually be converted into the above form. The proposition, "Horses eat oats," may be expressed in the form, "Horses are oat-eaters"; the proposition, "The sun melts the snow," into the form, "The sun is a-thing-which-melts-snow."

Relation of Judgment to Conception.—It would appear from the above examples that a judgment expresses in an explicit form the relations involved within the concept, and is, therefore, merely a direct way of indicating the state of development of any idea. If my concept of a dog, for example, is a synthesis of the qualities four-footed, hairy, fierce, and barking, then an analysis of the concept will furnish the following judgments:

A dog is { A four-footed thing.
A hairy thing.
A fierce thing.
A barking thing.

Because in these cases a concept seems necessary for an act of judgment, it is said that judgment is a more advanced form of thinking than conception. On the other hand, however, judgment is implied in the formation of a concept. When the child apprehends the dog as a four-footed object, his mind has grasped four-footedness as a quality pertaining to the strange object, and has, in a sense, brought the two ideas into relation. But while judgment is implied in the formation of the concept, the concept does not bring explicitly to the mind the judgments it implies. The concept snow, for instance, implies the property of whiteness, but whiteness must be apprehended as a distinct idea and related mentally with the idea snow before we can be said to have formed, or thought, the judgment, "Snow is white." Judgment is a form of thinking separate from conception, therefore, because it does thus bring into definite relief relations only implied in our general notions, or concepts. One value of judgment is, in fact, that it enables us to analyse our concepts, and thus note more explicitly the relations included in them.

Universal and Particular Judgments.—Judgments are found to differ also as to the universality of their affirmation. In such a judgment as "Man is mortal," since mortality is viewed as a quality always joined to manhood, the affirmation is accepted as a universal judgment. In such a judgment as "Men strive to subdue the air," the two objects of thought are not considered as always and necessarily joined together. The judgment is therefore particular in character. All of our laws of nature, as "Air has weight," "Pressure on liquids is transmitted in every direction," or "Heat is conducted by metals," are accepted as universal judgments.

Errors in judgment

Errors in Judgment due to: A. Faulty Concepts.—It may be seen from the foregoing that our judgments, when explicitly grasped by the mind and predicated in language, reflect the accuracy or inaccuracy of our concepts. Whatever relations are, as it were, wrapped up in a concept may merge at any time in the form of explicit judgments. If the fact that the only Chinamen seen by a child are engaged in laundry work causes this attribute to enter into his concept Chinaman, this will lead him to affirm that the restaurant keeper, Wan Lee, is a laundry-man. The republican who finds two or three cases of corruption among democrats, may conceive corruption as a quality common to democrats and affirm that honest John Smith is corrupt. Faulty concepts, therefore, are very likely to lead to faulty judgments. A first duty in education is evidently to see that children are forming correct class concepts. For this it must be seen that they always distinguish the essential features of the class of objects they are studying. They must learn, also, not to conclude on account of superficial likeness that really unlike objects belong to the same class. The child, for instance, in parsing the sentence, "The swing broke down," must be taught to look for essential characteristics, and not call the word *swing* a gerund because it ends in "ing"; which, though a common characteristic of gerunds, does not differentiate it from other classes of words. So, also, when the young nature student notes that the head of the spider is somewhat separated from the abdomen, he must not falsely conclude that the spider belongs to the class insects. In like manner, the pupil must not imagine, on account of superficial differences, that objects really the same belong to different classes, as for example, that a certain object is not a fish, but a bird, because it is flying through the air; or that a whale is a fish and not an animal, because it lives in water. The pupil must also learn to distinguish carefully between the particular and universal judgment. To affirm that "Men strive to subdue the air," does not imply that "John Smith strives to subdue the air." The importance of this distinction will be considered more fully in our next section.

B. Feeling.—Faulty concepts are not, however, the only causes for wrong judgments. It has been noted already that feeling enters largely as a factor in our conscious life. Man, therefore, in forming his judgments, is always in danger of being swayed by his feelings. Our likes and dislikes, in other words, interfere with our thinking, and prevent us from analysing our knowledge as we should. Instead, therefore, of striving to develop true concepts concerning men and events and basing our judgments upon these, we are inclined in many cases to allow our judgments to be swayed by mere feeling.

C. Laziness.—Indifference is likewise a common source of faulty judgments. To attend to the concept and discover its intension as a means for correct judgment evidently demands mental effort. Many people, however, prefer either to jump at conclusions or let others do their judging for them.

Sound Judgments Based on Scientific Concepts.—To be able to form correct judgments regarding the members of any class, however, the child should know, not only its common characteristics, but also the essential features which distinguish its members from those of co-ordinate classes. To know adequately the equilateral triangle, for instance, the pupil must know both the features which distinguish it from other triangles and also those in which it agrees with all triangles. To know fully the mentha family of plants, he must know both the characteristic qualities of the family and also those of the larger genus labiatae. From this it will be seen that a large share of school work must be devoted to building up scientific class notions in the minds of the pupils. Without this, many of their judgments must necessarily be faulty. To form such scientific concepts, however, it is necessary to relate one concept with another in more indirect ways than is done through the formation of judgments. This brings us to a consideration of *reasoning*, the third and last form of thinking.

REASONING

Nature of Reasoning.—Reasoning is defined as a mental process in which the mind arrives at a new judgment by comparing other judgments. The mind, for instance, is in possession of the two judgments, "Stones are heavy" and "Flint is a stone." By bringing these two judgments under the eye of attention and comparing them, the mind is able to arrive at the new judgment, "Flint is heavy." Here the new judgment, expressing a relation between the notions, *flint* and *heavy*, is supposed to be arrived at, neither by direct experience, nor by an immediate analysis of the concept *flint*, but more indirectly by comparing the other judgments. The judgment, or conclusion, is said, therefore, to be arrived at mediately, or by a process of reasoning. Reasoning is of two forms, deductive, or syllogistic, reasoning, and inductive reasoning.

Deduction

Nature of Deduction.—In deduction the mind is said to start with a general truth, or judgment, and by a process of reasoning to arrive at a more particular truth, or judgment, thus:

Stone is heavy;
Flint is a stone;
∴ Flint is heavy.

Expressed in this form, the reasoning process, as already mentioned, is known as a syllogism. The whole syllogism is made up of three parts, major premise, minor premise, and conclusion. The three concepts involved in the syllogism are known as the major, the minor, and the middle term. In the above syllogism, *heavy*, the predicate of the major premise, is the major term; *flint*, the subject of the minor premise, is the minor term; and *stone*, to which the other two are related in the premises, is known as the middle term. Because of this previous comparison of the major and the minor terms with the middle term, deduction is sometimes said to be a process by which the mind discovers a relation between two concepts by comparing them each with a third concept.

Purpose of Deduction.—It is to be noted, however, as pointed out in Chapter XV, that deductive reasoning takes place normally only when the mind is faced with a difficulty which demands solution. Take the case of the boy and his lost coin referred to in Chapter II. As he faces the problem, different methods of solution may present themselves. It may enter his mind, for instance, to tear up the grate, but this is rejected on account of possible damage to the brickwork. Finally he thinks of the tar and resorts to this method of recovery. In both of the above cases the boy based his conclusions upon known principles. As he considered the question of tearing up the grate, the thought came to his mind, "Lifting-a-grate is a-thing-which-may-cause-damage." As he considered the use of the tar, he had in mind the judgment, "Adhesion is a property of tar," and at once inferred that tar would solve his problem. In such practical cases, however, the mind seems to go directly from the problem in hand to a conclusion by means of a general principle. When a woman wishes to remove a stain, she at once says, "Gasoline will remove it." Here the mind, in arriving at its conclusion, seems to apply the principle, "Gasoline removes spots," directly to the particular problem. Thus the reasoning might seem to run as follows:

Problem: What will remove this stain?
Principle: Gasoline will remove stains.
Conclusion: Gasoline will remove this stain.

Here the middle term of the syllogism seems to disappear. It is to be noted, however, that our thought changes from the universal idea "stains," mentioned in the statement of the principle, to the particular idea "this stain" mentioned in the problem and in the conclusion. But this implies a middle term, which could be expressed thus:

Gasoline will remove stains;
This is a stain;
∴ Gasoline will remove *this*.

The syllogism is valuable, therefore, because it displays fully and clearly each element in the reasoning process, and thus assures the validity of the conclusion.

Deduction in School Recitation.—It will be recalled from what was noted in our study of general method, that deduction usually plays an important part during an ordinary developing lesson. In the step of preparation, when the pupil is given a particular example in order to recall old knowledge, the example suggests a problem which is intended to call up certain principles which are designed to be used during the presentation. In a lesson on the "Conjunctive Pronoun," for instance, if we have the pupil recall his knowledge of the conjunction by examining the particular word "if" in such a sentence as, "I shall go if they come," he interprets the word as a conjunction simply because he possesses a general rule applicable to it, or is able to go through a process of deduction. In the presentation also, when the pupil is called on to examine the word *who* in such a sentence as, "The man who met us is very old," and decides that it is both a conjunction and a pronoun, he is again making deductions, since it is by his general knowledge of conjunctions and pronouns that he is able to interpret the two functions of the particular word *who*. Finally, as already noted, the application of an ordinary recitation frequently involves deductive processes.

Induction

Nature of Induction.—Induction is described as a process of reasoning in which the mind arrives at a conclusion by an examination of particular cases, or judgments. A further distinguishing feature of the inductive process is that, while the known judgments are particular in character, the conclusion is accepted as a general law, or truth. As in deduction, the reasoning process arises on account of some difficulty, or problem, presented to the mind, as for example:

What is the effect of heat upon air?
Will glass conduct electricity?
Why do certain bodies refract light?

To satisfy itself upon the problem, the mind appeals to actual experience either by ordinary observation or through experimentation. These observations or experiments, which necessarily deal with particular instances, are supposed to provide a number of particular judgments, by examining which a satisfactory conclusion is ultimately reached.

Example of Induction.—As an example of induction, may be taken the solution of such a problem as, "Does air exert pressure?" To meet this hypothesis we must evidently do more than merely abstract the manifest properties of an object, as is done in ordinary conception, or appeal directly to some known general principle, as is done in deduction. The work of induction demands rather to examine the two at present known but disconnected things, *air* and *pressure*, and by scientific observation seek to discover a relation between them. For this purpose the investigator may place a card over a glass filled with water, and on inverting it find that the card is held to the glass. Taking a glass tube and putting one end in water, he may place his finger over the other end and, on raising the tube, find that water remains in the tube. Soaking a heavy piece of leather in water and pressing it upon the smooth surface of a stone or other object, he finds the stone can be lifted by means of the leather. Reflecting upon each of these circumstances the mind comes to the following conclusions:

Air pressure holds this card to the glass,
Air pressure keeps the water in the tube,
Air pressure holds together the leather and the stone,
∴ Air exerts pressure.

How Distinguished from, A. Deduction, and B. Conception.—Such a process as the above constitutes a process of reasoning, first, because the conclusion gives a new affirmation, or judgment, "Air exerts pressure," and secondly, because the judgment is supposed to be arrived at by comparing other judgments. As a process of reasoning, however, it differs from deduction in that the final judgment is a general judgment, or truth, which seems to be based upon a number of particular judgments obtained from actual experience, while in deduction the conclusion was particular and the major premise general. It is for this reason that induction is defined as a process of going from the particular to the general. Moreover, since induction leads to the formation of a universal judgment, or general truth, it differs from the generalizing process known as conception, which leads to the formation of a concept, or general idea. It is evident, however, that the process will enrich the concept involved in the new judgment. When the mind is able to affirm that air exerts pressure, the property, exerting-pressure, is at once synthesised into the notion air. This point will again be referred to in comparing induction and conception as generalizing processes.

In speaking of induction as a process of going from the particular to the general, this does not signify that the process deals with individual notions. The particulars in an inductive process are particular cases giving rise to particular judgments, and judgments involve concepts, or general ideas. When, in the inductive process, it is asserted that air holds the card to the glass, the mind is seeking to establish a relation between the notions air and pressure, and is, therefore, thinking in concepts. For this reason, it is usually said that induction takes for granted ordinary relations as involved in our everyday concepts, and concerns itself only with the more hidden relations of things. The significance of induction as a process of going from the particular to the general, therefore, consists in the fact that the conclusion is held to be a wider judgment than is contained in any of the premises.

Particular Truth Implies the General.—Describing the premises of an inductive process as particular truths, and the conclusion as a universal truth, however, involves the same fiction as was noted in separating the percept and the concept into two distinct types of notions. In the first place, my particular judgment, that air presses the card against the glass, is itself a deduction resting upon other general principles. Secondly, if the judgment that air presses the card against the glass contains no element of universal truth, then a thousand such judgments could give no universal truth. Moreover, if the mind approaches a process of induction with a problem, or hypothesis, before it, the general truth is already apprehended hypothetically in thought even before the particular instances are examined. When we set out, for instance, to investigate whether the line joining the bisecting points of the sides of a triangle is parallel with the base, we have accepted hypothetically the general principle that such lines are parallel with the base. The fact is, therefore, that when the mind examines the particular case and finds it to agree with the hypothesis, so far as it accepts this case as a truth, it also accepts it as a universal truth. Although, therefore, induction may involve going from one particular experiment or observation to another, it is in a sense a process of going from the general to the general.

That accepting the truth of a particular judgment may imply a universal judgment is very evident in the case of geometrical demonstrations. When it is shown, for instance, that in the case of the particular isosceles triangle ABC, the angles at the base are equal, the mind does not require to examine other particular triangles for verification, but at once asserts that in every isosceles triangle the angles at the base are equal.

Induction and Conception Interrelated.—Although as a process, induction is to be distinguished from conception, it either leads to an enriching of some concept, or may in fact be the only means by which certain scientific concepts are formed. While the images obtained by ordinary sense perception will enable a child to gain a notion of water, to add to the notion the property, boiling-at-a-certain-temperature, or able-to-be-converted-into-two-parts-hydrogen-and-one-part-oxygen, will demand a process of induction. The development of such scientific notions as oxide, equation, predicate adjective, etc., is also dependent upon a regular inductive process. For this reason many lessons may be viewed both as conceptual and as inductive lessons. To teach the adverb implies a conceptual process, because the child must synthesise certain attributes into his notion adverb. It is also an inductive lesson, because these attributes being formulated as definite judgments are, therefore, obtained inductively. The double character of such a lesson is fully indicated by the two results obtained. The lesson ends with the acquisition of a new term, adverb, which represents the result of the conceptual process. It also ends with the definition: "An adverb is a word which modifies a verb, adjective, or other adverb," which indicates the general truth or truths resulting from the inductive process.

Deduction and Induction Interrelated.—In our actual teaching processes there is a very close inter-relation between the two processes of reasoning. We have already noted on page 192 that, in such inductive lessons as teaching the definition of a noun or the rule for the addition of fractions, both the preparatory step and the application involve deduction. It is to be noted further, however, that even in the development of an inductive lesson there is a continual interplay between induction and deduction. This will be readily seen in the case of a pupil seeking to discover the rule for determining the number of repeaters in the addition of recurring decimals. When he notes that adding three numbers with one, one, and two repeaters respectively, gives him two repeaters in his answer, he is more than likely to infer that the rule is to have in the answer the highest number found among the addenda. So far as he makes this inference, he undoubtedly will apply it in interpreting the next problem, and if the next numbers have one, one, and three repeaters respectively, he will likely be quite convinced that his former inference is correct. When, however, he meets a question with one, two, and three repeaters respectively, he finds his former inference is incorrect, and may, thereupon, draw a new inference, which he will now proceed to apply to further examples. The general fact to be noted here, however, is that, so far as the mind during the examination of the particular examples reaches any conclusion in an inductive lesson, it evidently applies this conclusion to some degree in the study of the further examples, or thinks deductively, even during the inductive process.

DEVELOPMENT OF REASONING POWER

Development of Reasoning Power.—Since reasoning is essentially a purposive form of thinking, it is evident that any reasoning process will depend largely upon the presence of some problem which shall stimulate the mind to seek out relations necessary to its solution. Power to reason, therefore, is conditioned by the ability to attend voluntarily to the problem and discover the necessary relations. It is further evident that the accuracy of any reasoning process must be dependent upon the accuracy of the judgments upon which the conclusions are based. But these judgments in turn depend for their accuracy upon the accuracy of the concepts involved. Correct reasoning, therefore, must depend largely upon the accuracy of our concepts, or, in other words, upon the old knowledge at our command. On the other hand, however, it has been seen that both deductive and inductive reasoning follow to some degree a systematic form. For this reason it may be assumed that the practice of these forms should have some effect in giving control of the processes. The child, for instance, who habituates himself to such thought processes as AB equals BC, and AC equals BC, therefore AB equals AC, no doubt becomes able thereby to grasp such relations more easily. Granting so much, however, it is still evident that close attention to, and accurate knowledge of, the various terms involved in the reasoning process is the sure foundation of correct reasoning.

CHAPTER XXIX

FEELING

Sensuous and Ideal Feeling.—We have noted (Chapter XXIV), that in addition to the general feeling tone accompanying an act of attention, and already described as a feeling of interest, there are two important classes of feeling known respectively as sensuous and ideal feeling. When a person says: "I feel tired" or "I feel hungry," he is referring to the feeling side of certain organic sensations. When he says: "The air feels cold" or "The paper feels smooth," he is referring to the feeling side of temperature and touch sensations. These are, therefore, examples of sensuous feeling. On the other hand, to say "I feel angry" or "I feel afraid," is to refer to a feeling state which accompanies perhaps the perception of some object, the recollection or anticipation of some act, or the inference that something is sure to happen, etc. These latter states are therefore known as ideal feelings.

Quality of Feeling States.—The qualities of our various feeling states are distinguished under two heads, pleasure and pain. It might seem at first sight that our feeling states will fall into a much larger number of classes distinguished by differences in quality, or tone. The taste of an orange, the smell of lavender, the touch of a hot stove, the appreciation of a fine piece of music, and the appreciation of a lofty poem, seem at first sight to yield different feelings. The supposed difference in the quality of the feelings is due, however, to a difference in the knowledge elements accompanying the feelings, or to the fact that they are discriminated as different experiences. The idea of the music or the poem is of a higher grade than the sensory image of taste, and accordingly the feelings *appear* to be different. The feelings may, of course, differ in intensity, but in *quality* they are either pleasant or unpleasant.

CONDITIONS OF FEELING TONE

A. Neural.—The quality, or tone, of a feeling will vary according to the intensity of the impression. Great heat stimulates the nerves violently and the resultant feeling state is painful; warmth gives a moderate stimulation and the resultant tone is pleasant. Excessive cold also, because it stimulates violently, produces a painful feeling. Since the intensity of a stimulus varies according to the resistance encountered in the nervous arc, the quality of a feeling state must, therefore, vary according to the resistance. It is for this reason that an experience, at first very painful, may lose much of its tone by repetition. By repetition the nerve centres are adapted to the experience, resistance is lessened, and the accompanying pain diminished. In this way, some work or exercise, which is at first positively unpleasant, may at least become endurable as the organism becomes adapted to the occupation. From this point of view, it is sometimes said that any impressions to which we are perfectly adapted give pleasurable feelings, while, in other cases the resultant tone will be painful.

B. Mental.—The law of perfect adaptation also explains why ideal feelings may at one time result in a pleasant, and at another time in a painful, feeling tone. According to the principle of apperception, the new experience must organize itself with whatever thoughts and feelings are now occupying consciousness. It necessarily happens that a given experience does not always equally harmonize with our present thoughts and feelings. The recognition of a friend under ordinary circumstances is agreeable, but amid certain associations or in a certain environment, such recognition would be disagreeable. So, too, while an original experience may have been agreeable, the memory of it may now be disagreeable; and vice versa. For instance, the memory of a former success or prosperity may, in the midst of present failure and poverty, be disagreeable; while the recollection of former failure and defeat may now, in the midst of success and prosperity, be agreeable. What is it that makes a sensation, a perception, a memory, or an apprehended relation pleasant under some circumstances and unpleasant under others? The rule appears to be that when the experience harmonizes with our present train of thought, when it promotes our present interests and intentions, it is pleasant; but when, on the other hand, it does not harmonize with our train of thought or thwarts or impedes our interests and purposes, it is unpleasant.

Function of Pleasure and Pain.—From what has been noted concerning co-ordination between the adaptation of the organism to impression and the quality of the accompanying feeling, it is evident that pleasure and pain each have their part to play in promoting the ultimate good of the individual. Pain is beneficial, because it lets us know that there is some misadjustment to our environment, and thereby warns us to remove or cease doing what is proving injurious. In this connection, it may be noted that no disease is so dangerous as one that fails to make its presence known through pain. Pleasure also is valuable in so far as it results from perfect adaptation to a perfect environment, since it induces the individual to continue beneficial acts. It must be remembered, however, that so far as heredity or education has adapted our organism to improper stimuli, pleasure is no proof that the good of the organism is being advanced. In such cases, redemption can come to the fallen world only through suffering.

Feeling and Knowing.—Since the intensity of a feeling state is conditioned by the amount of resistance, an intense state of feeling is likely to be accompanied by a lowering of intellectual activity. For this reason excessive hunger, heat or cold, intense joy, anger or sorrow, are usually antagonistic to intellectual work. The explanation for this seems to be that so much of our nervous energy is consumed in overcoming the resistance in the centres affected, that little is left for ordinary intellectual processes. This does not, of course, imply that no one can do intellectual work under such conditions; nor that the intellectual man is always devoid of strong feelings, although such is often the case. Occasionally, however, a man is so strongly endowed with nervous energy, that even after overcoming the resistance being encountered, he still has a residue of energy to devote to ordinary intellectual processes.

Feeling and Will.—Although, as pointed out in the last paragraph, there is a certain antagonism between knowing and feeling, it has also been seen that every experience has its knowing as well as its feeling side. Because of this co-ordination, the qualities of our feeling states become known to us, or are able to be distinguished by the mind. As a result of this recognition of a difference in our feeling states, we learn to seek states of pleasure and to avoid states of pain or, in other words, our mere states of feeling become desires. This means that we become able to contrast a present feeling with other remembered states, and seek either to continue the present desired state or to substitute another for the present undesirable feeling. In the form of desire, therefore, our feelings become strong motives, which may influence the will to certain lines of action.

SENSUOUS FEELINGS

While the sensations of the special senses, namely, sight, sound, touch, taste, and smell, have each their affective, or feeling, side, a minute study of these feelings is not necessary for our present purpose. It may be noted, however, that in the more intellectual senses, namely, sight, hearing, and touch, feeling tone is less marked, although strong feeling may accompany certain tactile sensations. In the lower senses of taste and smell, the feeling tone is more pronounced. Under muscular sensation we meet such marked feeling tones as fatigue, exertion, and strain, while associated with the organic sensations are such feelings as hunger and thirst, and the various pains which usually accompany derangement and disease of the bodily organs. Some of these feelings are important, because they are likely to influence the will by developing into desires in the form of appetites. Many sensuous feelings are important also because they especially warn the mind regarding the condition of the organism.

EMOTION

Nature of Emotion.—An emotion differs from sensuous feeling, not in its content, but in its higher intensity, its greater complexity, and its more elaborate motor response. It may be defined as a succession of interconnected feelings with a more complex physical expression than a simple feeling. On reading an account of a battle, one may feel sad and express this sadness only in a gloomy appearance of the face. But if one finds that in this battle a friend has been killed, the feeling is much intensified and may become an emotion of grief, expressing itself in some complex way, perhaps in tears, in sobbing, in wringing the hands. Similarly, a feeling of slight irritation expressed in a frowning face, if intensified, becomes the emotion of anger, expressed in tense muscles, rapidly beating heart, laboured breathing, perhaps a torrent of words or a hasty blow.

Emotion and Instinct.—Feeling and instinct are closely related. Every instinct has its affective phase, that is, its satisfaction always involves an element of pleasure or pain. The satisfaction of the instincts of curiosity or physical activity illustrates this fact. On the other hand, every emotion has its characteristic instinctive response. Fear expresses itself in all persons alike in certain characteristic ways inherited from a remote ancestry; anger expresses itself in other instinctive reactions; grief in still others.

Conditions of Emotion

An analysis of a typical emotion will serve to show the conditions under which it makes its appearance. Let us take first the emotion of fear. Suppose a person is walking alone on a dark night along a deserted street. His nervous currents are discharging themselves uninterruptedly over their wonted channels, his current of thought is unimpeded. Suddenly there appears a strange and frightful object in his pathway. His train of thought is violently checked. His nervous currents, which a moment ago were passing out smoothly and without undue resistance into muscles of legs, arms, body, and face, are now suddenly obstructed, or in other words encounter violent resistance. He stands still. His heart momentarily stops beating. A temporary paralysis seizes him. As the nervous currents thus encounter resistance, the feeling tone known as fear is experienced. At the same time the currents burst their barriers and overflow into new channels that are easy of access, the motor centres being especially of this character. Some of the currents, therefore, run to the involuntary muscles, and in consequence the heart beats faster, the breathing becomes heavier, the face grows pale, a cold sweat breaks forth, the hair "stands on end." Other currents, through hereditary influences, pass to the voluntary muscles, and the person shrieks, and turns and flees.

Or take the emotion of anger. Some fine morning in school everything is in good order, everybody is industriously at work, the lessons are proceeding satisfactorily. The current of the teacher's experience is flowing smoothly and unobstructedly. Presently a troublesome boy, who has been repeatedly reproved for misconduct, again shows symptoms of idleness and misbehaviour. The smooth current of experience being checked, here also both a new feeling tone is experienced and the wonted nerve currents flow out into other brain centres. The teacher stops his work and gazes fixedly at the offending pupil. His heart beats rapidly, the blood surges to his face, his breathing becomes heavy, his muscles grow tense. In these reactions we have the nervous currents passing out over involuntary channels. Then, perhaps, the teacher unfortunately breaks forth into a torrent of words or lays violent hands upon the offender. Here the nervous currents are passing outward over the voluntary system.

These illustrations indicate that three important conditions are present at the appearance of the emotion, namely, (1) the presence of an unusual object in consciousness, (2) the consequent disturbance of the smooth flow of experience or, in physiological terms, the temporary obstruction of the ordinary pathways of nervous discharge through the great resistance encountered, and (3) the new feeling state with its concomitant overflow of the impulses into new motor channels, some of which lead to the involuntary muscles and others to the voluntary. The emotion proper consists in the feeling state which arises as a result of the resistance encountered by the nervous impulses as the smooth flow of experience is checked. The idea that I shall die some day arouses no emotion in me, because it in no way affects my ordinary thought processes, and therefore it in no way disturbs my nervous equilibrium. The perception of a wild animal about to kill me, because it suddenly thwarts and impedes the smooth flow of my experience through a suggestion of danger, produces an intense feeling and a diffused and intense derangement of the nervous equilibrium.

Development of Emotions.—The question of paramount importance in connection with emotion is how to arouse and develop desirable emotions. The close connection of the three phases of the mind's manifestation—knowing, feeling, and willing, gives the key to the question. Feeling cannot be developed alone apart from knowing and willing. In fact, if we attend carefully to the knowing and willing activities, the feelings, in one sense, take care of themselves. Two principles, therefore, lie at the basis of proper emotional development:

1. The mind must be allowed to dwell upon only those ideas to which worthy emotions are attached. We must refuse to think those thoughts that are tinged with unworthy feelings. The Apostle Paul has expressed this very eloquently when he says in his Epistle to the Philippians: "Finally, brethren, whatsoever things are true, whatsoever things are honest, whatsoever things are just, whatsoever things are pure, whatsoever things are lovely, whatsoever things are of good report; if there be any virtue, and if there be any praise, think on these things."

2. The teacher's main duty in the above regard is to provide the pupil with a rich fund of ideas to which desirable feelings cling. An impressive manner, an enthusiastic attitude toward subjects of study, an evident interest in them, and apparent appreciation of them, will also aid much in inspiring pupils with proper feelings, for feelings are often contagious in the absence of very definite ideas. How often have we been deeply moved by hearing a poem impressively read even though we have very imperfectly grasped its meaning. The feelings of the reader have been communicated to us through the principle of contagion. Similarly, in history, art, and nature study, emotions may be stirred, not only through the medium of the ideas presented, but also by the impressiveness, the enthusiasm, and the interest exhibited by the teacher in presenting them.

3. We must give expression to these emotions we wish to develop. Expression means the probability of the recurrence of the emotion, and gradually an emotional habit is formed. An unselfish disposition is cultivated by performing little acts of kindness and self-denial whenever the opportunity offers. The expression of a desirable emotion, moreover, should not stop merely with an experience of the organic sensations or the reflex reactions accompanying the emotion. To listen to a sermon and react only by an emotional thrill, a quickened heart beat, or a few tears, is a very ineffective kind of expression. The only kind of emotional expression that is of much consequence either to ourselves or others is conduct. Only in so far as our emotional experiences issue in action that is beneficial to those about us, are they of any practical value.

Elimination of Emotions.—Since certain of our emotions, such as anger and fear, are, in general, undesirable states of feeling, a question arises how such emotions may be prevented. It is sometimes said that, if we can inhibit the expression, the emotion will disappear, that is, if I can prevent the trembling, I will cease to be afraid. From what has just been learned, however, the emotion and its expression being really concomitant results of the antecedent obstruction of ordinary nervous discharges, emotion cannot be checked by checking the expression, but both will be checked if the nervous impulses can be made to continue in their wonted courses in spite of the disturbing presentations. The real secret of emotional control lies, therefore, in the power of voluntary attention. The effect of attention is to cause the nervous energy to be directed without undue resistance into its wonted channels, this, in turn, preventing its overflow into new channels. By thus directing the energy into wonted and open channels, attention prevents both the movements and the feeling that are concomitants of a disturbance of nervous equilibrium. By meeting the attack of the dog in a purposeful and attentive manner, we cause the otherwise damming-up nervous energy to continue flowing into ordinary channels, and in this way prevent both the feeling of fear and also the flow of the energy into the motor centres associated with the particular emotion. But while it is not scientifically correct in a particular case to say that we may inhibit the feeling by inhibiting the movements, it is of course true that, by avoiding a present emotional outburst, we are less likely in the future to respond to situations which tend to arouse the emotional state. On the other hand, to give way frequently to any emotional state will make it more difficult to avoid yielding to the emotion under similar conditions.

OTHER TYPES OF FEELING

Mood

Mood.—Our feelings and emotions become organized and developed in various ways. The sum total of all the feeling tones of our sensory and ideational processes at any particular time gives us our *mood* at that time. If, for instance, our organic sensations are prevailingly pleasant, if the ideas we dwell upon are tinged with agreeable feeling, our mood is cheerful. We can to a large extent control our current of thought, and can as we will, except in case of serious bodily disturbances, attend, or not attend, to our organic sensations. Consequently we are ourselves largely responsible for the moods we indulge.

Disposition

Disposition.—A particular kind of mood frequently indulged in produces a type of emotional habit, our *disposition*. For instance, the teacher who permits the occurrences of the class-room to trouble him unnecessarily, and who broods over these afterwards, soon develops a worrying disposition. As we have it in our power to determine what habits, emotional and otherwise, we form, we alone are responsible for the dispositions we cultivate.

Temperament

Temperament.—Some of us are provided with nervous systems that are predisposed to particular moods. This predisposition, together with frequent indulgence in particular types of mood, gives us our *temperament*. The responsibility for this we share with our ancestors, but, even though predisposed through heredity to unfortunate moods, we can ourselves decide whether we shall give way to them. Temperaments have been classified as *sanguine, melancholic, choleric,* and *phlegmatic*. The sanguine type is inclined to look on the bright side of things, to be optimistic; the melancholic tends to moodiness and gloom; the choleric is easily irritated, quick to anger; the phlegmatic is not easily aroused to emotion, is cold and sluggish. An individual seldom belongs exclusively to one type.

Sentiments

Sentiments.—Certain emotional tendencies become organized about an object and constitute a *sentiment*. The sentiment of love for our mother had its basis in our childhood in the perception of her as the source of numberless experiences involving pleasant feeling tones. As we grew older, we understood better her solicitude for our welfare and her sacrifices for our sake—further experiences involving a large feeling element. Thus there grew up about our mother an organized system of emotional tendencies, our sentiment of filial love. Such sentiments as patriotism, religious faith, selfishness, sympathy, arise and develop in the same way. Compared with moods, sentiments are more permanent in character and involve more complex knowledge elements. Moreover, they do not depend upon physiological conditions as do moods. One's organic sensations may affect one's mood to a considerable extent, but will scarcely influence one's patriotism or filial love.

CHAPTER XXX

THE WILL

VOLUNTARY CONTROL OF ACTION

TYPES OF MOVEMENT

Types of Movement.—Closely associated with the problem of voluntary attention is that of voluntary movement, or control of action. It is an evident fact that the infant can at first exercise no conscious control over his bodily movements. He has, it is true, certain reflex and instinctive tendencies which enable him to react in a definite way to certain special stimuli. In such cases, however, there is no conscious control of the movements, the bodily organs merely responding in a definite way whenever the proper stimulus is present. The eye, for instance, must wink when any foreign matter affects it; wry movements of the face must accompany the bitter taste; and the body must start at a sudden noise. At other times, bodily movements may be produced in a more spontaneous way. Here the physical energy stored within the system gives rise to bodily activity and causes those random impulsive movements so evident during infancy and early childhood. When these movements, which are the only ones possible to very early childhood, are compared with the movements of a workman placing the brick in the wall or of an artist executing a delicate piece of carving, there is found in the latter movements the conscious idea of a definite end, or object, to be reached. To gain control of one's movements is, therefore, to acquire an ability to direct bodily actions toward the attainment of a given end. Thus a question arises as to the process by which a child attains to this bodily control.

Ideas of Movements Acquired.—Although, as pointed out above, a child's early instinctive and impulsive movements are not under conscious control, they nevertheless become conscious acts, in the sense that the movements are soon realized in idea. The movements, in other words, give rise to conscious states, and these in turn are retained as portions of past experience. For instance, although the child at first grasps the object only impulsively, he nevertheless soon obtains an idea, or experience, of what it means to grasp with the hand. So, also, although he may first stretch the limb impulsively or make a wry face reflexively, he secures, in a short time, ideas representative of these movements. As the child thus obtains ideas representative of different bodily movements, he is able ultimately, by fixing his attention upon any movement, to produce it in a voluntary way.

DEVELOPMENT OF CONTROL

Development of Control: A. Ideo-motor Action.—At first, on account of the close association between the thought centres and the motor centres causing the act, the child seems to have little ability to check the act, whenever its representative idea enters consciousness. It is for this reason that young children often perform such seemingly unreasonable acts as, for instance, slapping another person, kicking and throwing objects, etc. In such cases, however, it must not be assumed that these are always deliberate acts. More often the act is performed simply because the image of the act arises in the child's mind, and his control of the motor discharge is so weak that the act follows immediately upon the idea. This same tendency frequently manifests itself even in the adult. As one thinks intently of some favourite game, he may suddenly find himself taking a bodily position used in playing that game. It is by the same law also that the impulsive man tends to act out in gesture any act that he may be describing in words. Such a type of action is described as ideo-motor action.

B. Deliberate Action.—Because the child in time gains ideas of various movements and an ability to fix his attention upon them, he thus becomes able to set one motor image against another as possible lines of action. One image may suggest to slap; the other to caress; the one to pull the weeds in the flower bed; the other, to lie down in the hammock. But attention is ultimately able, as noted in the last Chapter, so to control the impulse and resistance in the proper nervous centres that the acts themselves may be indefinitely suspended. Thus the mind becomes able to conceive lines of action and, by controlling bodily movement, gain time to consider the effectiveness of these toward the attainment of any end. When a bodily movement thus takes place in relation to some conscious end in view, it is termed a deliberate act. One important result of physical exercises with the young child is that they develop in him this deliberate control of bodily movements. The same may be said also of any orderly modes of action employed in the general management of the school. Regular forms of assembly and dismissal, of moving about the class-room, etc., all tend to give the child this same control over his acts.

Action versus Result.—As already noted, however, most of our movements soon develop into fixed habits. For this reason our bodily acts are usually performed more or less unconsciously, that is, without any deliberation as to the mere act itself. For this reason, we find that when bodily movements are held in check, or inhibited, in order to allow time for deliberation, attention usually fixes itself, not upon the acts themselves, but rather upon the results of these acts. For instance, a person having an axe and a saw may wish to divide a small board into two parts. Although the axe may be in his hand, he is thinking, not how he is to use the axe, but how it will result if he uses this to accomplish the end. In the same way he considers, not how to use the saw, but the result of using the saw. By inhibiting the motor impulses which would lead to the use of either of these, the individual is able to note, say, that to use the axe is a quick, but inaccurate, way of gaining the end; to use the saw, a slow, but accurate, way. The present need being interpreted as one where only an approximate division is necessary, attention is thereupon given wholly to the images tending to promote this action; resistance is thus overcome in these centres, and the necessary motor discharges for using the axe are given free play. Here, however, the mind evidently does not deliberate on how the hands are to use the axe or the saw, but rather upon the results following the use of these.

VOLITION

Nature of Will.—When voluntary attention is fixed, as above, upon the results of conflicting lines of action, the mind is said to experience a conflict of desires, or motives. So long as this conflict lasts, physical expression is inhibited, the mind deliberating upon and comparing the conflicting motives. For instance, a pupil on his way to school may be thrown into a conflict of motives. On the one side is a desire to remain under the trees near the bank of the stream; on the other a desire to obey his parents, and go to school. So long as these desires each press themselves upon the attention, there results an inhibiting of the nervous motor discharge with an accompanying mental state of conflict, or indecision. This prevents, for the time being, any action, and the youth deliberates between the two possible lines of conduct. As he weighs the various elements of pleasure on the one hand and of duty on the other, the one desire will finally appear the stronger. This constitutes the person's choice, or decision, and a line of action follows in accordance with the end, or motive, chosen. This mental choice, or decision, is usually termed an act of will.

Attention in Will.—Such a choice between motives, however, evidently involves an act of voluntary attention. What really goes on in consciousness in such a conflict of motives is that voluntary attention makes a single problem of the two-fold situation—school versus play. To this problem the attention marshals relative ideas and selects and adjusts them to the complex problem. Finally these are built into an organized experience which solves the problem as one, say, of going to school. The so-called choice is, therefore, merely the mental solution of the situation; the necessary bodily action follows in an habitual manner, once the attention lessens the resistance in the appropriate centres.

Factors in volitional act

Factors in Volitional Act.—Such an act of volition, or will, is usually analysed in the following steps:

1. Conflicting desires
2. Deliberation—weighing of motives
3. Choice—solving the problem
4. Expression.

As a mental process, however, an act of will does not include the fourth step—expression. The mind has evidently willed, the moment a conclusion, or choice, is reached in reference to the end in view. If, therefore, I stand undecided whether to paint the house white or green, an act of will has taken place when the conclusion, or mental decision, has been reached to paint the house green. On the other hand, however, only the man who forms a decision and then resolutely works out his decision through actual expression, will be credited with a strong will by the ordinary observer.

Physical Conditions of Will.—Deliberation being but a special case of giving voluntary attention to a selected problem, it involves the same expenditure of nervous energy in overcoming resistance within the brain centres as was seen to accompany any act of voluntary attention. Such being the case, our power of will at any given time is likely to vary in accordance with our bodily condition. The will is relatively weak during sickness, for instance, because the normal amount of nervous energy which must accompany the mental processes of deliberation and choice is not able to be supplied. For the same reason, lack of food and sleep, working in bad air, etc., are found to weaken the will for facing a difficulty, though we may nevertheless feel that it is something that ought to be done. An added reason, therefore, why the victim of alcohol and narcotics finds it difficult to break his habit is that the use of these may permanently lessen the energy of the nervous organism. In facing the difficult task of breaking an old habit, therefore, this person has rendered the task doubly difficult, because the indulgence has weakened his will for undertaking the struggle of breaking an old habit. On the other hand, good food, sleep, exercise in the fresh air, by quickening the blood and generating nervous energy, in a sense strengthens the will in undertaking the duties and responsibilities before it.

ABNORMAL TYPES OF WILL

The Impulsive Will.—One important problem in the education of the will is found in the relation of deliberation to choice. As is the case in a process of learning, the mind in deliberating must draw upon past experiences, must select and weigh conflicting ideas in a more or less intelligent manner, and upon this basis finally make its choice. A first characteristic of a person of will, therefore, is to be able to deliberate intelligently upon any different lines of action which may present themselves. But in the case of many individuals, there seems a lack of this power of deliberation. On every hand they display almost a childlike impulsiveness, rushing blindly into action, and always following up the word with the blow. This type, which is spoken of as an impulsive will, is likely to prevail more or less among young children. It is essential, therefore, that the teacher should take this into account in dealing with the moral and the practical actions of these children. It should be seen that such children in their various exercises are made to inhibit their actions sufficiently to allow them to deliberate and choose between alternative modes of action. For this purpose typical forms of constructive work will be found of educational value. In such exercises situations may be continually created in which the pupil must deliberate upon alternative lines of action and make his choice accordingly.

The Retarded Will.—In some cases a type of will is met in which the attention seems unable to lead deliberation into a state of choice. Like Hamlet, the person keeps ever weighing whether *to be or not to be* is the better course. Such people are necessarily lacking in achievement, although always intending to do great things in the future. This type of will is not so prevalent among young children; but if met, the teacher should, as far as possible, encourage the pupil to pass more rapidly from thought to action.

The Sluggish Will.—A third and quite common defect of will is seen where the mind is either too ignorant or too lazy to do the work of deliberating. While such characters are not impulsive, they tend to follow lines of action merely by habit, or in accordance with the direction of others, and do little thinking for themselves. The only remedy for such people is, of course, to quicken their intellectual life. Unless this can be done, the goodness of their character must depend largely upon the nobility of those who direct the formation of their habits and do their thinking for them.

Development of Will.—By recalling what has been established concerning the learning process, we may learn that most school exercises, when properly conducted, involve the essential facts of an act of will. In an ordinary school exercise, the child first has before him a certain aim, or problem, and then must select from former experience the related ideas which will enable him to solve this problem. So far, however, as the child is led to select and reject for himself these interpreting ideas, he must evidently go through a process similar to that of an ordinary act of will. When, for example, the child faces the problem of finding out how many yards of carpet of a certain width will cover the floor of a room, he must first decide how to find the number of strips required. Having come to a decision on this point, he must next give expression to his decision by actually working out this part of the problem. In like manner, he must now decide how to proceed with the next step in his problem and, having come to a conclusion on this point, must also give it expression by performing the necessary mathematical processes. It is for this reason, that the ordinary lessons and exercises of the school, when presented to the children as actual problems, constitute an excellent means for developing will power.

The Essentials of Moral Character.—It must be noted finally, that will power is a third essential factor in the attainment of real moral character, or social efficiency. We have learned that man, through the possession of an intelligent nature, is able to grasp the significance of his experience and thus form comprehensive plans and purposes for the regulation of his conduct. We have noted further that, through the development of right feeling, he may come to desire and plan for the attainment of only such ends as make for righteousness. Yet, however noble his desires, and however intelligent and comprehensive his plans and purposes, it is only as he develops a volitional personality, or determination of character which impels toward the attainment of these noble ends through intelligent plans, that man can be said to live the truly efficient life.

> Self-reverence, self-knowledge, self-control,
> These three alone lead life to sovereign power.

In this connection, also, we cannot do better than quote Huxley's description of an educated man, as given in his essay on *A Liberal Education*, a description which may be considered to crystallize the true conception of an efficient citizen:

That man, I think, has had a liberal education who has been so trained in youth that his body is the ready servant of his will, and does with ease and pleasure all the work that, as a mechanism, it is capable of; whose intellect is a clear, cold, logic engine, with all its parts of equal strength, and in smooth working order; ready, like a steam engine, to be turned to any kind of work, and spin the gossamers as well as forge the anchors of the mind; whose mind is stored with a knowledge of the great and fundamental truths of nature, and of the laws of her operations; one who, no stunted ascetic, is full of life and fire, but whose passions are trained to come to heel by a vigorous will, the servant of a tender conscience; who has learned to love all beauty, whether of nature or of art, to hate all vileness, and to respect others as himself.

CHAPTER XXXI

CHILD STUDY

Scope and Purpose of Child Study.—By child study is meant the observation of the general characteristics and the leading individual differences exhibited by children during the periods of infancy, childhood, and adolescence. Its purpose is to gather facts regarding childhood and formulate them into principles that are applicable in education. From the teacher's standpoint, the purpose is to be able to adapt intelligently his methods in each subject to the child's mind at the different stages of its development.

In the education of the child we have our eyes fixed, at least partly, upon his future. The aim of education is usually stated in terms of what the child is to *become*. He is to become a socially efficient individual, to be fitted to live completely, to develop a good moral character, to have his powers of mind and body harmoniously developed. All these aims look toward the future. But what the child *becomes* depends upon what he *is*. Education, in its broadest sense, means taking the individual's present equipment of mind and body and so using it as to enable him to become something else in the future. The teacher must be concerned, therefore, not only with what he wishes the child to *become* in the future, but also with what he *is*, here and now.

Importance to the Teacher.—The adaptation of matter and method to the child's tendencies, capacities, and interests, which all good teaching demands, is possible only through an understanding of his nature. The teacher must have regard, not only to the materials and the method used in training, but also to the being who is to be trained. A knowledge of child nature will prevent expensive mistakes and needless waste.

A few typical examples will serve to illustrate the immense importance a knowledge of child nature is to his teacher.

1. As has been already explained, when the teacher knows something about the instincts of children, he will utilize these tendencies in his teaching and work with them, not against them. He will, wherever possible, make use of the play instinct in his lessons, as for example, when he makes the multiplication drill a matter of climbing a stairway without stumbling or crossing a stream on stones without falling in. He will use the instinct of physical activity in having children learn number combinations by manipulating blocks, or square measure by actually measuring surfaces, or fractions by using scissors and strips of cardboard, or geographical features by modelling in sand and clay. He will use the imitative

instinct in cultivating desirable personal habits, such as neatness, cleanliness, and order, and in modifying conduct through the inspiring presentation of history and literature. He will provide exercise for the instinct of curiosity by suggesting interesting problems in geography and nature study.

2. When the teacher understands the principle of eliminating undesirable tendencies by substitution, he will not regard as cardinal sins the pushing, pinching, and kicking in which boys give vent to their excess energy, but will set about directing this purposeless activity into more profitable channels. He will thus substitute another means of expression for the present undesirable means. He will, for instance, give opportunity for physical exercises, paper-folding and cutting, cardboard work, wood-work, drawing, colour work, modelling, etc., so far as possible in all school subjects. He will try to transform the boy who teases and bullies the smaller boys into a guardian and protector. He will try to utilize the boy's tendency to collect useless odds and ends by turning it into the systematic and purposeful collection of plants, insects, specimens of soils, specimens illustrating phases of manufactures, postage stamps, coins, etc.

3. When the teacher knows that the interests of pupils have much to do with determining their effort, he will endeavour to seize upon these interests when most active. He will thus be saved such blunders as teaching in December a literature lesson on *An Apple Orchard in the Spring*, or assigning a composition on "Tobogganing" in June, because he realizes that the interest in these topics is not then active. Each season, each month of the year, each festival and holiday has its own particular interests, which may be effectively utilized by the presentation of appropriate materials in literature, in composition, in nature study, and in history. A current event may be taken advantage of to teach an important lesson in history or civics. For instance, an election may be made the occasion of a lesson on voting by ballot, a miniature election being conducted for that purpose.

4. When the teacher appreciates the extent of the capacities of children, he will not make too heavy demands upon their powers of logical reasoning by introducing too soon the study of formal grammar or the solution of difficult arithmetical problems. When he knows that the period from eight to twelve is the habit-forming period, he will stress, during these years such things as mechanical accuracy in the fundamental rules in arithmetic, the memorization of gems of poetry, and the cultivation of right physical and moral habits. When he knows the influence of motor expression in giving definiteness, vividness, and permanency to ideas, he will have much work in drawing, modelling, constructive work, dramatization, and oral and written expression.

METHODS OF CHILD STUDY

A. Observation.—From the teacher's standpoint the method of observation of individual children is the most practicable. He has the material for his observations constantly before him. He soon discovers that one pupil is clever, another dull; that one excels in arithmetic, another in history; that one is inclined to jump to conclusions, another is slow and deliberate. He is thus able to adapt his methods to meet individual requirements. But however advantageous this may be from the practical point of view, it must be noted that the facts thus secured are individual and not universal. Such child study does not in itself carry one very far. To be of real value to the teacher, these particular facts must be recognized as illustrative of a general law. When the teacher discovers, for instance, that nobody in his class responds very heartily to an abstract discussion of the rabbit, but that everybody is intensely interested when the actual rabbit is observed, he may regard the facts as illustrating the general principle that children need to be appealed to through the senses. Likewise when he obtains poor results in composition on the topic, "How I Spent My Summer Holidays," but excellent results on "How to Plant Bulbs," especially after the pupils have planted a bed of tulips on the front lawn, he may infer the law, that the best work is obtained when the matter is closely associated with the active interests of pupils. By watching the children when they are on the school grounds, the teacher may observe how far the occupations of the home, or a current event, such as a circus, an election, or a war, influences the play of the children. Thus the method of observation requires that not only individual facts should be obtained, but also that general principles should be inferred on the basis of these. Care must be taken, however, that the facts observed justify the inference.

B. Experiment.—An experiment in any branch of science means the observation of results under controlled conditions. Experimental child study must, to a large extent, therefore, be relegated to the psychological laboratory. Such experiments as the localization of cutaneous impressions, the influence of certain operations on fatigue, or the discovery of the length of time necessary for a conscious reaction, can be successfully carried out only with more or less elaborate equipment and under favourable conditions. However, the school offers opportunity for some simple yet practical experiments in child study. The teacher may discover experimentally what is the most favourable period at which to place a certain subject on the school programme, whether, for instance, it is best to take mechanical arithmetic when the minds of the pupils are fresh or when they are weary, or whether the writing lesson had better be taught immediately after the strenuous play at recess or at a time when the muscles are rested. He may find out the response of the pupils to problems in arithmetic closely connected with their lives (for example, in a rural community problems relating to farm activities), as compared with their response to problems involving more or less remote ideas. He may discover to what extent concentration in securing neat exercises in one subject, composition for instance, affects the exercises in other subjects in which neatness has not been explicitly demanded. This latter experiment might throw some light upon the much debated question of formal discipline. In all these cases the teacher must be on his guard not to accept as universal principles what he has found to be true of a small group of pupils, until at least he has found his conclusions verified by other experimenters.

C. Direct Questions.—This method involves the submission of questions to pupils of a particular age or grade, collecting and classifying their answers, and basing conclusions upon these. Much work in this direction has been done in recent years by certain educators, and much illuminating and more or less useful material has been collected. A good deal of light has been thrown upon the apperceptive material that children have possession of by noting their answers to such questions as: "Have you ever seen the stars? A robin? A pig? Where does milk come from? Where do potatoes come from?" etc., etc. The practical value of this method lies in the insight it gives into the interests of children, the kind of imagery they use, and the relationships they have set up among their ideas. Every teacher has been surprised at times at the absurd answers given by children. These absurdities are usually due to the teacher's taking for granted that the pupils have possession of certain old knowledge that is actually absent. The moral of such occurrences is that he should examine very carefully what "mind stuff" the pupils have for interpreting the new material.

D. Biographical Studies of Individual Children.—Many books have been written describing the development of individual children. These descriptions doubtless contain much that is typical of all children, but one must be careful not to argue too much from an individual case. Such records are valuable as confirmatory evidence of what has already been observed in connection with other children, or as suggestive of what may be looked for in them.

PERIODS OF DEVELOPMENT

The period covered by child study may be roughly divided into three parts, namely, (1) infancy, extending from birth to three years of age, (2) childhood, from three to twelve, and (3) adolescence, from twelve to eighteen. While children during each of these periods exhibit striking dissimilarities one from another, there are nevertheless many characteristics that are fairly universal during each period.

1. Infancy

A. Physical Characteristics.—One of the striking features of infancy is the rapidity with which command of the bodily organs is secured. Starting with a few inherited reflexes, the child at three years of age has attained fairly complete control of his sense organs and bodily movements, though he lacks that co-ordination of muscles by which certain delicate effects of hand and voice are produced. The relative growth is greater at this than at any subsequent period. Another prominent characteristic is the tendency to incessant movement. The constant handling, exploring, and analysing of objects enhances the child's natural thirst for knowledge, and he probably obtains a larger stock of ideas during the first three years of his life than during any equal period subsequently.

B. Mental Characteristics.—A conspicuous feature of infancy is the imitative tendency, which early manifests itself. Through this means the child acquires many of his movements, his language power, and the simple games he plays. Sense impressions begin to lose their fleeting character and to become more permanent. As evidence of this, few children remember events farther back than their third year, while many can distinctly recall events of the third and fourth years even after the lapse of a long period of time. The child at this period begins to compare, classify, and generalize in an elementary way, though his ideas are still largely of the concrete variety. His attention is almost entirely non-voluntary; he is interested in objects and activities for themselves alone, and not for the sake of an end. He is, as yet, unable to conceive remote ends, the prime condition of voluntary attention. His ideas of right and wrong conduct are associated with the approval and disapproval of those about him.

2. Childhood

A. Physical Characteristics.—In the earlier period of childhood, from three to seven years, bodily growth is very rapid. Much of the vital force is thus consumed, and less energy is available for physical activity. The child has also less power of resistance and is thus susceptible to the diseases of childhood. His movements are for the same reason lacking in co-ordination. In the later period, from seven to twelve years, the bodily growth is less rapid, more energy is available for physical activity, and the co-ordination of muscles is greater. The brain has now reached its maximum size and weight, any further changes being due to the formation of associative pathways along nerve centres. This is, therefore, pre-eminently the habit-forming period. From the physical standpoint this means that those activities that are essentially habitual must have their genesis during the period between seven and twelve if they are to function perfectly in later life. The mastery of a musical instrument must be begun then if technique is ever to be perfect. If a foreign language is to be acquired, it should be begun in this period, or there will always be inaccuracies in pronunciation and articulation.

B. Mental Characteristics.—The instinct of curiosity is very active in the earlier period of childhood, and this, combined with greater language power, leads to incessant questionings on the part of the child. He wants to know what, where, why, and how, in regard to everything that comes under his notice, and fortunate indeed is that child whose parent or teacher is sufficiently long-suffering to give satisfactory answers to his many and varied questions. To ignore the inquiries of the child, or to return impatient or grudging answers may inhibit the instinct and lead later to a lack of interest in the world about him. The imitative instinct is also still active and reveals itself particularly in the child's play, which in the main reflects the activities of those about him. He plays horse, policeman, school, Indian, in imitation of the occupations of others. Parents and teachers should depend largely upon this imitative tendency to secure desirable physical habits, such as erect and graceful carriage, cleanliness of person, orderly arrangement of personal belongings, neatness in dress, etc. The imagination is exceedingly active during childhood, fantastic and unregulated in the earlier period, under better control and direction in the later. It reveals itself in the love of hearing, reading, or inventing stories. The imitative play mentioned above is one phase of imaginative activity. The child's ideas of conduct, in this earlier stage of childhood, are derived from the pleasure or pain of their consequences. He has as yet little power of subordinating his lower impulses to an ideal end, and hence is not properly a moral being. Good conduct must, therefore, be secured principally through the exercise of arbitrary authority from without.

In the later period of childhood, acquired interests begin to be formed and, coincident with this, active attention appears. The child begins to be interested in the product, not merely in the process. The mind at this period is most retentive of sense impressions. This is consequently the time to bring the child into immediate contact with his environment through his senses, in such departments as nature study and field work in geography. Thus is laid the basis of future potentialities of imagery, and through it appreciation of literature. On account of the acuteness of sense activity at this period, this is also the time for memorization of fine passages of prose and poetry. The child's thinking is still of the pictorial rather than of the abstract order, though the powers of generalization and language are considerably extended. The social interests are not yet strong, and hence co-operation for a common purpose is largely absent. His games show a tendency toward individualism. When co-operative games are indulged in, he is usually willing to sacrifice the interests of his team to his own personal glorification.

3. Adolescence

A. Physical Characteristics.—In early adolescence the characteristic physical accompaniments of early childhood are repeated, namely, rapid growth and lack of muscular co-ordination. From twelve to fifteen, girls grow more rapidly than boys and are actually taller and heavier than boys at corresponding ages. From fifteen onward, however, the boys rapidly outstrip the girls in growth. Lack of muscular co-ordination is responsible for the awkward movements, ungainly appearance, ungraceful carriage, with their attendant self-consciousness, so characteristic of both boys and girls in early adolescence.

B. Mental Characteristics.—Ideas are gradually freed from their sensory accompaniments. The child thinks in symbols rather than in sensory images. Consequently there is a greater power of abstraction and reflective thought. This is therefore the period for emphasizing those subjects requiring logical reasoning, for example, mathematics, science, and the reflective aspects of grammar, history, and geography.

From association with others or from literature and history, ideals begin to be formed which influence conduct. This is brought about largely through the principle of suggestion. In the early years of adolescence children are very susceptible to suggestions, but the suggestive ideas must be introduced by a person who is trusted, admired, or loved, or under circumstances inspiring these feelings; hence the importance to the adolescent of having teachers of strong and inspiring personality. However, if the suggestive idea is to influence action, it must be introduced in such a way as not to set up a reaction against it. Reaction will be set up if the idea is antagonistic to the present ideas, feelings, or aims, or if it is so persistently thrust upon the child that he begins to suspect that he is being unduly influenced. To avoid reaction the parent or teacher should introduce suggestive ideas indirectly. For instance, while the mind is concentrated upon one set of ideas, a suggestive idea that would otherwise be distasteful may be tolerated. It may lie latent for a time, and when it recurs it may be regarded as original, under which condition it is likely to issue in action.

The adolescent stage is the period of greatest emotional development, and care should therefore be exercised to have the child's mind dwell upon only those ideas with which worthy emotions are associated. The emotional bent, whether good or bad, is determined to a large extent during this period of adolescence. So far as morality is the subordination of primitive instincts to higher ideas, the child now becomes a moral being. His conduct is now determined by reason and by ideals, and the primitive pleasure-pain motives disappear. It follows that coercion and arbitrary authority have little place in discipline at this period. Social interests are prominent, evidenced by the tendency to co-operate with others for a common end. The games of the period are mainly of the co-operative variety and are marked by a willingness to sacrifice personal interests for the sake of the team, or side.

INDIVIDUAL DIFFERENCES

While, as noted above, all children have certain common characteristics at each of the three periods of development, it is even more apparent that every child is in many respects different from every other child. He has certain peculiarities that demand particular treatment. It is evident that it would be impossible to enumerate all the individual differences in children. The most that can be done is to classify the most striking differences and endeavour to place individual children in one or other of these classes.

A. Differences in Thought.—One of the obvious classifications of pupils is that of "quick" and "slow." The former learns easily, but often forgets quickly; the latter learns slowly, but usually retains well. The former is keen and alert; the latter, dull and passive. The former frequently lacks perseverance; the latter is often tenacious and persistent. The former unjustly wins applause for his cleverness; the latter, equally unjustly, wins contempt for his dulness. The teacher must not be unfair to the dull plodder, who in later years may frequently outstrip his brilliant competitor in the race of life.

Some pupils think better in the abstract, others, in the concrete. The former will analyse and parse well in grammar, distinguish fine shades of meaning in language, manage numbers skilfully, or work out chemical equations accurately. The latter will be more successful in doing things, for instance, measuring boards, planning and planting a garden plot, making toys, designing dolls' clothes, and cooking. The schools of the past have all emphasized the ability to think in the abstract, and to a large extent ignored the ability to think in the concrete. This is unfair to the one class of thinkers. From the ranks of those who think in the abstract have come the great statesmen, poets, and philosophers; from the ranks of those who think in the concrete have come the carpenters, builders, and inventors. It will be admitted that the world owes as great a debt from the practical standpoint to the latter class as to the former. Let the school not despise or ignore the pupil who, though unable to think well in abstract studies, is able to do things.

B. Differences in Action.—There is a marked difference among children in the ability to connect an abstract direction with the required act. This is particularly seen in writing, art, and constructive work, subjects in which the aim is the formation of habit, and in which success depends upon following explicitly the direction given. The teacher will find it economical to give very definite instruction as to what is to be done in work in these subjects. It is equally important that instructions regarding conduct should be definite and unmistakable.

As explained in the last Chapter, there are two extreme and contrasting types of will exhibited by children, namely, the impulsive type and the obstructed type. In the former, action occurs without deliberation immediately upon the appearance of the idea in consciousness. This type is illustrated in the case of the pupil who, as soon as he hears a question, thoughtlessly blurts out an answer without any reflection whatever. In the adult, we find a similar illustration when, immediately upon hearing a pitiable story from a beggar, he hands out a dollar without stopping to investigate whether or not the action is well-advised. It is useless to plead in extenuation of such actions that the answer may be correct or the act noble and generous. The probability is equally great that the opposite may be the case. The remedy for impulsive action is patiently and persistently to encourage the pupil to reflect a moment before acting. In the case of the obstructed type of will, the individual ponders long over a course of action before he is able to bring himself to a decision. Such is the child whom it is hard to persuade to answer even easy questions, because he is unable to decide in just what form to put his answer. On an examination paper he proceeds slowly, not because he does not know the matter, but because he finds it hard to decide just what facts to select and how to express them. The bashful child belongs to this type. He would like to answer questions asked him, to talk freely with others, to act without any feeling of restraint, but is unable to bring himself to do so. The obstinate child is also of this type. He knows what he ought to do, but the opposing motives are strong enough to inhibit action in the right direction. As already shown, the remedy for the obstructed will is to encourage rapid deliberation and choice and then immediate action, thrusting aside all opposing motives. Show such pupils that in cases where the motives for and against a certain course of action are of equal strength, it often does not matter which course is selected. One may safely choose either and thus end the indecision. The "quick" child usually belongs to the impulsive type; the "slow" child, to the obstructed type. The former is apt to decide and act hastily and frequently unwisely; the latter is more guarded and, on the whole, more sound in his decision and action.

C. Differences in Temperament.—All four types of temperament given in the formal classification are represented among children in school. The *choleric* type is energetic, impulsive, quick-tempered, yet forgiving, interested in outward events. The *phlegmatic* type is impassive, unemotional, slow to anger, but not of great kindness, persistent in pursuing his purposes. The *sanguine* type is optimistic, impressionable, enthusiastic, but unsteady. The *melancholic* type is pessimistic, introspective, moody, suspicious of the motives of others. Most pupils belong to more than one class. Perhaps the two most prominent types represented in school are (1) that variety of the sanguine temperament which leads the individual to think himself, his possessions, and his work superior to all others, and (2) that variety of the melancholic temperament which leads the individual to fancy himself constantly the victim of injustice on the part of the teacher or the other pupils. A pupil of the first type always believes that his work is perfectly done; he boasts that he is sure he made a hundred per cent. on his examinations; what he has is always, in his own estimation, better than that of others. When the teacher suggests that his work might be better done, the pupil appears surprised and aggrieved. Such a child should be shown that he is right in not being discouraged over his own efforts, but wrong in thinking that his work does not admit of improvement. A pupil of the second type is continually imagining that the teacher treats him unjustly, that the other pupils slight or injure him, that, in short, he is an object of persecution. Such a pupil should be shown that nobody has a grudge against him, that the so-called slights are entirely imaginary, and that he should take a sane view of these things, depending more upon judgment than on feeling to estimate the action of others toward him.

D. Sex Differences.—Boys differ from girls in the predominance of certain instincts, interests, and mental powers. In boys the fighting instinct, and capacities of leadership, initiative, and mastery are prominent. In girls the instinct of nursing and fondling, and the capacities to comfort and relieve are prominent. These are revealed in the games of the playground. The interests of the two sexes are different, since their games and later pursuits are different. In a system of co-education it is impossible to take full cognizance of this fact in the work of the school. Yet it is possible to make some differentiation between the work assigned to boys and that assigned to girls. For instance, arithmetical problems given to boys might deal with activities interesting to boys, and those to girls might deal with activities interesting to girls. In composition the differentiation will be easier. Such a topic as "A Game of Baseball" would be more suitable for boys, and on the other hand "How to Bake Bread" would make a stronger appeal to girls. Similarly in literature, such a poem as *How They Brought the Good News from Ghent to Aix* would be particularly interesting to boys, while *The Romance of a Swan's Nest* would be of greater interest to girls. As to mental capacities, boys are usually superior in those fields where logical reasoning is demanded, while girls usually surpass boys in those fields involving perceptive powers and verbal memory. For instance, boys succeed better in mathematics, science, and the reflective phases of history; girls succeed better in spelling, in harmonizing colours in art work, in distinguishing fine shades of meaning in language, and in memorizing poetry. The average intellectual ability of each sex is nearly the same, but boys deviate from the average more than girls. Thus while the most brilliant pupils are likely to be boys, the dullest are also likely to be boys. It is a scientific fact that there are more individuals of conspicuously clever mind, but also more of weak intellect, among men than there are among women.

A Caution.—While it has been stated that the teacher should take notice of individual differences in his pupils, it may be advisable also to warn the student-teacher against any extravagant tendency in the direction of such a study. A teacher is occasionally met who seems to act on the assumption that his chief function is not to educate but to study children. Too much of his time may therefore be spent in the conducting of experiments and the making of observations to that end. While the data thus secured may be of some value, it must not be forgotten that control of the subject-matter of education and of the method of presenting that subject-matter to the normal child, together with an earnest, enthusiastic, and sympathetic manner, are the prime qualifications of the teacher as an instructor.

APPENDIX

Suggested Readings from Books of Reference

CHAPTER I

Bagley .... The Educative Process, Chapter I.
Colvin .... The Learning Process, Chapter II.
Strayer .... A Brief Course in the Teaching Process, Chapter I.
Thorndike .... Principles of Teaching, Chapter I.

CHAPTER II

Bagley .... Educational Values, Chapters I, II, III.
Strayer .... A Brief Course in the Teaching Process, Chapter III.
Thorndike .... Elements of Psychology, Chapter I.
Welton .... The Psychology of Education, Chapter VI.

CHAPTER III

Bagley .... The Educative Process, Chapters IV, XIV.
Colvin .... The Learning Process, Chapter I.
McMurry ..... The Method of the Recitation, Chapter I.
Raymont ..... The Principles of Education, Chapter XI.

CHAPTER IV

Bagley .... The Educative Process, Chapters II, XV.
Dewey .... The School and Society, Part I.
Raymont ..... The Principles of Education, Chapters VI, VII.
Strayer .... A Brief Course in the Teaching Process, Chapter XVIII.

CHAPTER V

Bagley .... The Educative Process, Chapter I.
Raymont ..... The Principles of Education, Chapter III.

CHAPTER VI

Bagley .... The Educative Process, Chapter III.
Dewey .... The School and Society, Part II.
Raymont ..... The Principles of Education, Chapters I, IV.
Welton .... The Psychology of Education, Chapter XIII.

CHAPTER VII

Landon ...... The Principles and Practice of Teaching, Chapter I.

CHAPTER VIII

Landon ...... The Principles and Practice of Teaching, Chapter I.
McMurry .... The Method of the Recitation, Chapter I.
Raymont ..... The Principles of Education, Chapter VIII.

CHAPTER IX

Kirkpatrick ... Fundamentals of Child Study, Chapter IV.
Landon ...... The Principles and Practice of Teaching, Chapter VII.
Dewey .... The School and Society, Part II.
Strayer .... A Brief Course in the Teaching Process, Chapter II.
Thorndike .... Principles of Teaching, Chapter III.

CHAPTER X

Betts .... The Mind and Its Education, Chapter VII.
McMurry .... The Method of the Recitation, Chapter VI.
Thorndike .... Principles of Teaching, Chapters IV, IX.

CHAPTER XI

Angell .... Psychology, Chapter VI.
Bagley .... The Educative Process, Chapters IV, V, IX.
Pillsbury ..... Essentials of Psychology, Chapter V.
Raymont ..... The Principles of Education, Chapter VIII.

CHAPTER XII

Betts .... Psychology, Chapter XVI.
Thorndike .... Principles of Teaching, Chapter XIII.
McMurry .... The Method of the Recitation, Chapter IX.

CHAPTER XIII

Landon . . . . . . The Principles and Practice of Teaching, Chapter VI.
McMurry . . . . The Method of the Recitation, Chapter VII.
Raymont . . . . . The Principles of Education, Chapter XII.

CHAPTER XIV

McMurry . . . . The Method of the Recitation, Chapter III.

CHAPTER XV

Bagley . . . . The Educative Process, Chapters XIX, XX.
Colvin . . . . The Learning Process, Chapter XXII.
McMurry . . . . The Method of the Recitation, Chapters VIII, X.
Strayer . . . . . . A Brief Course in the Teaching Process, Chapters V, VI.

CHAPTER XVI

Landon . . . . . . The Principles and Practice of Teaching, Chapter III.

CHAPTER XVII

Bagley . . . . The Educative Process, Chapters XXI, XXII.
Landon . . . . . . The Principles and Practice of Teaching, Chapter IV.
Strayer . . . . A Brief Course in the Teaching Process, Chapters IV, VIII, X.

CHAPTER XVIII

Landon . . . . . . The Principles and Practice of Teaching, Chapter VI.
Raymont . . . . . The Principles of Education, Chapter XII.
Strayer . . . . A Brief Course in the Educative Process, Chapter XI.

CHAPTER XIX

Betts . . . . The Mind and Its Education, Chapter I.
Pillsbury . . . . . Essentials of Education, Chapter I.
Raymont . . . . . The Principles of Education, Chapter II.
Welton . . . . The Psychology of Education, Chapter I.

CHAPTER XX

Angell . . . . Psychology, Chapter II.
Betts . . . . The Mind and Its Education, Chapter III.

Pillsbury ..... Essentials of Psychology, Chapter II.

Halleck ...... Education of the Central Nervous System.

CHAPTER XXI

Colvin .... The Learning Process, Chapters III, IV.

Kirkpatrick ... Fundamentals of Child Study, Chapter IV.

Pillsbury ..... Essentials of Psychology, Chapter X.

Thorndike .... Principles of Teaching, Chapter III.

Welton .... The Psychology of Education, Chapter IV.

CHAPTER XXII

Angell .... Psychology, Chapter III.

Bagley .... The Educative Process, Chapter VII.

Betts .... The Mind and Its Education, Chapter V.

Colvin .... The Learning Process, Chapters III, IV.

Thorndike .... Principles of Teaching, Chapter VIII.

Thorndike .... Elements of Psychology, Chapter XIII.

CHAPTER XXIII

Angell .... Psychology, Chapter IV.

Betts .... The Mind and Its Education, Chapter II.

Pillsbury ..... Essentials of Psychology, Chapter V.

Welton .... The Psychology of Education, Chapter VIII.

CHAPTER XXIV

Angell .... Psychology, Chapter XXI.

Betts .... The Mind and Its Education, Chapter XIII.

James .... Talks to Teachers, Chapter X.

Welton .... The Psychology of Education, Chapter VII.

CHAPTER XXV

Angell .... Psychology, Chapters V, VI.

Betts .... The Mind and Its Education, Chapter VI.

Pillsbury ..... Essentials of Psychology, Chapters IV, VII.

CHAPTER XXVI

Angell .... Psychology, Chapter IX.

Bagley .... The Educative Process, Chapters IV, XI.
Betts .... The Mind and Its Education, Chapter VIII.
Thorndike .... Elements of Psychology, Chapter III.
Pillsbury ..... Essentials of Psychology, Chapter VIII.

CHAPTER XXVII

Angell .... Psychology, Chapter VIII.
Betts .... The Mind and Its Education, Chapter IX.
Pillsbury ..... Essentials of Psychology, Chapter VIII.

CHAPTER XXVIII

Angell .... Psychology, Chapters X, XII.
Bagley .... The Educative Process, Chapters IX, X.
Betts .... The Mind and Its Education, Chapter X.
Colvin .... The Learning Process, Chapter XXII.
Pillsbury ..... Essentials of Psychology, Chapter IX.
Thorndike .... Elements of Psychology, Chapter VI.

CHAPTER XXIX

Angell .... Psychology, Chapters XIII, XIV.
Betts .... The Mind and Its Education, Chapters XII, XIV.
Pillsbury ..... Essentials of Psychology, Chapters XI, XII.

CHAPTER XXX

Angell .... Psychology, Chapters XX, XXII.
Betts .... The Mind and Its Education, Chapter XV.
Pillsbury ..... Essentials of Psychology, Chapter XIII.
Thorndike .... Elements of Psychology, Chapter VI.

CHAPTER XXXI

Bagley .... The Educative Process, Chapter XII.
Raymont ..... The Principles of Education, Chapter V.
Kirkpatrick ... Fundamentals of Child Study.

Printed by Libri Plureos GmbH in Hamburg,
Germany